D0402650

NOBODY CALLS ME
MR. KIRCK

NOBODY CALLS ME
MR. KIRCK

Harvey Kirck
with Wade Rowland

Collins Toronto

First published 1985
by Collins Publishers
100 Lesmill Road, Don Mills, Ontario

Canadian Cataloguing in Publication Data

Kirck, Harvey.
  Nobody calls me Mr. Kirck

Includes index.
ISBN 0-00-217466-9

1. Kirck, Harvey. 2. Broadcasters — Canada — Biography.
I. Rowland, Wade, 1944 –   II. Title.

PN1992.4.K53A37   1985   070.1'9'0924   C85-099396-2

Printed and bound in Canada by John Deyell Company

To Brenda — Thanks, Babe.

And for Chris,
who had the idea.

Foreword

Hold it right there! Before anybody turns another page I want to make something perfectly clear. I have not retired. First, I can't afford it and, second, I'm a little too young to lay down the cudgels just yet. I am growing weary of being greeted by strangers with, "Hey Harv, how's retirement?" (Nobody calls me "Mr. Kirck.") I am not now, nor have I ever been, retired. I have simply stopped being an anchorman.

I did my last network newscast on April 27th, 1984, and worked out a naive plan to take the summer off and just loaf. Then, I was invited by Collins Publishers to put down these scribblings in a book. I thought it would be easy, so I agreed. With wife, Brenda, and dog, T.J., I boarded our new boat, *Fair Passage*, and set off for what I imagined would be a long, lazy summer of cruising, pleasurably punctuated by occasional jottings of a few memories and anecdotes.

Not so. I found myself tied to my word processor and my boat tied to a dock. When the book was finished, I discovered that the network had a new project for me. It was to be called "Harvey's People," and the plan was for me to travel about Canada finding interesting people to be profiled as a special segment of *Canada AM*. It was a chance to do some light, interesting features with out-of-the-ordinary Canadians, the kind who have a story to tell, but rarely make the national media in the usual run of news. I would have Peggy Taylor, a sharp, energetic young story editor from *Canada AM* as field producer, and we'd be provided with a researcher. As a unit, we would be self-assigning—that is, we would pick our subjects and deal with them as we saw fit. We'd provide *Canada AM* with a finished product, six, seven, maybe nine minutes

1

long, for use every Friday morning. On paper, it sounded like a cinch.

That's how I came to be standing among the humungous boulders of the Frank Slide, with the wind whipping an abrasive mixture of sand and snow pellets around my shivering body, while I tried to shelter frail and wizened Arthur Graham, the last living survivor of the slide. The camera was recording what was supposed to be a nonchalant chat about that roaring, murderous morning when Turtle Mountain caved in. Furthermore, that's how I came to be trying to talk coherently into a microphone through chattering teeth on the dusty streets of a ghost town called Rowley, in Alberta, then warming myself in the cluttered surroundings of Sam's Saloon, a semi-legal bar where Rowley residents sometimes blew off steam. Later in the evening, I trudged with cameraman Gord Danielson along a wind-whipped snow-covered highway between Rowley and Drumheller. My prized Sam's Saloon hat was ripped from my head, and disappeared somewhere in a vast, unseen field of barley stubble.

It was a learning experience. I learned that an overweight, out-of-condition, ex-anchorman should never try to trek up a 45-degree mountain slope, looking for bighorn sheep with Andy Russell. On Grand Manan Island, while watching the Gray Cup game, I learned that it is possible to eat too many scallops. I learned humbling things about my abilities as a performer with Roy Thoreson, the world champion whistler, and with singer Carroll Baker. By the way, after you've spent most of your life trying to speak with reasonable clarity, try being an auctioneer.

I have a friend who once said he knew everything about television because he'd been watching it all his life. I'd thought I knew about television, too. But changes in technical equipment over the last few years amaze and astound me. What a joy it was to return through that snowstorm from Rowley, sit in the snug comfort of a hotel room, and watch what we'd done that day on a portable video playback pack. What a wonderful reassurance to know, when you leave a story, that you have all the ingredients for the telling. In the editing room, a choice is made, a computer is advised, tape machines whirr, and edits are accomplished in seconds. No cutting and splicing here. I still don't understand how all this new electronic gadgetry works, and I'm not sure I want to learn. But who knows what's in store. I've already been seduced by the delights of word processors. Maybe next year, I'll grab a pop can from a T-shirt and drink from it, or make T.J. into an image on a billboard, or make my car fly . . . .

Not likely. There is still some virtue in keeping it simple.

Chapter 1

Remember . . . ?

"Hello Canada, and hockey fans in the United States and Newfoundland . . . ."

"From out of the West come the thundering hoofbeats of the great horse Silver. The Lone Ranger."

"Knock!Knock! Who's there? It's the Happy Gang! Well, come o-o-o-n in!"

"It's the Johnson's Wax Program, with Fibber McGee and Molly."

I remember. I have learned that as you reach your fiftieth year, your affection for the past grows steadily more compelling. I suppose that's because of the uncomfortable realization that there's a lot more back there than there's likely to be up ahead. Those lines from the old radio shows play back vividly in my memory these days, evoking a world that draws irresistibly nearer to me the farther it recedes in time.

Stromberg-Carlson, Marconi, Stewart-Warner, Victor, General Electric . . . when you grew up in the Thirties in the dirt-poor clay belt of Northern Ontario, those names were all synonyms for liberation: passwords to fabulous new worlds. When the bitter winter winds howled through the poplars and tagalders, piling snow in four-foot drifts at the front door, inside, in the fragrant warmth of the old McClary cookstove, the radio was deliverance. To me, it was magic: the fascination began early and lasted a lifetime.

* * *

Uno Park is a tiny pinprick on the map of northeastern Ontario, a place where three roads converge about six miles outside New Liskeard. The Wabi River, the muddy Wabi, runs through the village and, many years ago, my grandfather owned a sawmill on its banks. Grandpa George Krick, his wife and two small children, and his brother Alf, had trekked north from the village of Winslow, in the Niagara Peninsula, in 1902. George and Alf established their sawmill, built a home, and for almost 14 years, prospered there as some of the first settlers on the northern frontier. It was in the house they built on the flats beside the river bank, just below the main street of the village, that my dad was born in 1905.

By 1916, the lumber business had begun to slump. I suppose it was because the initial building boom in the area had ended. When Alf lost an arm in a mill accident, the Krick brothers decided to sell the sawmill and their home. Alf headed west for British Columbia. Grandpa George bought a farm about a mile down the road.

It was a good-sized spread by the standards of the time. It had a drive shed and two big barns laid out in a T. The house had several bedrooms, a parlour, a dining-room, a kitchen, and a big summer kitchen. There were a couple of chicken-houses too, an ice-house, and another little building that sheltered the well. A long dirt lane led out to the main road to Uno Park, and where the trails met there was a three-room cottage that sat vacant for many years.

A mile or so further down the road, across the Wabi, was the Leverre farm. That's where my mother, Orphia May, was born in 1906. Where Grandpa Krick's farm was well-ordered and tidy, the Leverre place was anything but. I never met my Grandfather Leverre—he was dead before I arrived—but I think he may have had a blind eye for symmetry. There were buildings everywhere, with no apparent logic behind their placement. There was a rambling old farmhouse, and nearby, on the edge of a ravine, stood the milk-house. Beyond that were two barns, and behind them, a wagon shed. Across from the barns was the granary. Up the lane and across from the house stood the ramshackle machine shed.

On reflection, though, I may do an injustice to Grandpa Leverre: he died young after siring four strapping sons

5

and two daughters, and perhaps his children were partly responsible for the disjointed layout of their homestead. In any case, by the time I came along, it was the greatest place in the world for a kid to play.

My mother and father went to school together at Uno Park. Dad had a mile or so to walk: mother had three miles to go in summer, but only two in the winter when she could cross the ice on the Wabi. They were married in 1927, and moved into the little cottage at the end of Grandpa Krick's laneway. I was born in that cottage on October 14th, 1928.

* * *

There is no park in Uno Park, at least nothing worth naming a town after. Local folklore has it that the name derived from the Parker family, who were early settlers. Travellers in the area would ask: "D'ya know Parker?" Over the years this was corrupted to Uno Park. When I knew it, the village came close to being picturesque. That it failed was mainly due to the grey river: each spring its banks slipped untidily into the swollen stream in a tangle of broken trees, roots, brush, and huge clods of mud. The bridge in the village was an ugly black steel structure that was forever in need of paint. It was nonetheless a neat village, well-scrubbed, and perhaps even prosperous for the time and place.

Just at the top of the hill above the bridge, across the road from the general store, was a rambling frame house— part of a mixed farm that reached back in a narrow strip from the river bank. My parents moved into this house when I was just a few months old and my brother Rod was born there five years later.

My closest playmates were Harry and Martha Parker's girls, Shirley and Toots. I have a vivid picture in my mind of showing Shirley how to swim . . . in a large, muddy puddle in the Parkers' driveway. Shirley was impressed, but my mother, I seem to recall, was not.

Frank Rose's general store, across the road, carried everything you would expect to find in a country store in the Thirties. He had Bee Hive Golden Corn Syrup and

Sunlight Soap; Magic Baking Powder and Old Dutch Cleanser; bits of horse harness and assorted screws and nails. None of that was of much interest to me: what was important to this four-year-old was what Frank kept behind the counter in a flat, black and orange cardboard box. Licorice pipes and cigars! Even now, my mouth waters. And next in importance . . . the *Star Weekly*. Each weekend, it was my job to pick up the *Star Weekly* from Mr. Rose, and the first thing I'd do was check to make sure that the funnies were there, tucked into the glossy lithograph section: Tarzan the Ape Man, Maggie and Jiggs, Bronco Bill, Mandrake the Magician, Popeye, Dick Tracy, and Jimmy Frise and Greg Clark's "Bird's Eye Centre." What finer way is there for a young fellow to spend a Saturday afternoon than to sit with his father or mother reading the funnies?

A few minutes' walk on stubby legs from our front door, up past the manse and the United Church, stood Uno Park Public School. It was a frame building, painted white, with large, multi-paned windows on both sides. On a fine September morning in 1933, my mother took me by the hand and I became a student there. It was an adventure, but not a frightening one. The big slate blackboards between the side windows and across the front of the room, and the raised platform from which the teacher ruled, were a little intimidating, but all my friends were there with me, and I could look out the window and see my home. All in all, school was just dandy.

I was well into my first year when my father announced we were going to move—not just down the road, but five miles away, to another farm. When you're five years old, and your world has been contained in a comfortable and familiar radius of a couple of hundred yards, five miles is a long way! No longer would my school be within sight of home: no longer would we have the big, old house or Frank Rose's store just across the road. The new place was a long way from anywhere, and the house had just two rooms. One autumn day in 1934, the whole family climbed aboard the buggy and Dad drove us out toward the village of Hanbury.

Highway 11 must be one of the longest provincial roads anywhere. It starts at Yonge Street in Toronto and divides the province east and west for more than 300 miles. Then it begins a slow, 600-mile curve to the west that ends in a dip to the south and Thunder Bay. From there, it winds west again another 250 miles or so, until it runs off the Ontario map at the Manitoba border. Hanbury lay sprinkled along its shoulders six miles north of New Liskeard, 300 miles north of Toronto. A mile to the west, down a gravel sideroad at a point where it snaked along the banks of a steep gully, crossing three bridges within a quarter of a mile, was Earl Krick's new farm.

An 80-acre farm in that part of Northern Ontario automatically qualifies as poor. This one was not only poor, but it seems to me now to have had an air of weariness and resignation about it. The house was grey and run-down, perched on the brow of a hill overlooking one of the three bridges. It was a lovely site, but no effort had been put into making a real home of it. Waist-high grass, weeds, and scrub grew in an impenetrable tangle on all sides. Underbrush clung to the side of the ravine, spreading down the hill until it merged with the wood that bordered the stream. The path to the outhouse, which was secluded in the trees 100 or so feet away, was only faintly visible, and the trail to the barn appeared to me as a long corridor through the grass. The barn itself seemed tired. Its vertical board siding was weathered grey and some of the planks were missing, leaving gaping black portals that invited cautious exploration. Its most striking feature was its list: the old building seemed to be either leaning into a wind from the east, or wilting under the pressure of a westerly blow.

I know now that that scrub farm was a heartbreaker for both my mother and father. The soil was poor, so crops were sparse. When it rained, the grey mud became a sticky, slippery mess that could suck the rubber boots right off your feet. In summer, it baked into slabs, cracked and scarred. There was no machinery: ploughing, cultivating, harrowing, seeding, and harvesting were all labour-intensive, as they say nowadays, with my father supplying the labour and a pair of mismatched nags named King and Dan providing the horsepower. As Dad walked behind the single-share plough, he was jerked and twisted unmercifully in his fight with both the unyielding earth and the off-side pull of the team—one of them big, powerful, and rangy, the other short and stumpy. We bought some milk-cows, so fences had to go up. A chicken coop was built, and soon hens were scratching in the yard and we had our own eggs on the table. Dad built a pen along one side of the barn and that became home for the biggest, meanest pig I'd ever seen.

Mom went to work on the house and soon there was shiny new wall-to-wall linoleum on the floor, curtains in the windows, and wallpaper in bright floral patterns for the walls. The big black-and-white McClary cookstove dominated the room downstairs, taking up a good piece of the wall next to the back door. Beside it was an iron sofa-bed with a slightly lumpy, but not-uncomfortable cushion over unforgiving steel springs. In the corner was an easy chair, and beside that a cupboard fashioned from a couple of orange crates turned on end, nailed together and covered with a padded top and curtains. It was here that we kept the precious six-volt battery for the radio. Beside the window that overlooked the ravine, stood the wind-up Victrola. The gramophone rarely ran at a true 78 rpm, but the reedy sounds it produced were almost as miraculous as those we heard on the radio. We had a phone, too: it was the kind you see in antique stores now . . . a brown wooden box varnished shiny, with two big nickel-plated bells on top. We were on a party line, where everybody had a coded ring: maybe two longs and a short, or two shorts.

Another fixture was the DeLaval cream separator we kept near the back door, close by the coat hooks and the wooden box for wet or muddy boots. You filled the big stainless-steel basin that sat on top of the machine and as you turned a geared crank, the milk flowed through a series of screens that separated the thick, sweet cream into a smaller steel basin, while the skim milk was collected in pails. Turning the crank was one chore I relished.

In the centre of the room was a big, wooden table—a harvest table it'd be called today—that served a multitude of purposes. We ate from it, my mother sewed on it: bread was mixed and kneaded, and later cooled there. School work was done on it, and perhaps a million cribbage points pegged. My little brother was bathed, got his backside powdered with corn starch, and had hand-me-down diapers pinned on there.The wood surface was dented and scarred, but that didn't matter: it was always covered in brightly-coloured oilcloth, so slick and shiny it could be wiped clean with one swipe of a damp cloth and a little of the ubiquitous Sunlight Soap.

Upstairs, the house was a model of spartan simplicity. One room, two beds, a few cupboards, a dresser, and a gabled window at each end. It wasn't long before my father found the material to build a partition between Rod and me, and him and mother. After all, they were still young, and two small boys a few feet from your bed can be inhibiting.

The house was lit with coal-oil lamps, which threw off a pungent aroma that was somehow soothing. If you went outside after dark (or before dawn), you took along a lantern.

I haven't mentioned plumbing because there wasn't any. Water came from a well in the yard with an iron pump: it was brought inside and warmed in the McClary's copper reservoir, and bathing was done in a big porcelain basin upstairs. For my mother, that was a daily ritual: my father managed to avoid it unless they were going somewhere or having company. For day-to-day washing-up, there was the small enamel basin on a stand near the stove. The privy, a two-holer with solid door (no half-moon), was about ten seconds at a dead run from the back door—less, in really cold weather. Dad always tried to have something softer than the Eaton's catalogue on the shelf inside. In the summer, using the privy wasn't so bad, but in winter it was a trial. In the early days, I didn't have to worry about it very much. Being a youngster carried with it the privilege of using the chipped enamel potty that was under the bed.

A verandah was built along the front of the house and down one side—a big, comfortable place to sit after the day's work. Dad found time to clean up a small area around the house and to trim the grass, and that became lawn. My mother seeded flower beds and planted silver maple saplings, tending them all diligently. Surprisingly, most of what she planted grew, and she was rewarded with bright, blossoming beds of petunias, geraniums, irises, pansies, and shiny new leaves on the tiny trees.

Neighbours were important in any farm community in those days. We were lucky to have the Goddards on the place next to ours. Old Bill was a big-boned giant of a man, his face dominated by a long, hooking nose. He had a stern look about him, but was generous and kindly to a fault. His wife Lizzie was short and stout like a teapot, and a bit worn-down from looking after Bill and their five sons.

Bill had served in World War One, and was considered an expert on all manner of practical topics, notably medicine. The fact was, he did know something about doctoring, as we learned to our gratitude.

Kids' illnesses on the farm were usually treated with folk remedies handed down from generation to generation. If things got serious, a parent might call a doctor in town to ask for advice, but it was rare for the doctor to make a house call, even then. Few of us had cars, so in an emergency there was no question of rushing the patient to a hospital—you had to do the best you could with the resources at hand. When my brother Rod was about a year old, he came down with scarlet fever. My mother had been tending to him for hours and hours when she noticed his body suddenly stiffen, and then slowly begin to turn from fever-red to blue. He seemed to be holding his breath, and his limbs moved in jerks and spasms. He was in the grip of a convulsion. Mother raced for the door. She screamed twice . . . once for Father, and once for Bill Goddard. Dad was out on the land doing field work, and the Goddards' house was a couple of hundred yards away, across the ravine, but within moments, both men were at Rod's bedside. Bill took charge. He ordered our big, copper boiler filled with cool water, and then he lifted the stiffened body of my little brother and lowered him into it. The process was repeated several times, and slowly, the baby began to relax and the convulsion ended. Rod was still red from the fever, but he was out of danger.

When big jobs had to be done on the farms, they became co-operative efforts, or "bees." Threshing in the fall was one such occasion, and neighbours turned out with their teams and wagons to bring in the stooked sheaves from the fields and pitch them into the jaws of the threshing machine. Hundred-pound jute bags were filled, bounced a couple of times to settle the grain, topped up, tied with a flourish, and loaded on a wagon for transport to the family granary. When the crop was all off, there'd be a big communal supper. Then the man with the machinery would hook his thresher onto his tractor and move on to the next farm, where the process would be repeated.

There were also bees for special jobs. On our farm, there was a "slash," a scrubby tangle of bush that ran along the south line. It took up maybe ten or twelve acres, and on an 80-acre farm that was too much. Stuff would grow on that land if the willows and poplars and tagalders could be removed.

From neighbouring farms, Goddards and Overtons and Pettifers and Loaches, and a gaggle of Kricks and Leverres converged to attack the bush with teams, logging chains, scrapers and axes. When the job was done, we had several cords of firewood, Dad had a new field to work, and I could walk straight across our land to the Pettifers' place to see my friend Clifford.

We had another bee at our place: this one was no hack and slash affair, but an enterprise requiring considerable delicacy and precision. Our house was going to be moved! Just why requires some explaining: my mother was a good cook, and some of her finest efforts went into her preserves. She would "put down" everything in season. I had a particular fondness for her pickles—including the best pickled beets I've ever tasted — and there were fruit preserves made from wild strawberries, raspberries, even chokecherries. All these delicacies needed to be stored in a cool place, however, and our new house had no cellar. After much discussion, the decision was made to dig a cellar and move the house onto it. Dad figured the house was too far from the barn anyway, so it was a matter of killing two birds with one stone.

Dad did most of the preparatory work himself, digging the pit, lining its walls with a stockade of small logs, and putting down a wood floor. A new foundation was made of heavy timbers laid in a deep trench and spiked together. When it came time to shift the house, Dad called on Bill Goddard—this time in his capacity as resident engineer. Under Bill's supervision, the men who had gathered in our yard early one morning jacked up the house and slid huge logs underneath for skids. Two teams were hitched up, one to each skid. Horse leaned into harness, the traces strained, and with a groan, the house began to move. There was a lot of creaking and snapping, but the teams were held to an even pull and the skids were long enough to smooth out any bumps. Before long the building was being lowered onto its new foundation. All that was left to do was to cut a trap door in the kitchen floor, and my mother had her cold cellar.

* * *

Many years later, I visited the old homestead to discover the cellar had caved in, a victim of dampness and wood rot. Some years after that, the old house caved in, too. It's sad to think of all that effort gone for nought. For in the end my father would give up trying to scratch a living out of the farm and go out to work instead. Yet, for me, those years on the farm were pure gold, and the memories never fail to bring a fond smile. The Great Depression, which we were struggling to survive, meant little to me. At worst, it was the sadness in my parents' voices in overheard conversations about Dad's friend, or mother's cousin, going off on the "grain train" to work on the harvest somewhere "out west." There were government make-work projects then, but we didn't know them as such. A big drainage ditch was dug to take water out of the swampy "flats," through the back of some of the farms and into the Wabi. Some men got work building roads or cutting timber; but mostly they stuck tenaciously to their farms, as my parents did. We were poor, all right, but I'm not sure we were aware of it. All of us in that area at that time were in the same boat, and none of us really knew anything different.

I don't believe anyone went hungry: the farms provided basic food for the table, and there was wild game, and an uncle might stretch a net across the Wabi to supply fish for neighbours and relatives. When we needed extra cash, there were farm goods that could be marketed. My father travelled to New Liskeard every Saturday, through all kinds of weather, taking chickens, eggs, and garden vegetables, in season. Some of our neighbours marketed in a big way in Kirkland Lake. For that, though, they had to get up at three in the morning, travel to the station at Uno Park by wagon or sleigh, and catch the Temiskaming and Northern Ontario Railway train to Kirkland Lake.

One way or another they survived, all of them, through hard work, their own ingenuity, and sheer, stubborn farmers' pride. I believe there are few of them who today would not look back with fondness on those years.

Chapter 2

Hanbury school was about a mile from our farm—a cavernous, one-room building with a big basement that was used as a lunch room and play area. Its grounds were enormous: there was a baseball diamond, a soccer field, a couple of swings, and a deep, wooded ravine out back that provided good ski trails in winter and a wilderness battlefield for cowboys and Indians in the summer. Directly across Highway 11 was the general store and post office, owned by Mrs. Routliffe. Together with the six or eight farmhouses close by, these buildings comprised the village of Hanbury. It was in this setting that I met the kids that I would live and learn with for the next five or six years: the Newmans, Clifford and Margaret Pettifer, Orville Hines, Margaret Hamilton, Arden and Harvey Conners, Don and Darryl Plaunt, a gang of Loaches, Morley Hetherington, Will Nickle, Albert Healy, and more names lost to time.

Mrs. Routliffe was a kindly, long-suffering lady who somehow tolerated the gang of rowdies who crowded into her store each day just after four o'clock. Her stock of soft drinks was stored in one corner of the store, and more often than I care to admit a crowd of us would gather at her counter to block her view while others slipped bottles of Coke or Orange Crush under their jackets. We'd all get together later to share in the spoils; there's no denying, the flavour of that stolen pop had a special piquancy. That was about the extent of our delinquent behaviour, though we were a pretty rambunctious roughneck bunch.

The first fight I ever had, apart from constant battling with my brother Rod, was with a fellow named Orville Hines. We were arguing about something or other as we made our way home from school one winter afternoon.

15

Orville was a little guy and in frustration he heaved a ski pole at me, pointed end first. I dodged, pulled the pole from the snow and, with a wild swing, bent it over poor Orville's back. As bamboo will, it splintered in many places. Orville was most unhappy, but we never again had strong words for each other.

Another fracas involved an older boy, a tough young kid who liked to run the schoolyard his way. One day, I took exception to his bullying ways and we got into a tussle. Before long, he had me on the ground and I knew I was doomed as I watched him wind up for a real hay-maker. I closed my eyes and prepared for the worst. I felt an almighty thump, but then I heard a howl of pain and when I opened my eyes, the bully was rolling on the ground holding his hand. He'd dislocated his thumb and sprained a finger. Harvey's hard head became a legend, the bully became a laughing stock, and violence in the schoolyard settled down to routine name-calling and threats.

As though in answer to the fervent, if misguided, pray-ers of us young ruffians, our school burned down one bleak December day in 1939, after everyone had gone home. From our farm, we could see the flickering glow in the sky as the old building crackled and roared, finally collapsing in a spectacular shower of sparks. We kids were jubilant, but not for long. Classes were set up in the basement of the United Church up the hill, and for most of us that meant a longer trek each morning and evening—for my brother and me about a mile more each way. Harley Town-ship was not a prosperous area, but the board of education went to work quickly, and within a few weeks a new school rose on the old foundation, and it was back to business as usual. Well, perhaps not *quite* usual. The move back to the school brought an outbreak of cowboy and Indian warfare the likes of which Hanbury had never seen. Carpenters had left dozens of triangular bits of left-over lumber scat-tered around the schoolyard and these were immediately requisitioned as Colt .45s, Navy .44s, "hawglegs" or what-ever else our blood-thirsty little imaginations could conjure up. Stuck in your belt, they were great for the fast draw and the shoot-out. The smaller ones could be concealed in your shirt, for use when captured. Or, in the event you were tagged to be the bad guy, for "dirty killin'."

* * *

Along about 1939, the MacNamara Construction Company inadvertently provided our little community with some wonderful recreation facilities. Contracted to provide a blacktop surface for Highway 11 between New Liskeard and Englehart, they dug a huge limestone quarry about a mile north of our school, for aggregate. Soon after the job had been finished, it filled up with spring water and became a gigantic swimming hole. The gravel road used by the trucks to get to the bottom of the pit provided a gentle slope into the deep end for the timid and, for the more daring, there were steep cliffs where you could jump 20 or more feet into the water. We had rafts and diving boards, and we even hauled a couple of abandoned construction shacks to the water's edge to serve as changing rooms.

In winter, the quarry was big enough for two or three skating rinks, if you could find enough shovels and strong backs to keep the snow cleared. Many of us learned to skate on the quarry at Hanbury. There was always a pick-up hockey game when you had the time. Equipment was rudimentary: rolled-up newspapers or Eaton's catalogues (fastened with binder twine or sealer rings) served as shin pads, and if no puck were available, frozen horse buns worked pretty well. In fact, they were a lot easier to raise when you took a shot.

Our construction shack change-houses were a godsend in that often bitter climate, but they were rough, dangerous buildings. In the jostling that took place there, I was pushed off-balance against the wall one day. I slid to the floor, and on the way down encountered the pointy end of a protruding nail. It took a gouge out of my backside and the scar is still there as a reminder.

In summer, the newly paved highway, lacking any serious volume of traffic, became an ideal bicycle track. There was a rock cut just north of Hanbury where a steep hill had been shaped down to a long, gradual grade. Pedalling up the hill was something of a chore, but what came next made it worthwhile. We'd mount our bikes, pedal like mad down the hill until we'd reached a predetermined point, and then, we'd coast! On a good day, with a tailwind, we could speed down the highway well past the store. If you really had your speed up, you could even get past the dip by the Alderdice home and out onto the flat section beyond, coasting for nearly two miles without touching the pedals.

In winter, we skied. Our skis were the old-fashioned type held on with a simple leather toe-strap, and few of us had ski poles. Jack Goddard—my closest friend at the time—was the best skier in the school, with the most absurd skis imaginable. They'd cost 98¢ out of the Eaton's catalogue, and before he'd had them very long, one began turning up at about the point where the toe-strap was fastened until its forward tip was seven or eight inches off the ground. The other ski just as quickly lost what curl it had had and ended up as a virtually flat board. Still, Jack could make those sticks perform! Gliding along the hard-packed shoulders of those country roads, he could set a pace that no one could match. On the hills, he raced along swiftly, taking drifts and gullies with ease. He was always the one who broke the trails, and there was never a challenge to his status.

Everyone, young and old, skied in winter. Soon after the first snow, the countryside would be criss-crossed with an elaborate network of trails. My uncle Clifford carefully considered all of this and decided he would go into the ski-making business, crafting them from two-by-four stock. I believe they were about seven feet long, and the tips were turned up by soaking them in boiling water. They were so heavy and they slid so poorly that you needed legs of steel to move them. The wood he used didn't have much give to it so that a sharp dip in the snow meant a dry snap and a busted ski. Needless to say, Uncle Clifford didn't make a lot of skis.

Getting around on skis during the worst of the winter weather could be a bone-chilling business. But once you were home, the evening chores done, and snug in your little house, there was a wonderful feeling of comfort and security. The aromatic oil lamps flickered, creating a magic-lantern show of shadows on the walls. The radio crackled with the distant sounds of CFRB Toronto, KDKA Pittsburgh, or WSM in Nashville: the clear-channel stations that brought us the familiar voices of Jack Armstrong, Don Winslow, Jack Benny, Fred Allen, Cecil B. DeMille, Wilf Carter, and the Grand Ole Opry.

It would be difficult to overstate the importance of radio in the rural Canada of the Thirties and Forties. It played an indispensable role in our lives, and while it was one thing to devour all the books you could find (don't forget Big Little Books), the radio provided not only entertainment but a direct and immediate link with the wide world outside. My dad made it a habit to tune in CFRB every evening to hear the familiar bugle herald, Jim Hunter, and the news.

Our "local" station was CJKL in Kirkland Lake, which carried CBC programs, including the Saturday night hockey games. Dad and Grandfather developed a ritual around these broadcasts. My father was a fan of the Toronto Maple Leafs and Grandpa was a fan of any team that was *not* the Leafs. Saturday nights when the Leafs won, my dad would call Grandpa on the phone and there would be a lot of teasing and chortling. If the Leafs lost, the phone would ring and my dad would stand there, receiver to his ear, stoically absorbing the ribbing that came from the other end of the line. That good-natured rivalry continued for years.

Those hockey broadcasts, incidentally, were responsible for one of the best merchandising schemes ever to hit this country. Is there a middle-aged man anywhere who did not collect Bee Hive Golden Corn Syrup hockey photos in his youth? I had a collection a couple of inches high, and right on top were Syl Apps, Gordie Drillon, and Bob Davidson. Then there was Turk Broda and Sweeney Shriner, the Metz brothers, Red Horner (the bad boy), and Wally Stanowski—all glorious action pictures, with the players cutting in front of the camera, sticks low and poised, skates sending up a shower of ice that seemed to leap right out at you.

I wonder if Foster Hewitt was ever included in that series of pictures. He certainly ought to have been. Even more than the star players, Foster was a vital part of every *Hockey Night in Canada* broadcast for the vast majority of Canadians who never had, and perhaps never would see the teams in action. He made Maple Leaf Gardens—"where the Boston Bruins are defending the north end to my left and the Toronto Maple Leafs are defending the south end to my right"—palpably real for us.

Mail was also very important to us. Ours was pretty reliable, thanks in large measure to Tommy Drinkle and Dickie Russell. Tommy Drinkle was a weather-beaten, slow-moving, bandy-legged little man with a horse to match. When Tommy came into view down the road, there was always plenty of time for a stroll out to the roadway where the mailbox stood. He used a buggy in summer, equipped with a canopy against the rain and a comfortable leather seat. Tommy snoozed there: his horse, familiar with the route, would trudge along, then stop at a mailbox. Tommy would come awake with a jerk, drop off the mail, and then resume his nap as the horse plodded on to the next stop. Sleep was a bit more difficult in the winter: Tommy's cutter was enclosed in a tent-like affair, and there was a little paper-burning stove inside that had to be stoked from time to time.

Tommy was eventually replaced by Dickie Russell, who was decidedly more modern—he delivered the mail in a Model A Ford. The Model A was not a powerful car. Its little four-cylinder engine would chick, chick, chick, right along on the level, but on the hilly country roads it pooped out as often as not. Dickie had a ritual that took place at the bottom of the hill that separated our place from Goddards'—he'd turn the Model A around, and with easy aplomb, back up the hill. Reverse was the only gear low enough to get him to the top, and even then it was touch-and-go.

* * *

Looking back, I can see how the isolation that had been a defining characteristic of our part of the world was rapidly breaking down during the years of my childhood. The radio helped, but improved communication was also bringing us into closer physical contact with the outside world. Our family's experience of this was, I believe, typical.

In 1937, Dad bought a car. It was a 1929 Whippet, two-tone blue and black with wood-spoked wheels and a spare tire mounted on the back. It had a huge wooden steering wheel, and there were spark and throttle levers on the steering column. The four-cylinder engine would pull it along at a respectable 25 or 30 miles an hour.

It wasn't much of a car in real terms—this was the time of Hupmobiles, Hudson Terraplanes, DeSotos, and Packards: the Model B Ford was as popular as the A had been, and Dodge, Plymouth, and Chevrolet were beginning to make heavy inroads. A Whippet, even then, was something of an antique.

It was, nonetheless, our pride and joy, for now it was a simple 20 or 30 minute drive to New Liskeard. That new mobility made a great change in our lives. I believe it was the beginning of the end of farming for my father. No longer dependent on horses for transportation, I think he began to foresee the day when he would make his living elsewhere, away from home.

For a few more years Father continued to scrabble in the hard clay, bucking the odds, refusing to give up on what he'd put so much sweat into creating. He made his trips to market each week, and the return continued to be meagre. He spent a couple of months each winter in the logging camps to the north of us as well—a harsh way of salting away a little money for the next season. While he was away, Mother, Rod, and I tended the farm, feeding and watering the animals and cleaning their stalls. My mother watched over Rod and me . . . caring, loving.

I saw my first motion picture and met my first genuine, honest-to-goodness celebrity during this period. The movie came first: a temperance organization arrived in a dusty convoy of cars from the south on a swing through Northern Ontario, preaching the evils of drink. I didn't know much about that, but I desperately wanted to see the picture they were going to show in the Hanbury United Church basement.

It turned out to be a faded print of a tear-jerker called *Ten Nights in a Bar-room*. The plot concerned a little girl who missed her father terribly because, after his store closed, he was staying out late . . . at the bar-room. In a plaintive voice, she sang:

"Father, dear father, come home with me now;
The clock in the steeple strikes one.
You said you were coming right home from the shop,
As soon as your day's work was done."

The father became debauched, of course, but then found salvation and returned to his sanctimonious family.

Now that we owned a car, the focus of our summertime outings shifted in the direction of New Liskeard. New Liskeard beach was renowned as one of the best in Northern Ontario. It had a wide stretch of sand, clean, clear water, a race track for trots with a big grandstand, pavilions and hot dog stands, and all sorts of modern conveniences. Companies from as far away as Kirkland Lake held their staff picnics there. It was at a Lakeshore Gold Mine picnic that I met my first celebrity, Whipper Billy Watson. "The Whip" had been wrestling professionally for only a few years, but he was fast becoming one of the country's top attractions. On this occasion, he appeared in a ring set up on the beach baseball diamond, and quickly dispatched his opponent. As the match ended, my father pushed me toward Whipper's corner. As he climbed over the ropes, I reached up and grabbed his hand. He was dripping sweat, his body glistening, and his hand was soft and wet and clammy. I let go. Whipper looked at me and said something like, "Good to see ya, kid," and went on his way. I was thrilled.

Years later, when we were both involved in celebrity snowmobile races, or some such foolishness, I told him the story. He growled, "Couldn't have been me. I'm not that much older than you, Kirck." So naturally whenever we meet now I needle him about that . . . from a safe distance, of course.

Outings to town remained infrequent, however. Our social life revolved around a few close neighbours, and family. Most weekends, we'd visit either Grandma Leverre's house, or the Krick's.

At the Krick house, our behaviour was always a little restrained: I do believe the Kricks considered themselves just slightly above the prevailing social level at Uno Park. That didn't stop Rod and me from having a good time. Over the years, Grandpa had filled the porch on the back of his house with souvenirs and mementoes, and my brother and I never tired of searching for goodies in drawers and cupboards. That's where I got my first pipe. My grandpa kindly gave me an old clay pipe he'd had for years—it was to be used for blowing soap bubbles. It worked for that, too. It also worked well a little later when I discovered that dried-out red clover heads burn almost as well as tobacco.

The atmosphere was less formal at the Leverre farm. My grandmother Leverre was called Mommy by everyone—not "mummy", but "maw-mee." She's been dead for years, but her family still refers to her that way. She was short and fat, with the kind of wrinkled face that has crinkles in the corner of the eyes. She was tough: a shout from her and a swipe of her broom could shoo a hog from the front yard in double-quick time. She could be gentle as an angel when she was drying tears from a kid's cheeks.

Most of my uncles on my mother's side had a wonderful touch with musical instruments. They could all saw away on a fiddle, pick guitar and banjo, play mouth organ, and pound out a tune or two on the piano. Saturday afternoon at Leverre's could develop into a real hoedown. Clayton and Kenny turned out jigs and reels on the fiddles ("Little Burnt Potato" and "Orange Blossom Special"), Maillie whacked away at his guitar, someone else would get out the banjo, and my dad, who was as musical as a crutch, played his jew's-harp. There might even be a bottle of whiskey to sip from. Grandma would soon be out in her kitchen, cooking up a mess of salt pork and fried potatoes, and a big loaf of fresh bread.

Oh, happy days!

Chapter 3

When my father finally decided to give up farming, he got himself a job in New Liskeard driving a snowplough for the Department of Highways. That was in 1939. It wasn't long before we'd sold our livestock and what little we had in the way of farm implements. For the first time, there was a bit of money available.

Rod and I were not eager to leave the farm, but change was inevitable if we were to seek out better opportunities. We moved first to a small house out on the highway: I was close to finishing public school, and my parents thought it would be best to remain near Hanbury until I'd completed senior fourth class (the equivalent of today's grade eight).

The change was not entirely for the worse. Our new home was comfortable, and it was just a short walk from school. I still had my school chums, and Clifford Pettifer was still my buddy. That was important, as I'll explain. I had become a bad smoker. It started with dried clover heads in my grandfather's pipe and despite some unpleasant experiences, I persisted. Once, my mother caught me lighting up in the haymow of our old barn. One spark and the building would have been a goner, and along with it all the hay. I got caught swiping cigarette money from my father's pants pocket. He chased me all over the yard, swinging at me with a willow branch, catching me about every third swipe. He bellowed dire threats . . . I screeched through my tears, more frightened than hurt.

Clifford was a real "friend in need." He was Mrs. Routliffe's nephew or grandson, I can't remember which. At any rate, he had access to the shelves behind the counter in her store, and he could occasionally slip a ten-cent pack of Turrets, Sweet Caporals, or Buckinghams into his pocket.

We'd find a convenient hiding place and puff away like real men, often turning green in the process.

All of that I remember with complete clarity; on another subject, that of my singing career, I'm at a loss. I'd always liked to sing and I had good pitch and tone, though not much control. Somehow, I got singing lessons; and, somehow, I wound up in a music festival and made the front page of the *Temiskaming Speaker*. The date is May 14, 1942, and the headline reads:

HIGH PRAISE GIVEN HANBURY BOY VOCALIST

High tribute to the work of one of the contestants from the country districts who took part in the special Rural Classes at the Temiskaming Festival of Music was paid by the Vocal Adjudicator, George Lambert of the Toronto Conservatory of Music. Speaking of the singing of Harvey Krick of Hanbury, who carried off honours in the Boys' Solo, 14 years and under, and who sang at the concert which concluded the Festival, Mr. Lambert declared this young vocalist possesses what he describes as a "cathedral voice." The adjudicator said that if the boy were living nearer a city he would recommend him to a choir master because of the quality of his singing. Harvey Krick is a son of Mr. and Mrs. Earl Krick and a member of a pioneer family of the Temiskaming District.

As they say in show business, that's probably the best notice I ever had. "Stop look and listen,/ Err you cross the street,/ Use your eyes and ears then,/ Err you use your feet." Could that be the song? I believe it was.

When the school year ended, my family prepared to move into New Liskeard, and I went to work on my grandfather's farm, which was by that time pretty much run by my uncle Cliff.

I guess I was never meant to be a farmer. I could never, for instance, get the hang of building a load of hay. Whenever Cliff pitched and I loaded, we'd get halfway back to the barn and my load would sigh gently and slide down over the sides of the racks onto the ground. This usually happened when we were crossing the log bridge that spanned a small creek, and often the hay would end up in the water. After this had happened a few times, I was permanently assigned to the far tougher job of pitching the hay up onto the wagon, where Cliff would build the load. Once back at the barn, I'd be sent up into the haymow to spread the stuff around as it dropped from the big loading fork. It was hard, dusty, itchy work. The fork would take its big bite of hay from the wagon, rise up to the rafters, and then as often as not glide along the track until it was directly over me, at which point someone on the ground would trip it before I could scramble out of the way. I'd be half-suffocated by the time I'd dug my way out. Times like that, it was easy for me to forget any warm feelings I may have had about farming.

Friday was always get-ready-for-market day. That meant killing chickens. Cliff sold a lot of fresh poultry at the time. I learned how to do the job in a relatively humane way, by inserting the small blade of a jack-knife through the chicken's mouth into its brain. Then you'd cut its throat with a quick flick, to bleed it. Those of you who are still with me may be interested to know that there was a practical, as well as a humanitarian reason for this method. Because it was killed instantly, the bird had no time to tense its muscles, which meant the feathers could be plucked more easily. So it was flick, flick, and a flurry of feathers, through 20 or 30 chickens every Friday. Cliff would keep me entertained through all of this unpleasant work, reciting poems like "The Cremation of Sam McGee" and "The Face on the Bar-room floor." He had a regular storehouse of poetry in his head, and I never ceased to be spellbound by his renditions.

When the haying was completed, it was time to spread the year's accumulation of manure on the field—also my job, of course. At first, it wasn't too bad: I'd back the team and the manure spreader as close to the pile as possible, and work off the top. The stuff was drier and lighter up there. The spreader loaded, I'd take it down the lane to the back field, put the machinery in gear, and the load would spray out the rear, propelled by a steel-toothed cylinder. Now and then a big chunk would get caught in a tooth and spray forward instead of backward. Where I sat driving the team was right on the flight path of these missiles. They were on target often enough. But the drive back for the next load would be a pleasure; draft horses don't move quickly at the best of times, so we'd make our way to the barn at a pleasant amble, the spreader's machinery turned off, its steel wheels crunching on the gravel road, the sun warm and lazy.

Then it was back to the mountain of ooze and its indescribable odour. I swore to Cliff that there must be an accumulation of many years' manure in that pile. He suggested that if that were the case, I might find something interesting at the bottom, so I'd better keep at it. I did, but I didn't find anything.

As the new school year approached, I said goodbye to everyone on the farm and headed for New Liskeard, a bit of hard-earned cash in my pocket and full of excitement at the prospect of beginning high school. Over the holidays, Dad, Mother, and Rod had moved into a big second-storey duplex and were now town folks.

* * *

In the early 1940's, New Liskeard had a population of about 4000. While mainly a farming town, it had two major industries—a lumber company and a foundry. The town had a snobbish air about it, which still seems to me to have been justified. Of the towns in the region (Cobalt, Haileybury, and Englehart were all nearby), New Liskeard had the tidiest streets, the nicest houses, the best stores, and the most affluent population. In preparing this book, I recently spent a few days in the region, and I found no reason to revise my opinion. It's still the prettiest of the lot, and the only one that's seen much growth in the intervening 40 years.

For a young teenager from the farm, town life was a wonder. I revelled in walking on sidewalks, riding my bike on paved streets, and having a store only a five-minute walk away. The high school was just three blocks down the street from our home, and Anderson's soda bar and Greenwood's restaurant were much more interesting hangouts than Mrs. Routliffe's general store.

Our home-room teacher, Zia Crete, was a tall, raven-haired Greek-born lady with a fearful temper. She kept us in line by firing wood-backed blackboard brushes at us when we did something wrong—and she had a deadly arm. Despite her best efforts, I was never to be a particularly good student in high school. I'd done well in public school, but when we moved to town I fell in with a group of boys about my own age and we were always able to find better things to do than study. We played hockey together in winter. I was a big, ungainly defenceman, and I suppose it was my size that kept me on the team because I couldn't handle the puck. In summer we had a baseball team. My spot was second base, where my height was an asset.

By far the most popular organized sport was skiing. The town had a first-class club complete with a comfortable clubhouse, a jump, and a good variety of runs. The only convenience we lacked was a ski lift, but that didn't seem to bother anyone—we herring-boned our way up the hills with the same exuberance that we displayed on the way down.

Those New Liskeard ski hills were the setting for the beginnings of a romance. She was the belle of the high school, a self-assured beauty with a mane of long, dark hair and eyes that sparkled with excitement and a knowledge I could only guess at. Her figure was full and mature, and she had a retinue of lusty young fellows who followed her every move with expectant eyes. Of course, she knew how to use her obvious attractions to pick her companions on her terms; and there were occasional glances in my direction! I was a couple of years younger, and about as debonair and sophisticated as you'd expect a big, clumsy teenage farm kid to be.

There was a long, winding ski trail, far from the centre of the club's activities. She happened to be following me, in a line of several skiers. As we reached an open stretch about half a mile from the clubhouse, I fell. Then she fell, virtually into my arms. The other skiers glided by, and we were left alone. Acting on an impulse of inspired good sense, I grabbed her and kissed her right on the lips. Now the fat was in the fire. There was a lot of groping and tugging and giggling, and some more kissing. But it's not easy to get anything serious going when you're in six feet of snow and bundled up in ski clothes.

For the next year or so, she and I spent a lot of time together exchanging love-lorn looks, sighing, talking, necking, sighing, and talking. She was determined she was going to "save herself" for her marriage . . . and she probably did. In spite of my best juvenile efforts, when I left New Liskeard for Toronto, as far as I know her virtue was still mostly intact.

I joined the New Liskeard High School Band. (My singing career had ended when my "cathedral" voice began to change to something more suited to the shower.) My dad owned a tenor horn: where it came from, I have no idea, but when I announced to the school band leader that I had it, I was immediately enlisted. I learned to read music in a minimal way, and became quite proficient at the marches we played. There was, I admit, an ulterior motive for my enthusiasm: The New Liskeard High School Band wore magnificent uniforms. They were black and gold, topped off by a military-style peaked cap that was white with a black band. The really glorious part was the swirling black cape, lined with gold satin. We were a sight to behold in any parade, our uniforms spotless, our instruments glistening, our marching . . . well, not bad. It was a grand thrill to head up a parade down Whitewood Avenue, the crowds along the sidewalk waving, strains of "Colonel Bogey" echoing through the air.

Much as I was enjoying life in town, there was something missing, though I'm not sure I recognized it at the time. On the farm, home had been the centre of life. Outside activities were generated from home, and usually involved family or close neighbours. The demands of work were more or less constant, and when you did take a break, entertainment consisted of radio, books, and perhaps card games. On the rare occasions when there was an organized activity—a Christmas concert at the school, for instance—it was attended by people for miles around.

In town, there seemed to be more things to do, and at the same time, fewer. While there were plenty of organized events, we seemed to spend a lot of time walking up and down Whitewood Avenue or Armstrong Street looking in shop windows, hanging out in Anderson's Drug Store and Soda Bar, or in Greenwood's restaurant. Another regular time-waster was a walk to the T&NO station to watch the night train arrive, disgorge its passengers, and then move out toward points further north. There were also the bowling alley and the pool room; while few of us had money to play, we spent hours watching those who did. I found it hard to adjust to the aimlessness of town life. The cohesive influence of home and family, so important in rural life, was missing.

Money was still scarce around our house, and I think my dad was beginning to consider moving south. He had a new job, working at the lumber yard, but it had as little future as driving a snowplough. He certainly had no intention of returning to farming, so a move to Toronto seemed logical. My father was a methodical man, and at this stage, he was still thinking about it.

I got a part-time job as a "printer's devil" at the *Temiskaming Speaker*. Cec Bond was the publisher then—overweight, bald, steel-rimmed glasses—and the paper was one of those weeklies that had a small but wide-ranging circulation. It was full of personal columns: "Brethour Township Happenings," or "Thornloe News." Reports on Ladies' Aid meetings were a staple, too, and there were usually a couple of pages of want ads.

Being a printer's devil was not exactly a glamorous newspaper job. It involved mostly cleaning the shop's ancient presses, and my mother would raise Cain with me when I came home, my clothes covered in black, indelible printer's ink. I got some variety when an occasional job printing contract came up. We printed the local telephone books, for instance, and when that happened my job was to run the guillotine that sliced off the ragged edges of the books as they came off the presses. This too was drudgery, though there was a certain thrill in watching that big blade slice through the books like butter, your fingers just inches away from dismemberment. For a while, I envied the staple machine operator, who seemed to me to have a more interesting task on our little assembly line. He got to run a machine that held a magazine of staples that were anywhere up to an inch long; when he pushed a pedal, it fell on the book like a tiger, fired the staples through the paper and folded them behind. My enthusiasm for that job vanished when I saw an operator put a staple through the end of his finger. His hand came away from the bench with a phone book attached.

When I'd grown tired of printer's ink, I got a summer job as caddy master at the New Liskeard Golf Club. I was responsible for cutting and watering the fairways and greens, and looking after the caddy shack, which sold soft drinks, candy bars, and golf balls. I was also supposed to keep track of the young kids who occasionally caddied for the more affluent members.

What I liked most about the job was being able to drive the weird and wonderful tractor that was used to haul the mowers. It was a Model A Ford, cut down so that there was about four feet between the front and rear axles. Wide steel bands had been welded to the rims of the back wheels, and these were studded with short spikes. It was a beautiful contraption, the work of Perry Armstrong, a local garage owner. Not only did I get to drive it while mowing the fairways, but I was given special permission to take it downtown periodically for servicing. After I'd scrounged some golf clubs and learned to play a little, I used it as a golf cart. It was a perfect job, and I might still be there if it hadn't been for the caddy shack. That was what did me in. It didn't take in a great deal of money, but the executive board of the club naturally wanted as much as was theirs. I had too many friends, I think. We'd hang around the shack, sipping pop and eating chocolate bars, and my mind would be on anything but business. When it came time to take stock, there was always a terrible shortfall for which I would be duly, though not too severely, chastised.

* * *

In 1944, my dad had made his decision: he would go to Toronto to look the situation over and see what his prospects were. If he found satisfactory work, he'd send for Rod and me and Mom when he'd had a chance to get established. There were some tearful farewells. Dad had spent many winters in logging camps when we were on the farm, but he had never been very far away. He was always able to come home for the occasional weekend, or if there was some emergency; but this was something different. Our anxiety was coloured by a feeling of anticipation: if Dad were moving to Toronto, could we be far behind?

My father's entry into the work force in Toronto was hardly cause for drumrolls and fanfares. An unskilled labourer from Northern Ontario doesn't make much of a splash in a city bustling with war-time activity. He made an early decision which he always considered one of his shrewdest: he reasoned that many of the positions then available in war plants would disappear when the conflict ended, so he decided to avoid the temptation of an easy job and concentrate instead on finding one that did not depend on the fighting for its future.

His first job was wheeling a big transport rig between Toronto and Montreal: night driving, mostly. That ended one snowy morning when he rolled into the east end of Toronto after an all-night drive. His rig skidded out of control on a grade down to a railway underpass. The trailer jack-knifed and the rig then rolled, coming to rest on its side. Dad crawled out unhurt. When the truck was righted, he continued on to the terminal, picked up his wages and never returned. He continued to drive trucks, but now it was strictly short trips. Hendrie Cartage carried on business handling freight locally for Canadian National Railways, and Dad landed a job there. Before long he became foreman in the department that specialized in moving heavy machinery, a position he was to hold for the next ten years.

With some stability in Dad's job outlook, the rest of the family prepared to move to Toronto. There was high excitement in that old house on Niven Street as my mother, brother, and I prepared for the great adventure. It was a big, big city, and the little I knew about it made it seem the centre of the universe. Foster Hewitt lived in Toronto; the Maple Leafs played there; Jim Hunter worked there.

I had visions of walking the shining streets in the glare of millions of lights reflecting in the huge display windows of a thousand stores. Eaton's and Simpsons were there . . . no more ordering from their glossy catalogues for us. There would be streetcars and buses, like the ones you saw in the pictures in the *Star Weekly*. I might even get to meet Greg Clark and Jimmy Frise. Anything was possible in Toronto!

Bleak reality intruded briefly: it was a time for saying goodbye to the familiar people and places of my childhood—my grandparents' farms, Frank Rose's store, the old farms at Hanbury and the quarry, New Liskeard and all the friends I'd made there.

Ours was a do-it-yourself world, and so while my father worked, a relative drove a borrowed truck up to New Liskeard where Uncle Ken and Uncle Maillie helped us carry our worldly possessions down the long flight of stairs. Loaded up, we immediately set out for the south, my brother and me riding comfortably in the back of the truck on a fat chesterfield.

We moved into an upstairs flat in a house at 1 Classic Avenue, about halfway between Bloor and College Street, a block or two east of Spadina. It was a neat, clean, dead-end street, and a garage right beside our front door served as a backstop for neighbourhood kids who used the pavement as a playground. Ours was the best-looking house on the block. Like the others, it was a big, two-storey brick structure, and the owner, who was Dutch, hadn't lost his old-country passion for paint and scrub brushes. The place sparkled, inside and out. We shared a common entrance, and upstairs, our family had a kitchen, a bathroom, a bedroom, and a living-room, reading from back to front. The living-room doubled as a bedroom for Rod and me. It was small, but it had all the requirements for beginning a home. We'd made it to Toronto.

Soon after we moved in, we had a family conference. This was unusual; Dad had always made most of the decisions without much consultation; but all of our futures were concerned this time. We decided that the first goal would be to get a house of our own, as soon as possible. That would take money.

So it was that I went to work, rather than back to school. I'd been in New Liskeard High School for almost three years, I was big and healthy, and there was no reason why I couldn't help out with the family finances. Mom, too, would find work. Rod, of course, would continue on at school, and he was enrolled forthwith at the Huron Street Public School.

I got a job as a helper on a Hendrie Cartage truck, on my dad's recommendation. It was tough; aside from my summer jobs, I'd never worked a lick in my life, and here I had to answer not only to my boss, but to my father as well. Added to this, I was finding Toronto to be a lonely and intimidating place. I hated getting on the streetcar every day—I felt everyone was staring, sizing up this big, hick kid, so obviously fresh off the farm. That was to improve somewhat when I received my Hendrie hat. It was black and had an official uniform-type air about it. Hendrie Cartage was spelled out in bold letters across the front, just above the peak. When I wore that hat, I swaggered a little.

I had few friends: my school chums had all been left behind in New Liskeard and I was uncomfortable about seeking out places where kids my age might congregate. So I became something of a loner. There was a small theatre down on College Street, and I spent many hours there with John Wayne and Gary Cooper and Jimmy Cagney, indulging my teenage fantasies.

Working for Hendrie was not exactly fulfilling my dreams about life in Toronto either, though there were some interesting times. On one occasion, the driver suggested I back the truck into the loading bay at the Front Street CN sheds. I did so with such enthusiasm that I took a great chunk out of the dock and almost drove the bed of the truck through the cab. I didn't drive much after that. I had another driver whose taste for strong drink almost got us both fired. On a warm summer afternoon, we were sent to Gilbey's Distillery for a load of booze—cases and cases of the stuff. Naturally, one case was dropped. Gin, I think. As the broken bottles slowly leaked onto the truck bed, the driver yelled at me: "C'mon, we can't let this go to waste!" In seconds, we had the tops of our thermos bottles in hand and, while I held the leaking case, he caught the leaking liquor. Now, I wasn't the expert on hard drink that I am today, but this stuff was downright awful. Filtered through the heavy cardboard case, it had a flavour that would knock the palate out of an old Bay Rum drinker. My driver seemed to enjoy it, however, and how was I to say I didn't? It was not one of my better days. On the way back to the sheds, my stomach did a dance at every bump, and turning corners was an ordeal. Finally, I fell asleep in the cab as the truck was unloaded.

Onward and upward: a few months later, I got a job at Standard Casing, a small company on Sorauren Avenue whose business was packing casings for sausages. Where they got all those miles of gut, I never learned. My job was simply to pack wooden pails with the stuff: a layer of casing, a layer of salt, a layer of casing, a layer of salt. Pack it down tight, then seal the pail by hammering a wooden lid in place.

The job was anything but memorable, but it provided my first encounter with an "older woman." She was a voluptuous lady, several years my senior—divorced, I think, and even to me, clearly in need of male companionship. There were a few steamy, though tentative, encounters among the sausage casings in the warehouse and, in due course, I was invited to her apartment. As I had no experience at this kind of thing—none at all—I looked forward to our tryst with a great deal of trepidation. I made it as far as her street, and then walked back and forth outside her place a couple of times. Finally, I screwed up my courage and, stomach churning, walked up the sidewalk to her verandah. I stood there for a moment, and then bolted.

Next morning, with head bowed, I mumbled a shifty-eyed apology and offered some lame excuse for standing her up. Dumb though I was, I caught the frost in the air, and it was clear I'd missed my big chance. Such is life.

Chapter 4

It's 1944: Allied armies are hammering their way across Europe and up the Italian boot. Rifles from Long Branch are firing through French hedgerows; bren-gun carriers from Toronto roll along the dikes of Holland; and the big Lancasters from Malton cloud the skies over Germany wearing RAF roundels. Hurricanes from Fort William, intelligence experts from Camp X at Oshawa, bond drives and scrap drives across the country, all support Canadian soldiers slogging their way toward Germany. The story of Canada's war was being brought to us by men like Charlie Lynch, Bruce West, Ross Munro, and Matthew Halton. Walter Cronkite rode on U.S. daylight bombing missions and wrote purple prose that reached our newspapers through the United Press wire service.

I was learning the intimate details of the war from the likes of Robert Taylor and John Wayne and Spencer Tracy . . . and, incidentally, absorbing massive doses of propaganda in the process. Hollywood created attitudes that were as black and white as its movie prints: Krauts and Japs were bad; everyone else was good. Those movies, with help from the other media, were responsible for creating such racism and intolerance toward the Japanese that there was little or no remorse when Hiroshima and Nagasaki were obliterated by atomic bombs. Only later, when the extent of the pain became known, was there a recognition that perhaps the Japanese were human beings, too.

But in 1944, with the war in Europe mostly won, they were the enemy: brutal, villainous, sub-human—candidates for extermination. And exterminated they were, on thousands of flickering screens across North America. These were action pictures with a geography lesson. We learned about Guadalcanal and Corregidor, about Bataan and the

Marshall Islands and Iwo Jima. And who would ever have thought that Robert Taylor's last stand behind that old Vickers was actually taking place on the back lot of a Hollywood movie studio?

What really riveted me, though, was the voice of the movie newsreel. Win Barron narrated the Canadian version, and his booming voice was one I would later try to emulate. Like Lorne Greene, who was known on CBC radio as "the voice of doom," Barron was an early hero.

I was coming up to my sixteenth birthday, and was working now in the mail room of the *Toronto Star*. There were three classes of workers in the mail room: the mailers, who made a good living wrapping, tying, and labelling bundles of newspapers; the apprentice mailers, who stood to make a good living when they met union qualifications; and the others, who had no status at all. I was one of the others. My job was to snatch papers from the conveyor belts that rumbled through from the pressroom in long, overhead lines and dump them onto steel-sheathed tables at which the mailers worked. Every fiftieth paper was turned at a slight angle, and the belt was unloaded 50 at a time. They were stacked in piles of a hundred, and shoved in the direction of the nearest mailer. A few whips of twine, the snick of a curved knife, worn like a ring on the little finger, the slap of a label, and the papers were slid the length of the table and down a chute to the waiting delivery trucks.

Our foreman, "old Bob," took me in hand and showed me the ropes. He taught me how to maintain a rhythm on the conveyor so my back didn't break, for there was no stopping a press run once it had started, and there were thousands of papers in each edition. Ink right off the presses was still wet, so old Bob warned me to always wear an apron, showed me how to fold paper armbands which protected you from wrist to elbow, and how to make the square paper hats that were worn at a cocky angle by everyone in the mail room.

Later, I moved to the night shift at the *Star*, and was put to work on the *Star Weekly*. It was printed in sections, and our job was to put them together, then count out the papers into bundles for the mailers to tie and label. It was lighter work than on the daily, and there was less supervision. Best of all, we all got to read the colour comics about three days before they hit the streets.

As my personal fortunes improved, so did those of the family. My brother was doing well in his first Toronto school, and my mother had a job. She worked at Connaught Laboratories, which was turning out massive quantities of the new drug, penicillin, for which there was heavy demand in devastated Europe. Dad was already a senior employee at Hendrie Cartage, and he was getting to be an expert in the movement of heavy machinery, working with a crew and a big truck that had all sorts of rollers and cables and winches and other specialized equipment. He liked his work and it was to lead him eventually to the job he would have for the rest of his life.

* * *

I was never much of a fighter, but I learned a little about handling myself at the *Star*. I got into a shoving match one day with a young fellow who was a member of the Junction Gang in Toronto's west end. (Remember street gangs?) There was a jab or two, then some thrashing around on the mail-room floor. Suddenly, I saw the flash of a knife. Others stepped in and ended the fight before any damage was done, but that knife sure as hell scared me, and I didn't mess with him after that. Fortunately, he didn't mess with me, either. Word of the scuffle got around, though, and before long Harry "One-Punch" Stransman paid me a visit. Harry was a pressman at the *Star* who promoted small-time club fights around the city.

"Hey, kid," he said. "Whyn'cha come down to da gym and we'll look yas over."

My total knowledge of boxing amounted to an idea that you kept your left hand out in front of you, and your chin behind your right, but I went off to the gym anyway . . . it was something to do. With Harry looking on, I learned how to keep the light bag swinging and how to land left-right combinations into the heavy bag. I learned how boxers wrap their hands, and that you don't walk in a ring, you shuffle. I even did a little sparring with some of the other hopefuls in Harry's stable.

Happily or unhappily, I had no inclination to hammer anyone else into oblivion. I didn't even want to cut anyone; no killer instinct and lazy to boot. Harry "One-Punch" Stransman abandoned me, and my career as a boxer ended. What little I did learn would stand me in good stead some time later. I'd been having a continuing wrangle with one of my workmates. Frank was a big guy, all muscles you could see, and we just couldn't get along. Rather than go through another rassling match in the mailroom, we decided to be civilized and have it out in the ring. On the chosen night, a gang of us descended on the Broadview YMCA. We took over the ring, chose a referee, and got into the gloves. I wore a pair of shiny satin trunks, and they gave me a kind of professional look, which helped my confidence.

Someone rang a bell, and we shuffled out to the centre of the canvas, waltzing around very stylishly, but not doing a great deal else for the first round. In the second round, Frank threw a punch that connected flush with my nose. I lost my balance and one glove looped in the air, coming down on Frank's head. It wasn't a punch, really, but it set his legs to wobbling. We stood there, my bloody nose, his wobbly legs, and decided that was enough. We became fast friends after that, and remained so until I left Toronto to begin my career in radio.

* * *

Though I had no firm career goal at that time, I was certain that I didn't want to spend the rest of my life as a labourer. I fancied myself sometimes as a writer, working in far-away places—maybe a foreign correspondent. That probably came from reading Ernest Hemingway in *Life*. I thought flying an airplane might be a nice job; that came from seeing *Test Pilot*. It was something different every day. Through it all, though, was a continuing fascination with *those guys*: Wes McKnight, Jim Hunter, Foster Hewitt . . . and the American announcers: Harry Von Zell, Don

Wilson . . . . Being "on the radio" held a persistent appeal, if only as a remote dream.

Unfocussed though my ambitions were, I was nonetheless bent on self-improvement. I listened carefully to the way English was spoken publicly, and on the radio and in the movies. I read avidly and indiscriminately, and often I read aloud, practising my pronounciation and diction. Before long, I was able to express myself with reasonable clarity, and cover up my lack of formal schooling. I had also enrolled in a night course at Shaw Business Schools, where I was supposed to learn how to keep books and type with all ten fingers. I'm still typing with two fingers, but I did manage to absorb the rudiments of bookkeeping.

That landed me my first white-collar job. It was a very junior position at the Imperial Bank of Canada. The branch where I was to work was at Dundas and Jarvis Streets, right on the edge of Toronto's red-light district. It was an area of grotty hotels, the kind that kept a few dingy rooms open upstairs to meet the qualifications for a beverage-room licence. Down-at-the-heel hustlers, no longer able to make the grade further north where the real prostitutes worked, used those rooms by the hour, and pensioners rented them by the month. Sprinkled among the hotels were run-down rooming houses where the poorest of the poor eked out a meagre existence. They were forbidding buildings, and I couldn't imagine what life might be like inside.

On a Monday morning, I arrived at nine o'clock sharp, dressed in a starched white shirt, spiffy tie and suit, and shiny black shoes. The bank was small: to the left of the entrance was the manager's office; straight ahead there was a counter and a teller's cage—a real cage with high bars all around and a wire door at the back that was kept locked. There was an opaque glass screen beside it, and the current account ledger-keeper worked behind that. Then the counter took a sharp turn to the right and hard against the wall was the savings account area, where I would spend the next year of my life.

My job was to maintain the ledger for all the savings accounts, and to keep passbooks up to date. It caused me more than one sleepless night, since books had to be balanced every month-end, and any money lost came out of my own pocket. On a ledger-keeper's salary, it was hard enough to find the money for room and board, let alone pay off a bookkeeping error. (My branch manager was fond of saying the small salary I was earning would be more than made up for when I got my own branch, in maybe 25 years.) Fortunately, I learned quickly to use an adding machine without even looking at the keys, and that undoubtedly saved me a great deal of money, given my congenital incompetence in simple arithmetic.

There were a couple of ancient revolvers in the bank, relics of the days before alarm systems and the police were able to provide adequate protection against hold-ups. Neither had been cleaned in God knows how long and the brass cartridge cases had spread green tarnish over the backs of the cylinders. One of them figured in a minor incident that brought some excitement to our lives, and, in the process, taught me something about myself. One afternoon, just before closing, a man in a threadbare topcoat shoved a note at our teller, announcing a stick-up. The teller, who fancied himself something of a man's man, fumbled around in the till while the hold-up man grew more and more agitated and finally turned and fled. The rest of us looked on, stunned, as Teller grabbed one of the rusty old revolvers from under his counter and kicked open the cage door behind him. By this time, Bandit was outside, scrambling into a car parked at the curb. Teller vaulted the counter, bounded across the lobby, swung open the door and leaped outside onto Dundas Street, gun aimed in the best one-handed Hollywood firing position at the getaway car speeding up Jarvis. We held our breath, waiting to see if he would actually fire. He didn't, and he returned to his cage. The bank was closed, and the staff spent the rest of the afternoon answering police questions. None of us was much help; we'd concentrated more on the teller's futile pursuit than we had on the bad guy. I found that, far from admiring my co-worker's derring-do, I was appalled at his foolishness. Had he fired the gun, it probably would have blown up in his face. And if it hadn't blown up, he would likely have felled some innocent bystander. I decided: no heroics for this banker.

41

Many of our customers were pensioners who could afford nothing better than the cheap rooms in the local hotels and rooming houses. It wasn't long before I was able to put names and faces together, and I'd carry on long and interesting conversations with some of these old-timers while putting their bank books in order. The down-and-outers among them would cash their cheques, bank enough money to pay for necessities for a month, and take the rest in cash, which they would blow on booze. Through one of these unfortunate old men I got to see the inside of one of the infamous Jarvis Street rooming houses.

It was the end of the month. Len Macklem, who kept the current account ledger, and I were working late, trying to pull balances. He was almost as bad at adding and subtracting as I was and so there was a certain empathy between us. Finally, our work done, we closed up the bank and headed home. There was a sloppy, wet snow falling and the grey slush splashed from our galoshes with every step. As we approached the basement entrance of the beverage room of one of the hotels, there was a crash! An old man burst through the door, staggered up the four or five cement steps to the street, and then sagged, face down, to the sidewalk at our feet. Len and I knelt, and rolled him over. He wore a faded greatcoat, stained now from the fall. He had a bump on his forehead which bled a little, and he was drunk as a skunk. We recognized him as one of our regular pensioners and we got him to tell us, through spittle and loose false teeth, where he lived. It turned out to be one of the rooming houses.

We dragged him to his feet and, propping him between us, managed to steer him to his front door a couple of blocks away. Neither Len nor I had any great enthusiasm for actually entering the building, but we couldn't leave our man on the street—he was too drunk to make it inside on his own. So we manhandled him up the stairs and through the front door. The smell inside made me want to gag, and the only light came from a bare bulb halfway down the wide hallway.

"There," the old man said, and he gestured down the hall. As we helped him along, we must have been making a fair bit of noise, because we hadn't gone more than a few steps when a door suddenly opened and a woman stepped out in front of us. She was about 30 and her long, unkempt hair fell over the shoulders of a shabby house-dress, beneath which she was quite obviously wearing nothing at all. She was carrying a dirty-faced baby in diapers on her hip.

"Waddya want?" she asked aggressively.

"We're bringing the old man home." I explained in as friendly a tone as I could muster.

She gave Len and me the once-over.

"Okay . . . in here." She jerked her head to the open door beside her and stepped back, clearing the way.

We stepped into an environment that was so utterly alien to me, it made an impression that has remained vivid for nearly 40 years. There was a living-room, but there was so little light I couldn't make out much detail. We followed on through into the kitchen, where a bare bulb hung from twisted wires. The floor was bare wood and appeared to have been that way forever. The only furniture was a round table, draped by a worn oilcloth, with two chairs tucked under. On the table was a chipped plate that held a dried-out slice of bologna, curling around the edges, and a half-eaten slice of brown bread. A sticky fly strip hung in a corner of the room.

We helped the old man to his room, which was off the kitchen. There was a small iron bed, a cheap dresser and a tattered arm chair, and that's all. No personal effects; nothing on the walls. It was the room of a drowning man, and it made me shiver. Len and I laid him out on the mattress, pulled off his shoes and beat our retreat. As we hurried down the gloomy hallway, the woman called out.

"Say, thanks."

In our fear and ignorance, we didn't answer.

* * *

Our family's years of hard work and sacrifice began to show dividends in the spring of 1946, when Mother and Dad bought a house. We said goodbye to 1 Classic Avenue, and moved to 1057 Davenport Road. It was a narrow house in the Toronto Victorian style, three stories high with a

43

big main-floor verandah and a two-storey screened porch on the back. It cost $3,500—$500 down and the rest on a mortgage.

Dad rented the second floor to a young couple, Jim and Kay Bryant. Jim was an upholsterer's apprentice who played a virtuoso harmonica. I remembered a few chords on the guitar from the old farm days, and we had some wonderful times. Downstairs, Dad moved furniture around until he and Mom had a bedroom where the dining-room had been. My brother and I inhabited the attic. It was an old house, cramped and constantly in need of repair. Still, it provided us with a sense of security we hadn't enjoyed since leaving the farm.

Chapter 5

Banking was becoming boring, and for an 18-year-old, the prospect of a branch of my own in 25 years sounded less and less like a career opportunity, and more and more like a life sentence. An advertisement in the *Star* caught my eye: it was for someone to train as a bookkeeper at a wholesale grocery firm. I found the offices of Higgins and Burke Limited in a row of dingy brick buildings in one of the oldest parts of Toronto, on Front Street east of Yonge. I presented myself to the receptionist and enquired about the ad, and a few minutes later was interviewed by the office manager, Mr. Rippon, and the chief accountant, Mr. Racicot. The session must have gone all right because I was hired as the firm's junior bookkeeper.

It didn't take long to learn that it was not a prestige position. My main task, initially, was to stamp a date alongside a name whenever a cheque came in from an account. My relationship with Mr. Racicot fluctuated according to his mood, and his mood varied according to whether or not I did as I was told, quickly and correctly. Frequently, I would feel a prickle on the back of my neck as I sat hunched over some ledger. Turning, I would catch his baleful, bespectacled glare. As his temper rose, his physical presence seemed to grow until he loomed over me, tufts of his grey hair quivering at the temples, his teeth clenching his pipe stem until I figured either his molars or the stem would have to cave in. At his desk, my error would be pointed out in icy detail, and corrections made slowly and deliberately. I would then be dismissed with a sharp nod. Mr. Racicot was a man of few words.

The building where Higgins and Burke conducted their business had been built when Front Street was one of Toronto's main centres of commerce. The treads on the stairways had been worn hollow by the thousands of work boots that had scuffed up and down over the years, and the old wooden floors creaked and groaned under the weight of tons of cases of foodstuffs. I enjoyed roaming through its many-scented rooms and passageways, for it seemed to be a living remnant of the city's past. Mother Parker's Tea and Coffee was a division of Higgins and Burke, and one corner of the building was pervaded by the rich fragrance of coffee beans being roasted, ground, and blended. In another spot, you were greeted by the tangy smell of fresh teas from around the world. Nearby was the office of Mr. Bain, the tea taster, on whom rested responsibility for the distinctive taste and bouquet of the Mother Parker's blend. I was never made privy to his methods, but it was fascinating to peek through his door while he was at work. He always seemed to have many cups of tea lined up on a long table. He would move slowly down the line, pick up a cup, pinkie cocked in the best finishing school manner, and bring it to his lips. Then would come a decidedly unmannerly sound, an astonishing kind of *sssswwwwwwoooooossshh*, as he drew the tea into his mouth. If that noise happened to catch you off-guard as you walked past Mr. Bain's office, it could give you quite a turn. Now, I suppose, it's all done silently by chemistry and electronic gizmos.

My work was more interesting and varied than it had been at the bank, and I enjoyed it, especially when the company moved to new, modern headquarters in north Toronto, and installed an IBM punch-card inventory system. I was one of a number of employees sent to the new location several weeks before it opened, to help install and test the new equipment. I knew nothing about electronics (and still don't), but I was pretty good at pulling cards from bins, running the sorting machine and pushing the buttons that provided a print-out. Primitive though it may have been in today's terms, it was a far cry from Tony Racicot's fat ledger books. We had a lot of spare time between test runs, and some of us took to racing the forklift trucks in the still-vacant warehouse. This highly entertaining pastime ended when some damage was done and we were all docked several days' pay.

It was during this period that I married for the first time, at the tender age of 18. Maggie had been transferred to Toronto from a small Ontario town where she'd worked as a secretary, and, like me, she'd found difficulty in meeting new people and assimilating. We were both used to the easy friendships of small-town life, and weren't yet able to see that Toronto was really just an agglomeration of small communities. The city's sheer size overwhelmed us. Like many a country-bred couple before us, and I'm sure many to follow, we clung to each other in our loneliness and lack of sophistication. There is comfort, but there are also drawbacks to such an alliance. Horizons narrow and opportunities offered by the city are lost. The real world tends to become more, rather than less, frightening. Later, when the growing-up process widens horizons and adult pressures and responsibilities begin to impinge, the walls of the secure little world you've created inevitably begin to crack. The piper must be paid and the results are often heart-breaking.

When we were married, in late 1947, it seemed an ideal match—and we did have a few good years together. But as we grew up, we grew apart: as we developed some assurance of our individual worth in the world at large, our worth to each other was diminished. We were divorced in 1956 after a long separation, and Maggie went on to new and better things.

One would think that with a new and reasonably interesting job, not to mention a new bride, my life would be full enough. Yet, much as I was enjoying myself, the old radio itch was starting up again. I'd been reading about Lorne Greene and his new Academy of Radio Arts, a training school for actors and announcers he'd set up in a building across the street from the CBC studios. John Drainie, Mavor Moore, and Bud Knapp were among the talented performers there who were teaching people how to "go on the radio." From the first, the school's close ties with the CBC almost guaranteed anyone with a modicum of talent a shot at some work for the Corporation. It was also expensive—too expensive for me on my bookkeeper's salary.

47

Then I discovered the CKEY Drama Workshop. Its stated purpose was to encourage young people to enter the broadcasting profession. Knowing that station owner Jack Kent Cooke seldom made an investment without expecting a return, it seems safe to conclude that there was an unstated purpose as well—to provide the station with free talent for its weekly dramas. Not that that would have concerned me then—what was important was that the workshop seemed ideally suited to my aims, my free time, and my means. Especially my means: it cost nothing. It met once a week at the Trinity Church auditorium, on Trinity Square in downtown Toronto, and after the work sessions, casting took place for a radio play which would be broadcast later that week. Members shared in production chores, as well as making up the cast.

The whole thing was the brainchild of Howard Milsom, an actor, director, and producer of vast experience. Physically, he was an unlikely subject for hero-worship. He was pear-shaped and baggy, and the top half of his round face was mostly obscured by black-rimmed glasses. He was, nonetheless, ideally suited for the role of guru to an extremely diverse group of young people who shared one ambition—to be household names on the radio. Always soft-spoken, he controlled sometimes rowdy sessions in a gentle but firm manner, correcting misinterpretations, improving a line here, and reworking a characterization there. Howard inspired respect, and when he made a suggestion, it was heeded. Although he'd acted with and directed some of the best talent in the country, he was at the same time outside the acting establishment of the day (perhaps "clique" might be a better term), and that added to his stature in our eyes, for we were all outsiders trying to get in.

He gave occasional impromptu talks, but there were no lectures and little concern for theory and formalism. It was a "learn-by-doing" experience. The budget for the entire operation was about $1.98: scripts were all in the public domain, so there were no royalties to pay, and CKEY provided the theatre for workshop sessions and rehearsals, and the studio and air time for our broadcasts.

We students were a pretty motley crew, too. There was Les Rubie, a little round man whom I'm sure looked old the day he was born. Lately, he's become famous as Mr. Hall, the shopkeeper, in television ads and billboards for one of the lotteries. Larry Solway was with us for a while: he was to spend many years as one of the best—and most notorious—talk show hosts in the country. There was Stephanie Wiseman, who was to gain such notoriety in England when, as Stevie Wise the jazz singer, she married the Governor-General of Ghana, Lord Listowell, and became a countess. Jim Barron and Claude Rae, Hazeldine Hall and Iris Cooper all achieved a measure of success in radio and television in later years.

Perhaps the most famous alumnus of the workshop is Harold Town. I've always felt that a truly talented person will be gifted in not just one, but many disciplines. I think Harold would have become famous no matter what route he chose. Even then, he was becoming well known for his paintings, and at the same time was a fine, professional-calibre actor, even in this amateur milieu. There was a commanding presence about him, and it gave him a certain domination over our small group in much the same way, I suspect, as it has given him a dominant position in the artistic community for 30 or more years.

The workshop sessions went on for about three hours, with groups of us reading aloud from dog-eared scripts, prompting and coaching each other. Senior members took the lead, with Howard hovering in the background. After a short intermission, Howard would break out the scripts for that week's broadcast, and the casting process would begin. We all held our breath, hoping for a part, however small, so we could tell the folks at home we were going to be on the radio. Those selected would do a quick read-through, and rehearsal time would be set.

I had apparently some aptitude for all this, because within a few months I was taking part in almost every play presented. It became a serious grind. I worked and lived about an hour's streetcar ride from both the Trinity Square theatre and the CKEY studios (Maggie and I had rented a basement flat in Weston), and it meant I was devoting three full evenings a week to workshop, rehearsal, and the broadcasts. After a year and a half of this, plus a full-time job, I was beginning to wear a little thin at the edges.

By the spring of 1948, I had begun asking some serious questions about the direction my life was taking. Being an actor was a pretty precarious career at that time. I had no feel for stage work, and radio drama was a domain almost exclusive to CBC, where a tight cadre of talented people dominated most productions. It was a virtual closed shop. More and more, my thinking reverted to what I'd wanted to do in the first place—work at a radio station as an announcer. I discussed my misgivings with Les Rubie, who by this time had developed into a fine character actor and was fiercely determined to become a professional. Les volunteered to write on my behalf to a friend of his who'd recently become manager of a radio station in Sault Ste. Marie. The man's name was Basil Scully. I talked this over with Howard, who agreed with me that a solid job in the radio business was a great deal better than an occasional freelance acting call. So I asked Les to write the letter.

Within a few weeks, we had a reply. Les and Howard's glowing recommendations had obviously had an impact: yes, Mr. Scully would like a letter from Mr. Kirk, and an audition, please.

That spelling and pronunciation of my name, incidentally, was the direct responsibility of Howard Milsom. After I'd known him for a couple of weeks, he began calling me Kirk. He didn't make an issue of it; he simply refused to recognize that my name was Harvey Krick. Well, Kirk stuck, until several years later I decided I'd better settle on one name or the other. As a compromise, I transposed a couple of letters in Krick, and it came out Kirck. It was legally changed later.

Howard arranged for me to cut an audition at CKEY. This was before the days of tape, and recordings were all done on acetate discs. I practised and practised, because I'd been warned that once the cutting needle had been dropped onto the disc, there would be no turning back. My mistakes would be permanently and irredeemably etched in the acetate.

I don't remember what I recorded; probably some commercials, some news, and maybe introductions to some records. That's usually the way auditions went. I do recall the sweat on my palms and the trembling of my script as I sat in the CKEY studio—the same studio where some of the best radio people in the country worked. When it was done, I took my precious record, bundled it into a heavily-wrapped parcel and, for better or worse, shipped it off to the Sault.

The wait for a reply was interminable, and with each passing day, the anxiety tightened. When a letter bearing the call letters of the radio station finally arrived, my hands shook so badly I could hardly open the envelope. And then there was a great, euphoric flood of satisfaction, joy, and pride—all those emotions that accompany the realization that a dream is about to come true. Yes, the letter said, there was a staff announcer's position open at CJIC. When could I start?

I went straight out and bought a car—a 12-year-old wreck of an Oldsmobile convertible. After all, I was a radio announcer, so I couldn't very well ride the streetcar; I needed something that would reflect my new status in life. I celebrated with Maggie. I celebrated with my family—my mother full of optimism, my father skeptical, my brother glad to be done with my badgering. I celebrated with my co-workers at Higgins and Burke, and with my friends at the CKEY Drama Workshop, where any success for one was encouragement for all.

My last broadcast for the workshop was a memorable one. It was a play called *A Cask of Amontillado*, and it was a sort of private detective story. Harold Town was a Nero Wolfe-style character, and I played his assistant. Perhaps it was my good fortune that moved the whole cast to a looseness we seldom felt. In any case, Town, self-assured and feeling rascally, began ad-libbing lines to me, and I'd try to reply in kind. He strode around the studio, sometimes off-mike, and I had no choice but to follow. Others in the cast joined in, until poor Howard Milsom, who was producing, threw up his hands. Les Rubie, at the sound effects board, had no idea what to expect next. There was a kind of controlled chaos in the studio, with stifled giggles and the noise of shuffled paper as actors frantically tried to find their places. It worked out right on time, thanks to the genius of Harold Town, whom I suspect knew exactly what he was doing and where he was going. It gave us all an exercise we'd never forget, and it came to be known as one of the best shows the workshop produced.

* * *

Finally, on a bright July morning in 1948, Maggie and I loaded our worldly goods into the '36 Olds, and left Toronto for Sault Ste. Marie.

Chapter 6

In 1948, Sault Ste. Marie was an industrial town of about 25,000 people, most of them dependent on Algoma Steel, Abitibi Lumber, or the Algoma Central Railway for their livelihood. Despite the heavy industry, the city enjoyed a picturesque setting. The St. Mary's River rises out of Lake Superior here, and along the city's waterfront a steady procession of giant freighters, either on their way to, or just back from, the Soo Locks and Lake Huron, crept cautiously through the narrows that separated it from Sault, Michigan. West of the city, the highway meandered along the still-untamed north shore of Lake Superior.

The Windsor Hotel stood in the heart of the Sault commercial district and was one of the city's landmarks. It had started as a country inn but had grown along with the town into a sprawling structure with several wings. It was owned by Algoma Steel, and in its penthouse lived the principal owner of the steelworks, Sir James Dunn. He was seldom seen in town; one presumes his many business interests kept him occupied elswhere, in more salubrious surroundings.

Brock Street ran along one side of the hotel (down to the ferry dock where you caught the boat to Michigan), and it was there that I found the entrance to CJIC, right next to the door to the hotel beer parlour.

My heart sank a little. I'd been expecting something more imposing. But a chat with Basil Scully soon restored my enthusiasm. Although he hadn't been in the business very long, Bas exuded confidence, and left you with the impression he knew everything there was to know about broadcasting.

I had the station tour—it took about four minutes. There was one large studio with one big RCA microphone on a boom, and another suspended over a small wooden desk. A grand piano of uncertain vintage was parked in a corner. Behind a large, double-glazed window was the control room. It was the real working bridge of the radio station. There were two massive turntables, designed to spin the big, 30-inch transcription records from which much of our programming originated. Between them was the operating console. Announcers at CJIC were expected to be their own operators, and so the first thing I had to learn was how to use the control-room machinery. You sat between the turntables, facing the console where there were some dials and switches for controlling levels and opening mikes. There were moments when you needed a little dexterity to place a record on the turntable, cue it to the music, and talk at the same time; but, mostly the cueing was done while the other turntable was in use, and so it was a matter of "announcing," letting the record spin, and then adjusting a pot (or rheostat) to the desired output level. Sounds a little complicated, but it wasn't.

The staff at CJIC was a large one for the size of the station, populated with the kinds of characters you were likely to find at just about any small-town radio station in those days. Grant Hyland was the owner and general manager. He was about as tight-fisted as the rest of his breed, and he had an idea that to pay the production staff more than $30.00 a week would be to set a dangerous precedent. (I was pulling down $27.50.) Dave Irwin was our producer, and he sometimes doubled as announcer: a big, bony man with a smile like sunshine and a heavy thatch of corn-blonde hair. Our news staff consisted of Lionel McAuley, who also worked at the *Sault Star*. He didn't talk in plummy tones, but he knew more about what was happening in the Sault than anybody else. Don Ramsey, who by now must be one of the longest-running country music personalities in broadcasting was also on staff. He had a bad habit of showing up at the station just as he was being introduced on air. There were others, but that will give you the idea.

I quickly found out that at a small radio station, the new guy did everything. I worked the morning show when the regular man was away, handled Don Ramsey's country show when he didn't show up, and also did a lot of " duty announcing," which tended to be pretty humdrum. Since CJIC was a CBC affiliate, we carried the afternoon soap operas, and there would be a tedious stretch when all there was to do was make a station break every 15 minutes. Dave Irwin and I developed a system to combat the boredom. We found that we could make a station break, race downstairs to the hotel beer parlour, belt back a draft, and be back in the studio in time for the next break. Sometimes we alternated, which meant we had time for two drafts. I began to see the wisdom of having the station entrance right next to the hotel beverage room.

Often there was other work to be done during network air time: records were filed, commercials recorded, and sometimes we made sales calls. There was copy to be written, either for newscasts or commercials. Then there were the "Birthday Train"—15 minutes of kids' birthday greetings—and the funeral announcements, sponsored by one of the funeral parlours in town and always done in sonorous, solemn tones.

I'm indebted to Bas Scully for jogging my memory about some of these old friends. He offered me one other thumbnail sketch which I should include here: "Harvey Kirck . . . long and lean, with an excellent voice and delivery, even while learning the ropes. Was often invited to play golf with the boss (Scully) because he was the one the boss was most likely to beat." There is some truth in that assessment—I suspected at the time, and still do, that one of the reasons I was hired was so that Scully would have someone he could order to join him for golf. We played at a place named The Root River Golf Course; we called it "The Pasture," and that's about what it was.

Gradually, I settled into a dream shift, partly because of Scully's passion for golf. I worked over the noon hour as a sort of duty announcer and read a major newscast at 12:30. After that, I was free to do as I wanted until five, except on fine summer days when Scully would frog-march me to the Pasture for a round or two. I had to be back at the station to cover the supper hour and do another newscast at seven.

It was at CJIC that I first learned about the terrible tricks that are played on announcers. A newscaster could be destroyed if the script was left in front of the mike with just the top page loose and the rest stapled firmly to the desk. An unexpected shock could be just as disastrous: on one occasion Dave Irwin fitted a couple of conical wooden spools from the ends of teletype rolls under his glasses, crawled on hands and knees into the main studio, then rose like some spectre from the deep to stare through the control room glass at Don Ramsey, who was on the air with his western music show. Ramsey jumped about a foot in the air, then began to laugh and continued to do so through most of the time slot. The program went on as virtually uninterrupted music, but there was hell to pay the next day about lost commercial time.

Small-town radio was special. There was a close and important relationship with the audience, who depended on you for all sorts of information and for much of their entertainment. And even the young announcers serving apprenticeships became well-known figures—big fish in a small pond, I guess. When Lord Thomson of Fleet was just plain Roy Thomson, he coined a famous aphorism. He owned a string of small stations and he referred to each of them as, "a licence to print money." That turned out to be true for him, but I've always felt it indicated a thoughtless disregard for the audience which identified so closely with those stations.

Although we enjoyed all the fun, those of us who were young and full of ambition took our work very seriously. We had our sights set on jobs in the big time; in Toronto or Vancouver or Montreal, or maybe even New York. We would spend a lot of time practising—reading aloud and learning to lift the words from the paper, a process someone has described as seeing the word, putting it through your brain, and letting it out your mouth as your own, unique utterance. We also spent time trying to emulate the real pros. I learned a lot from two CBC announcers: Earl Cameron and Harry Mannis. Both had the big voices associated with newscasting, and both had cadence, rhythm, and pacing that were wonderful to hear. As a result of my trying to imitate them, CJIC would have a 12:30 newscast with a young voice that sounded vaguely like Harry Mannis, and a newscast at seven read by an "Earl Cameron" in training.

It wasn't professionalism at its best and maybe it sounds a bit slap-dash compared to the way things are done today at the generously equipped schools of broadcast journalism at our community colleges and universities, but that informal apprenticeship program run by the nation's small-town radio stations served its purpose well for hundreds of aspiring young broadcasters.

* * *

Just before my first anniversary at CJIC, I took a vacation, heading south to visit my family in their new house in Ajax, just outside Toronto. On the way, I passed through Barrie, a pretty little town that made its living servicing the resort areas to the north and east, around Georgian Bay and the Kawartha Lakes.

I knew there was a brand-new radio station in Barrie (CKBB), and on the spur of the moment I decided, "why not?" Maybe they had a job for a snappy young announcer. I could by then read a pretty good newscast, and I'd honed my interview skills with perhaps half a dozen celebrity interviews in the Sault—people like Hank Williams, Tony Pastor, and Rosemary Clooney. That, and my experience hosting a live country-and-western music show, I felt, made me an admirable candidate for employment.

CKBB's offices were up a steep flight of stairs, on a second floor of a building on Dunlop Street, whose main floor was occupied by a branch of the Household Finance Company. I introduced myself to the station owner, Ralph Snelgrove, who was universally known as The Boss. It was an appropriate tag: he was a prematurely bald, bustling, bundle of energy, who'd started CKBB from scratch. He ran everything: no matter what title anyone else had at the station, Ralph was really in charge. Only the sales department, headed by the redoubtable Art Harrison, was exempt from the Boss's constant scrutiny.

Ralph Snelgrove didn't believe in fancy auditions.

"You want a job, young fellow?"

"Yes sir," I replied.

"Okay. There's a show on at 1:30. I'm going home for lunch and I'll listen to you. I'll talk to you when I come back."

I was stunned; but before panic could set in, I was hustled off to a meeting with program director Dick Mungham, and the two of us began immediately to set about organizing this show I was to do. We picked some music and I read through the commercials, my mind doing wheelies all the while.

1:30 arrived all too soon, and I found myself sitting in the announce booth, facing Dick through the control room glass. He opened my mike and I started the program. That went fine. Then it was time to introduce the first record, something up-tempo by Percy Faith. With appropriate gusto, and in my most mellifluous announcer's voice, I began: "Here's a rousing virgin of . . . ." Dick winced, and I felt the colour drain from my face. I was devastated. An on-air audition, and I'd blown it in the first two minutes! The rest of the program went reasonably well, with no major gaffes, and I left the announce booth bathed in sweat, to await the return of The Boss.

Ralph came barrelling through the door.

"Come on in here with me," he said, indicating his office. I'd barely settled in my chair when he snapped, "I liked your show. When do you want to start?"

I swallowed the whoop of joy that was struggling to get out. We agreed on a starting date three weeks hence, so that I could give proper notice to the people who'd been so good to me at CJIC. And then, with more than a little trepidation, I broached the subject of money.

"Mr. Snelgrove, what can I expect to be paid here?"

The rest of the conversation is gone from memory, but I can still see the slow transfiguration of Snelgrove's face into a convincing mask of tragedy. I was to learn this was his standard tactic when dealing with staff about money. We settled on a figure—I think it was $35 a week—that was better than what I'd been earning in Sault Ste. Marie and I was thus embarked on the second stage in my apprenticeship.

It was not easy saying goodbye to CJIC and the Sault: I liked the town and I was grateful to Bas Scully and the rest for accepting me into their tight little family. At the same time, it was accepted that ambitious young people like me would inevitably move on, and my resignation was accepted with good grace. So we packed up, Maggie and I, stowing our household stuff on a moving truck, and our personal things in our beat-up '36 Olds.

CKBB was an independent station with no network affiliations, which meant that from sign-on at six a.m. to sign-off at midnight, all its programming was produced internally, using the station's own facilities and talent. Announcers were expected to fill a lot more air time than we'd had to at CJIC, where CBC programming had eaten up a lot of time each afternoon and evening. Music was the staple, but the Barrie station was the most community-oriented of any I worked for. This was an enormous boon to me, because it guaranteed I'd have a wide variety of duties—exactly the kind of experience I needed.

I was assigned to the morning shift. That meant signing on the station at six a.m., doing the wake-up show, reading the news on the hour and doing a major, ten-minute newscast at eight. News again at nine, then off for awhile. Breakfast. Then, over the noon hour, a fifteen-minute newscast and whatever else needed to be done. That was the basic shift, but the work didn't end there.

CKBB had a summer program called "Voices on Vacation," which became my responsibility. It involved running around to the various hotels and resorts, interviewing visitors. The station had some of the new-fangled tape recorders that were just making their appearance, and the raw interviews were brought back to the station to be spliced together to make an hour-long program. Depending on how well you planned, that could amount to a three or four-hour chore. And then there was "A Penny for Your Thoughts." When I arrived, it belonged to Tom Daley, a big, heavy-set fellow of 22 or 23, on his way like me to eventual stardom. When Tom left Barrie for London, Ontario, I inherited the show and the task of cornering passersby on the street and getting them to answer the question of the day. They got a penny for their trouble. Hot stuff!

PFYT travelled around a lot. It would go to strawberry festivals, to high-school functions, to Camp Borden and Oro Station and Egbert and a lot of other little places in the region. I'd head out in the station's 1949 Ford wagon and try to get the program done before it got too late, because I had to be at work at five the next morning to sign the station on at six.

Pete Griffin, who nowadays is perhaps best known as half of the Pete 'n' Geets craziness in Toronto, worked the night shift at CKBB. I quickly learned he was not to be trusted. One night after signing off the station, he opened all the pots and switches so that every microphone in the place was live. Next morning, anyone who happened to have a radio on before the normal sign-on time was treated to the sound of me opening the front door, trudging up the long flight of stairs, whistling, banging doors, ripping wire copy, greeting the cleaning lady with idle chit-chat, walking into the control room and then muttering expletives to myself as I noticed the VU meters wagging their needles at the slightest sound. The cleaning lady and I were news all over town that day.

Pete and I both got a sample of Ralph Snelgrove's explosive temper one night when I'd returned late to the station after taping PFYT. I leaned over the desk toward Pete's mike and we had a little on-air conversation between records. It went on for ten or fifteen minutes. Later on, as I was about to leave for home, we heard a crash as the front door opened. Then, footsteps pounded up the stairs and down the hall and finally a red-faced Snelgrove burst into the control room. He didn't think much of the conversation we'd had, and he spent the next ten minutes letting us know how stupid, inane, idiotic and nonsensical he thought it had been. Then he stalked over to his office and slammed the door. For the next ten minutes, Pete and I went quietly and sheepishly about our business. Then Snelgrove yanked open his office door and barged into the control room again, his face merely pink now. He growled: "If you two clowns have to have one of your dumb conversations, at least get close enough to the microphone to be heard. I drove all the way in from Minet's Point, and all I could hear was mumbling."

With that, The Boss walked out, and we never heard about the incident again.

* * *

If Sault Ste. Marie was a good place to start a career, Barrie was an ideal waypoint. Many of those who'd worked at CJIC had been locals, with little or no interest in moving on, but almost everybody at CKBB was from somewhere else, and we were all looking for ways to further our careers.

Bill Hewitt was a case in point. He was CKBB's sportscaster when I arrived, paying his dues for when he'd take over from his father, Foster, as the play-by-play voice of *Hockey Night in Canada*. I felt a twinge of nostalgia when I was introduced to him: when Bill was just a little guy growing up, Foster would occasionally bring him to the gondola at Maple Leaf Gardens and get him to call a few minutes of the game. On a couple of those occasions, I'd been listening back home on the farm, consumed with envy.

Bill's successor was a skinny blonde kid who was hired on the basis of his self-advertising as an expert on play-by-play hockey commentary. Dave Wright was brash and full of confidence, and it wasn't until later that we learned he'd never called a hockey game in his life. By that time he'd become so good at it that nobody minded the lie. Dave was unstoppable: in one of the OHA towns, he discovered there was no place in the arena for him to set up his mike, so he climbed into the roof beams and did his play-by-play from up there. Dave is now a mainstay of the CHUM group, working in Halifax.

Bill Maynard was the odd man out in our upwardly mobile crew. He was a local boy, who did a country-and-western disc-jockey show. He had to be one of the worst announcers ever to get on the air. I guess somebody finally told him that because he eventually left the business, which I suppose was a good thing for him; but at the same time his leaving made me a little sad. He was a great, big ploughboy with heart and soul, he loved what he was doing, and his homely attitude could have been an asset

61

to the industry, if it could only have found a place for him. He later became a successful oil company executive.

There were others, but the special person for me was Pete Griffin. He had a sense of humour even then that could only be described as bizarre. Compared to him, I was straight as an arrow, but we became friends and have remained so through the years. Pete applied for a job in Calgary, at CKXL, a station that was patterning itself after CKEY in Toronto, which in turn was using a very successful formula developed in New York. It was the disc jockey as celebrity, with the music taking a back-seat role to the on-air personality; lots of time and weather checks, news on the hour, and a strictly controlled amount of chatter. His application was accepted—apparently the management in Calgary knew very little about this brilliant, but undisciplined young announcer they were hiring. In any case, after long and beery goodbyes, he climbed aboard a train and headed west.

After Griffin's departure late in '49, life at CKBB wasn't the same for me. I enjoyed the work—but living at the poverty line was beginning to get me down. I couldn't even afford a car. You'd have had a hard time convincing me then, but I realize now that the experience I was gaining was worth more than money. Ralph Snelgrove and his brother Bert (the station's general-manager) ensured that if there was something happening within range of its transmitters, CKBB was there. No doubt they recognized the potential value of their market, and in time they had a very lucrative operation on their hands. That does not detract from the fact that they built it with class and an admirable sense of community responsibility.

As for me, pushed by lusty ambition, I was anxious to move onward and upward.

Chapter 7

A letter arrived. It was from Jack Stewart, who said he was program manager at CKXL in Calgary and had been hearing some great things about me from a young man he'd recently hired—Peter Griffin by name. Would I agree to submit an audition tape? He was offering a good salary, and he said the station was looking for someone who could become the "Keith Sandy of Calgary," hosting a prime-time program of recorded music.

My God! They wanted me for that? Keith Sandy was one of the biggest names in Toronto radio in the early Fifties, the host of CKEY's "Make-Believe Ballroom." Impossible! But here was the offer, in black and white: I had to give it a shot.

I worked up an audition, copying a segment of the "Ballroom" from CKEY, and including a couple of commercials and some bits of newscasts. I sent it off; and within a couple of weeks I had a firm offer, which I accepted by return mail.

Once again, though, I was to find it difficult to leave my friends and colleagues. Barrie had been a delightful place to live, within sight of some of the finest resort country in Canada and only about 45 minutes from Toronto. It was obvious even in 1949-50 that it would grow into a colourful and interesting community. I still remember my days in Barrie as some of the finest I've spent in the broadcasting business.

I was also, I admit, feeling apprehensive. I had less than two years' experience, and yet I was going as a key member of CKXL's staff to a major city where there were a number of competing stations. I was acutely aware that there were hundreds of other young people out there, just as eager and perhaps better qualified than me. Then there was the matter of moving a couple of thousand miles away from all that I was familiar with. I'd never been anywhere outside Ontario, and I had no idea what to expect. I was about as sophisticated as a pup-dog.

Cockiness won out in the end, though it was a qualified victory: we decided that Maggie should stay behind with my parents while I headed west to scout the lay of the land and find a place to live. She was interested in a writing career, and I was to check out the possibilities at the local newspapers.

Even on my new salary, there was no question of buying a car or flying to Calgary; it was to be a three-day trip by train, chugging through Northern Ontario, past the flatlands near my home town, into the bush on the north shore of Lake Superior, through the Lake of the Woods wilderness, and on toward Winnipeg and then Calgary.

My friend Pete Griffin met me at the railway station. He was bubbling with excitement, and in retrospect I think it was more than the simple pleasure of being reunited with an old friend—he was just glad to be greeting another Easterner. We traded gossip, but all I could get Griffin to say about Calgary was: "Strange town." That disturbed me some.

We went directly to the studios on Ninth Avenue, kitty-corner to the magnificent, old Palliser Hotel. There were some railway tracks across the street and, looking south, the older part of the city—"the other side of the tracks." I noted that the radio station was perilously close to the dividing line. It occupied a two-storey building, with sales and general offices on the main floor, and the studios and production facilities on the second. Pete turned me over to Jack Stewart, the program manager who'd written me in Barrie. He was a man of indeterminate age, soft and bulky, with a smile that was almost shy. His eyes hung low in their sockets and were underlined with dark smudges; he combed his black, brilliantined hair straight back like a silent movie villain.

"Welcome," he said, and gripped my hand.

My confidence was somewhat shaken when he took me on the mandatory station tour. If Jack Stewart was a man who appeared to have been run over by a few of life's sixteen-wheelers, he had nothing on the station. It was not a bad plant, in terms of its equipment. But it had a shabby look about it, as if it had been roughed up by an Alberta dust storm. This was particularly true of the production areas; the offices on the main floor were better maintained. There was a tendency in some radio operations to consider the production side the part that spends money, and the sales and executive side the part that brings money in. The decor I was seeing seemed to me to reflect that attitude.

I met some of the staff. Fred Shaw was the general manager, a man in his late forties. He was something of an enigma to the production staff upstairs, who were bemused by his habit of slapping his thigh, hand in pocket, while muttering "Dynamite!" for no apparent reason.

The sales manager was Bruce Alloway, a cool, dapper young fellow who was always immaculately groomed. I found him a little stand-offish at the time, but when I met him years later as president of CFRN-TV in Edmonton, I discovered an affable and generous man.

The announcers I would work with were a motley crew, some of them young and ambitious, some older and prone to cynicism and nostalgia. Guy Vaughan was one of my favourites. He was the chief newscaster, and he spoke in a very loud, authoritative voice, affecting a *veddy* British accent. When he emphasized a word, spittle would fog the air in front of him. I always felt that Guy should have wiped off the microphone and desk when he finished a broadcast. He was a big man, massive in head and shoulders with a bristling moustache and a commanding manner, and so I never made the suggestion. Guy spent a lot of his time in company with the Mills Brothers, a couple of hard-case tag-team wrestlers who kept in shape by spending afternoons in a saloon near the station, slugging back draft beer. For all his idiosyncrasies, Guy was a fine newsman, and he really wasn't as ferocious as he seemed. Pete LaValley was the other half of the news team, and, at least in appearance, he was a suitable match for Guy: a swarthy, raw-boned man, he had a bad scar on his face that made him look a little frightening.

Then there was Steve Woodman, *aka* Squeaky, the Elf. Steve was a dinky little guy who couldn't have weighed more then 120 pounds; but he had a big voice and a strange and wonderful sense of humour. He was a talented musician, and each afternoon, he did a program in which he played the piano and organ, and carried on crazy conversations with his friend Squeaky and some of Squeaky's elfish friends. Normally, Steve did all the voices, but he'd occasionally call on the assistance of that other irrepressible crackpot, Pete Griffin. The hour was a wonderful bit of improvised nonsense. On one of the rare occasions when I was invited to participate, I spent the whole time panting and barking like a dog. (Don't ask me what for.)

I found it interesting, and a little puzzling, moving to a station populated by radio personalities that were very well known in the West. Some of them had been around for years, and yet I'd never heard of them—nor, I suspect, had anyone else in the East. These men and women tended to stay in their own backyard, gaining their education and experience in the West and remaining there throughout their careers. They had a certain mobility, but it stopped at the Manitoba border. George Collins was a prime example. He was a fine announcer who'd knocked around in the business for years out west. He could have worked in any metropolitan centre, yet he chose to stay close to home.

I found a grimy little apartment on the south side of town, near the Stampede grounds. The fancy Stampede Corral had yet to be built, and the neighbourhood was a close approximation of a slum. Maggie arrived and found herself a secretary's job, while waiting for a chance at one of the city's two newspapers.

My work went well, though I wasn't really happy being a disc-jockey. I put on the smoothest delivery I could muster and "Make Believe Ballroom" rolled along satisfactorily through two hours in the morning and two more over the supper hour. That was a lot of air time for a green announcer, but it was just what I needed. I had no intention of staying in Calgary for long; my plan was to move to a major broadcasting centre as soon as I was ready, and I meant to be ready soon.

* * *

In the meantime, I was learning a thing or two about the business they didn't teach me in Barrie or the Sault.

Ken Foss was our sports man, an acerbic, pug-nosed guy who looked as though he should have been—perhaps had been—a prize fighter. He was an absolute genius at what was called"recreated sports." It was a penny-pinching way to cover sporting events in distant cities, and it involved obtaining a coded summary of the action by ticker-tape supplied by a trained telegraph operator. The sportscaster would call the game, play by play, based on what the tape was telling him, while a sound-effects record provided the crowd noise. The sound of a bat striking a ball could be simulated by rapping the announcer's desk with a pencil. (Ronald Reagan likes to reminisce about doing recreated sports early in his career.)

One evening, Foss was calling a particularly lacklustre hockey game and decided to get it over with a little early. He wound up the game two minutes before the clock had run out, and went into his three-star selection. At the distant arena, however, the game had picked up, and a goal was scored. Confusion. Panic. Then Foss cranked up the canned crowd noise and said something like this:

"Ladies and gentlemen, there is some confusion on the ice . . . it seems there is a problem with the official clock. No . . . yes . . . there is time left . . . there is another two minutes left in the game! It seems to be cleared up, and we're ready for the face-off."

He then went on to call the last two minutes of the game. As far as I know, there wasn't a soul in the audience any the wiser—except those admiring young guys at the station.

There were groupies in those days, though we didn't call them that. One who comes immediately to mind is the Plumber's wife. She was an attractive woman of perhaps 40, who fell in love with each of us in turn. Her adventures had an abrupt ending when her latest conquest among the staff was taking her home late one night in a cab. The Plumber was supposed to be out on a job, but he appeared in full, roaring fury in the doorway of the house as the two were climbing out of the car. The announcer leaped back in the cab and departed at high speed, and the Plumber's wife never came by again.

The cab in question had been driven by Old Nev (I never knew his real name), who ran a cab stand from a tiny office on the main floor of the CKXL building. He was short and pear-shaped from years of sitting in a car, and he had a great heart. When any of us needed a couple of bucks before pay-day, we knew Nev was good for a touch. Few of us could afford cars, so Nev was called to the rescue in rain or in snowstorms, or if we were late for an early shift.

The other survival unit in the district was McCrohan's Restaurant. It was a clean, no-nonsense place, across the street from the Palliser, and they served a hearty and delicious chili with lots of crackers on the side. I have little doubt that if McCrohan's had not been there, more than a few CKXL announcers would have starved to death.

As he has wherever he's worked, it was Peter Griffin who created the true legends at CKXL. The station's chief engineer, a man named Ross, had a proprietary love of his equipment, and probably would have been happier as curator of a museum. At any rate, he kept it in top condition, and permitted the production staff to use it only because he had to. His pride and joy was an old RCA ribbon microphone that he'd sent to Toronto for reconditioning and then lovingly installed in the main studio, where it shone like the day it was minted. Pete and Steve Woodman were doing their afternoon nonsense one day while a terrific dust storm swirled outside, rattling the studio windows overlooking Ninth Avenue. One of them mentioned how windy it was, and that sparked off a series of ad-libs that ended when one of them said: "Why don't we show the folks just how windy it is?"

With that, they yanked open a window and stuck the shiny microphone out into the gale. A ribbon mike is a delicate instrument, the four-inch strip of metal—the ribbon—mounted with precision to pick up the minute vibrations in the air caused by an announcer's voice. The wind outside snapped it into an arc so extreme that no sound at all registered. Ross, listening in his office, went apoplectic. Fortunately, the thing continued to function when Griffin and Woodman brought it back inside, and the only real harm done was to Ross's nerves.

That was, I believe, the beginning of Griffin's decline from favour at CKXL. Of course, the Goolies didn't help. Pete invented them one night on the graveyard shift. To ease the boredom, he reported to his listeners that funny little "things" were overrunning his control room. He never described them, but after that he got to blaming all sorts of problems on them. The Goolies caused technical hitches and dead air. They were what caused the wrong records to come up, and they incited giggling fits in announcers. It was pure lunacy, but the listeners ate it up, and Goolies worked their way into Calgary folklore. The station manager was less appreciative than the audience. The bosses saw it as another example of the dangerous antics of a loose cannon.

It was an incident in which Griffin was entirely innocent that finally stretched management's limits of tolerance to the breaking point. It happened during another boring overnight shift. Griffin was the only person in the station, and he needed a lunch break. CKXL possessed a Webcor tape recorder, but the engineers never allowed it to be employed for any useful purpose, like recording a half-hour program to give an announcer a break. For that purpose, they'd make up instead a 15-minute acetate disc, which gave Griffin just enough time to run downstairs, sprint over to McCrohans, pick up coffee and doughnuts, and get back to the studio before the record ended. On the night in question, the main door locked behind him on the way out. Pete didn't notice this until he returned, loaded down with coffee and a sandwich, and found he couldn't get back inside. He had to think fast, because there wasn't much time left on the disc. Stashing his food, he raced across to the Palliser, burst into the lobby and demanded to see the janitor. Night clerks at the Palliser didn't take kindly to wild-eyed young men making strange demands in the dead of night: there was some delay.

Pete checks his watch . . . two minutes left on the record.

Finally, a janitor is found, and Pete explains the problem: he needs a ladder to get to the open window of the second-floor studio.

The janitor is skeptical, but he shuffles off dutifully into the bowels of the hotel and, minutes later, reappears with a long ladder.

By now, the record has reached its end. Listeners are hearing *kshew, kshew, kshew, kshew,* as the needle drops off the end of the grooves at the centre of the disc.

About ten minutes later, Griffin and the janitor reach the street below the window and Griffin scrambles up the ladder.

Kshew, kshew, kshew, kshew.

With poise and aplomb, Griffin gives a time check, a station break, and continues on as though nothing had happened.

Soon after that, he was fired. But his adventures didn't stop. Pete had relatives in Vancouver, and he decided to pay them a visit. Out of work, he used the only method of transportation he could afford—he hitch-hiked. It was a season of bad forest fires in Alberta and B.C. In the foothills of the Rockies, he was picked up by a man driving a half-ton truck.

The driver turned out to be a forestry officer, and he promptly drafted Griffin into his fire-fighting crew.

A day's drive into the bush, Pete was put to work. He was a bad fire-fighter, so they made him assistant cook. His chores were relatively simple, he had all the food he could eat, and he was a comfortable distance from the fire front. There was even a certain romance about being shanghaied into a fire-fighting outfit. But misfortune struck: he spilled a tub of hot soup over his foot and wound up in hospital. Pete was shipped back to Calgary, where he faced the task of explaining to his friends how he came to be burned while several miles from the fire he was fighting.

He did eventually make it to Vancouver, and when his visit ended, he decided it would be a lot simpler to make the return trip to Calgary by rail. Of course, he couldn't afford a ticket, so he hopped on a flat-bed rail car that was laden with steel bars. The sun was shining and the steel radiated a pleasant warmth as the train rumbled into the mountains and began its long ascent, smoke from the coal-burning engine billowing overhead. Higher and higher it strained, as Pete dozed contentedly, lulled by the rocking of the flatcar and the clickity-clack of its wheels. He awoke with a start some time later, to see the gaping maw of a tunnel looming up, and before he could react, he was inside it. The smoke no longer billowed picturesquely overhead—it was all around him, thick, choking, rancid, and full of great chunks of soot.

For miles, the train laboured in darkness, while Pete hung on and tried to keep from suffocating.

Then, just when he thought he was a goner, he was bathed in light as the train emerged suddenly into blinding sunlight, high up in a snowy alpine meadow. Just as suddenly, it was freezing cold.

In my apartment in Calgary, Maggie and I were spending a quiet evening at home. There was a knock at the door. I opened it to find an apparition standing before me. It was so black I could scarcely make it out against the darkness in the street. I could see clothing, but that was black too. A pair of eyes showed, and a flash of white teeth. Then, a familiar voice.

"Mind if I use your shower?"

Pete peeled off his clothes, Maggie tossed them in the garbage, and he had his shower. It took most of the rest of the night for him to recount his adventure.

* * *

Through all the fun and games, I continued to work diligently at my craft. "Make Believe Ballroom" (MBB) had been dropped in a format change, and I was assigned to another shift, which included a couple of newscasts. That was fine with me: I'd never considered myself much of a DJ, though the MBB had given me several months of long hours on the air and a chance to hone my delivery on the many commercials it carried. I still practised, as I had before, reading aloud whatever came to hand, but my self-education program was beginning to take on a slightly different focus. I realized that my lack of formal schooling would become a handicap if I was to realize some of my dreams. I started a new round of reading—better books by better authors, and I began to seriously study their style. I read every page of the newspapers, and spent hours in the newsroom, rewriting wire copy, learning the basics of newswriting. I learned from my more-experienced colleagues, watching, listening, asking questions. I listened with an increasingly critical ear to every voice on the radio, especially on the CBC and those big American stations, studying tone, inflection, and pacing.

71

Gradually, my self-consciousness left me, and I was able to open a mike and experiment with style and technique. Read this part fast, slow the pace here, emphasize this word, throw that one away. By scratching the backs of the engineers, I was able to use the tape recorder, recording and playing back, and then doing it over again, doing it better.

I found I didn't like the sound of my voice. It seemed thin and tinny: it lacked timbre and resonance. I told myself that this was normal, that few people like the way they sound on tape, because what they hear is very different from the sound they're used to, mediated by the bones and cavities of the head. That rationalization worked for a while, but the quality of my voice was to become such an obsession that, a few years later, I took some singing lessons at the Royal Conservatory of Music, in Toronto. My teacher put me through the scales and gave me all the big Broadway songs to sing: "Some Enchanted Evening," and "Oklahoma!" It was supposed to improve my range. I don't know whether it did or not. I certainly didn't learn much about singing.

* * *

The 1950 Calgary Stampede came and went, and I had a front-row seat, since every radio station in town competed with remote broadcasts from the grounds. I interviewed everyone from bronc busters to Indian chiefs to tourists from Arizona. I watched chuckwagon races and wore a Stetson. I learned a lesson in Western boosterism: during the Stampede, everyone in town affected a Texan drawl and wore high-heeled boots and Roy Rogers shirts. It was a time when the newly rich oil capital went back to its origins, unabashedly displaying its cow-town roots. I had one big complaint, which I made public on the radio. I said that the chuckwagons that dotted downtown intersections were selling half-cooked bacon and soggy flapjacks. It was true, but no one would back me up. After all, this was the Calgary Stampede, and everything was great!

Looking back, I suppose that experience, trivial though it may seem now, contributed to my growing restlessness, to the longing to return to the part of the country where

I felt most at home, to what we called "Back East." I found myself thinking of Calgary as a pretentious prairie town that would still be a collection of grain elevators and feed-lots, were it not for the incredible oil windfall of Leduc.

I taped some work that I felt would make a good audition, then asked our engineer if he'd cut it to a disc. At that point, I was still speculating as to where I'd send it.

Back in the Drama Workshop days, I had met CKEY's program manager, Don Insley. I'd heard since that CKEY had a management contract with a station in Ottawa, CKOY. I mulled that over for several days. Ottawa might not be bad. I hadn't a hope of getting on at a Toronto station at this stage, but a job at CKOY might be a good jumping-off point for later on. I wrote a long letter, outlining my vast experience as a broadcaster—all two-and-a-half years of it. Then I crossed my fingers and mailed the letter, along with the audition disc, to Insley. I didn't hold out much hope, but it made me feel better to have taken a step toward going back home—to have made a kind of commitment to myself.

In due time, a reply arrived, signed by Insley. I had to read it twice before it registered: he was offering me a job in Toronto! There was no opening at CKOY at the moment, he said, but CKEY was in need of a duty announcer. Would I be interested?

"Interested" was a woefully inadequate word to describe my reaction. Here was what every young announcer dreamed of . . . a job in the Big Time (even if I didn't exactly know what a "duty" anouncer was). I was going from $50 a week to who knew how much money. And at CKEY—*the* station, home of Stu Kenny, Keith Sandy, Mickey Lester, Frank Armstrong, Howard Cooney, Joe Crysdale, Hal Kelly, Lorne Greene, Joel Aldred. The best . . . and I was going to be one of them!

Chapter 8

This time, Toronto felt like home. Hell, I wasn't a country kid anymore—I'd been around. And I was a radio announcer.

If Toronto no longer intimidated me, the idea of competing with the likes of Jack Dennett, Wally Crouter, Gordon Sinclair, Wes McKnight, John Rae, and Elwood Glover, did. I was scared stiff. The fact that I was joining a Jack Kent Cooke operation did nothing to ease my anxiety. Cooke owned CKEY, the Toronto Maple Leaf baseball team, a Triple-A club, *Liberty* magazine, and God knows what else. He'd been in radio from its earliest days, and he had a reputation for breathing fire and brimstone on anyone who did not measure up 100 percent of the time.

CKEY's studios were squeezed into a long, narrow, three-storey building on University Avenue, just below Dundas. The basement housed news, engineering, and Don Insley's office; the main floor, reception, studios, copywriters, traffic; the second and third floors, sales and the inner sanctum of Jack Kent Cooke.

I walked up the couple of steps to the front door and pulled it open. Inside, were two or three more steps up to the reception area where, seated primly at a small telephone switchboard console, was a striking blonde with laughing eyes, and the biggest chest I'd ever seen.

She smiled at me. "What can I do for you, young man?"

I thought of a lot of things. When I opened my mouth to speak, nothing came out. I tried again.

"I'd like to see Mr. Insley, please."

She plugged a patch cord into her switchboard and told someone there was a young man to see Don.

A moment later, Insley was there—young, stocky, blonde brushcut, a round and pleasant face—his hand outstretched.

"You must be Harvey Kirck. Welcome."

I decided then and there that if I were going to entrust my budding career to anyone, this would be the man. My first impression was borne out when I got to know him. Don Insley was the kind of man who took a paternal interest in everyone on the staff: he was not only the program director; he was father confessor, Dutch uncle, and advisor to anyone who needed help.

Aware of my nervousness, he started the conversation easily.

"That's Miriam." He nodded in the direction of the receptionist. "Everyone who comes in here goes a little vacant when they speak to her."

I began to relax a little.

Insley led me down a flight of stairs and along a narrow corridor to his tiny office. It was littered with newspapers, magazines, and back issues of *Billboard* and *Variety*. The walls were hung with plaques and photographs, including a picture of a very pretty woman whom he said was his wife, Marnie.

He assigned me to the afternoon shift, from four to midnight, and told me I'd start off by making station breaks.

"But we'll give you a few days to look around and meet the fellows. I'll tell you when you start."

That was the first sign I was involved with a truly professional operation. I took note of the second during the time I spent hanging around the studios, watching and learning: this station didn't have any operator-announcers. Here, the announcer sat in a studio at a small desk that was equipped with a microphone, and a switch to turn it on and off, along with a "cough button." An operator sat beyond a large, double-glazed window, and he did the production work, cueing records and setting up commercial discs. The announcer's job was to keep track of the log, make sure that commercial spots went in on time, and . . . be charming.

It seemed to me to be the height of luxury, but in fact the arrangement made sound operating sense. Radio time was not cheap, and the system allowed the person on the air to use it to best advantage. He could give his undivided attention to the job he was trained to do—to sell the advertiser's product effectively, and to provide the audience with polished, professional entertainment and information.

After three days of observing, word came from Insley that I was to start work. I was to read a 30-second commercial at the bottom of the clock, then make a station break leading into Keith Sandy's "Make Believe Ballroom." As the second hand whittled away the last few moments, and I fought to control my nervousness, my mouth went dry and my tongue seemed to be developing a case of *rigor mortis*. Then, my cue, and I snapped into automatic pilot, reading through the spot without a hitch. A pause, and then: "Dial 580, CKEY, Toronto."

I'd done it and it hadn't hurt a bit! I was excited, and very, very pleased with myself.

For the next two hours, I sat opposite Keith Sandy, marvelling at his manner at the mike. The program was divided into a series of ten to fifteen-minute segments, each featuring a band and guest vocalist. The musicians were supposedly on a revolving bandstand, and Sandy would bridge from one to the other. I'd read a commercial during each break, and do a station ID.

Sandy was a man who could only be described as "suave." Not a hair on his head was out of place, and he sported a neat, black moustache. His clothes fit with a perfection only an expensive tailor can achieve. When he spoke, the flow of words was smooth and controlled, with just the right emphasis. He sounded as though his throat had been lubricated with 10W30. He could sell anything from deoderant to bank loans with equal aplomb, and I seriously doubt whether we'll ever again see a staff announcer of equal skill.

If you take an average ball player and move him into a pennant-winning team, chances are pretty good that he'll perform up to the standards of his new team-mates—and better than his own average. Until I joined CKEY, my working relationships had been generally with people of my own calibre: young people just starting out in broadcasting, or others who had decided just to coast along to retirement. Suddenly, I was thrown in with men and women who were at the pinnacle of their careers, in the country's major broadcasting centre. The result was that my work improved rapidly, and I gained more and more confidence. Don Insley pushed me into work I had no idea I could do. I became the number-one utility man, filling in whenever anyone was absent.

I sat in for "The Ole Redhead," Stu Kenny. At six a.m., Stu would shout: "Wake up, Ontario," and thousands did just that. His voice was too thin, but he had a style and quality to fit the times, and he was the undisputed king of morning radio. My own "Wake up, Ontario," seemed to lack some of Stu's electricity.

Once a week, I worked an overnight shift, filling in for Johnny Williams on the "All-Night House Party." On that shift, you not only introduced the records, you also read a newscast every hour. It was busy.

I worked with Mickey Lester, a wonderful snarky old man who could have been cast in "Fiddler on the Roof," and whose trademark show-opener was: "Hi there, m'friendly." He'd sit hunched in his chair behind the mike, an old black fedora perched on the back of his head, mangling the language and chuckling 'way back in his throat at his own jokes. It was said that the bookkeeping department had to get after Mickey periodically because he never cashed his pay cheques.

I even did occasional colour commentary on live baseball from the old Maple Leaf Stadium, working with sportscasters Joe Crysdale and Hal Kelly. They were an oddly mismatched team: Crysdale short, dark, spindly and bespectacled; Kelly a blonde, burly, hard-living Irishman. I once watched from the control room while the two of them coped magnificently with one of the minor disasters which tended to crop up in the strange business of recreated sports broadcasts. The ticker-tape, feeding information back to the studio from some out-of-town stadium, suddenly stopped functioning, halfway through a ball game.

Crysdale signalled the operator to bring up the recorded crowd noise.

"What's this, Hal?"

"I'm not sure, Joe. There seems to be some disturbance on the field." That was the standard routine to cover tape breakdowns.

More crowd noise, but still no tape. Joe took the plunge. "Wait a second. I think I see what's happening. Well, will you look at that. There's a dog on the field!" During the next five minutes, the two of them concocted an elaborate and very funny running commentary on umpires, players, and coaches running around the stadium, trying to grab a short-legged but agile little mutt. When the ticker-tape was restored, they allowed the dog to be captured and escorted from the field, to the accompaniment of enthusiastic fans conveniently whirling around on a record in the control room.

* * *

I was having the time of my life, and making a little money for a change. Not much, in terms of direct salary, but CKEY had a supplementary fee system. We were paid anywhere from 25 to 60 cents for each commercial we read, and if you read a lot of them, it added up.

Insley kept on pushing. He made suggestions, gave advice, was tough when I screwed up, and unstinting with his praise when he thought I deserved it. But the initial excitement and euphoria had to end somewhere, and when it finally did, I came down to earth with a dull thud. It happened about the time I'd begun taking singing lessons to improve my voice. I'd listen to the other announcers at the station, then record something myself, and I'd think: "I'll never make it." It got so bad, I began thinking of getting out of the business and trying something else.

The Bell Telephone office was just up University Avenue. I thought, "Maybe I could be a PR man for Ma Bell." I went in and picked up an application for employment. At home that night, I tore it up.

The next morning I talked with Insley, and as usual, he knew just what to do.

"How'd you like to work on news for a while?"

And that's how I became an ambulance chaser.

CKEY had a solid reputation for news in those days, which it had earned not through any special effort at news gathering, but through the abilities of its newscasters: Howard Cooney, Franklin Armstrong, and Lorne Greene.

Howard and Frank did the hourly newscasts, ripping wire copy, re-writing some of it, scalping newspaper stories, and making phone calls. Lorne Greene did a newscast during the supper hour, for which he had a marvellous writer, Harry Rasky. (Rasky has since gone on to well-deserved fame and glory as a documentary film-maker.) All three newscasters had the kind of authority that made you believe in them and in what they said. So, despite a lack of staff and facilities in the newsroom, CKEY held the respect of its audience.

My role was to run around with a tape recorder to provide spot news: I met and interviewed politicians and entertainers and celebrities. I interviewed trembling tellers after bank robberies, taciturn cops involved in homicide investigations, and the grieving mothers and fathers of accident victims. I went to fires, and saw the anguish of families who'd lost everything they had. Once, I chased a police radio call to the waterfront. Three small boys had disappeared two weeks earlier, and the police thought they had located their bodies. I found a group of men on the beach beside an old tarpaulin. There was something under the tarp, and I asked a cop I knew what it was. Without a word, he flipped a corner, and there were the three small corpses, bloated and unrecognizable. I went behind my car and threw up.

One of the most disturbing broadcasts I've ever done was made during that period. Johnny Williams and I were assigned to cover the air show at the 1953 Canadian National Exhibition—we were to watch the spectacle on the waterfront, record our impressions, and get the tape back to the station so that it could be aired as soon as possible after the fact.

September 19, 1953 was not a good day for flying. The air was laden with moisture, and there was low, heavy cloud cover. An F-86 screamed across the waterfront, just a few yards above the slate-grey water of Lake Ontario. A beautiful plane, I thought, sleek and menacing . . . perhaps the prettiest fighter since the Spitfire. I knew this was the only F-86 in the show, and I also knew, from an earlier briefing, that the pilot's wife was in Toronto for a brief visit with her husband. He came back for a low pass right in front of the grandstand and then pointed the plane's nose straight up . . . up, and then into a graceful loop over the top, just below the blanket of cloud. And then , straight down. The crowd gasped and held its breath.

I had the mike and was describing what I was seeing. The pilot seemed to be leaving his pull-out awfully late . . . and then suddenly there was a great ball of black smoke, and a split second later the dreadful sound of the impact. I couldn't bring myself to say the plane had crashed.

"He's hit the water!" I cried. "He's hit the water!"

There was a terrifying hush along the waterfront. Then came the screams of women and the frightened shouts of men. I thrust the mike at Johnny and raced to a rescue helicopter. A crewman pulled me aboard just as the chopper left the pad. It took about 30 seconds to reach the spot where the plane had hit. There was nothing there but a few scraps of wreckage.

Back at the station, I was given a hero's welcome. My tape was being played over and over. Gordon Sinclair, in his radio column in the *Star*, likened my broadcast to the famous live report on the fiery crash of the airship Hindenburg in New Jersey in the Thirties.

It was strong stuff. My interest in news up to that time had been less than consuming. Now, I was beginning to appreciate the appeal of being where the action was, of knowing what was happening before most others did, of seeing events unfold first-hand, and then describing and interpreting them.

At the same time, I was finding there was a Jekyll and Hyde aspect to life at CKEY. On the one hand, there was a wonderful camaraderie among the staff. The old pros had no reservations about giving newcomers like me (and Carl Banas, who'd just arrived) advice and encouragement. The bosses in the front office were generous in their efforts to promote the younger talent. There was little or no status consciousness in the place.

On the other hand, Jack Kent Cooke was a hard-driving man, and he rode his staff insistently. There was a constant demand for higher productivity, and woe betide the announcer who blew a commercial and forced a "make good"—a free spot. The maintenance of the highest standards of professionalism was a rigid requirement of every minute of air time.

That kind of pressure led to some hard living.

We had a yacht club, and I remember being introduced to it by Hal Kelly. When he issued his off-hand invitation one afternoon, I had no idea what he was talking about, but I had some free time and decided to go along. We drove to the nearest liquor store, bought a mickey of rye, stopped at a variety store for some Coke, then continued on to the waterfront where Kelly found a secluded spot among the warehouses. As he turned off the ignition, Kelly said: "Okay, kid, this is the yacht club."

I was a little disappointed at first, but as we sat there in the warm sun, with the water slopping around the piers, I decided it was pretty nice, after all. I figured this was a signal that I'd really been accepted, and that pleased me no end. Kelly cracked the mickey and we split the Coke. It promised to be a nice lazy afternoon.

Our quiet conversation was interrupted when a police cruiser pulled up alongside. I frantically tried to hide my drink, but Kelly said, "Don't worry," and greeted the cops as old friends. Then, by God, he offered *them* a drink. I was weighing my chances of getting away if I cut and ran; but to my astonishment, the cops merely declined the offer.

"We're supposed to be on Bloor Street," they said. "We decided to come down here to cool off for a while."

We chatted with the policemen for perhaps half an hour, and then Kelly turned to me:

"I've gotta go to the ball park." He leaned across to my window and said to the policemen: "Would you mind dropping this guy off at the station?"

They agreed, and I moved into the back seat of the cruiser. At the station, I made a fast exit, hoping no one would see the new announcer arriving for work with a police escort.

Keith Sandy and I got into a routine that had all the dubious attractions of living dangerously. At seven p.m., Sandy's "Ballroom" show would be interrupted for a ten-minute newscast read by Lorne Greene. Keith would sign off the segment, then race for the studio door as I read a commercial and made a station break. He'd have his car at the front door, and I'd be climbing in by the time Joel Aldred had finished introducing Greene. Then it was a quick trip to the Nanking, a Chinese restaurant a couple of blocks away on Elizabeth Street. The bartender would see us coming, set up two beers, and we'd enjoy them rather hurriedly, before leaping into the car and racing back to the station just in time for Greene's sign-off. Keith would roll into his usual smooth intro for another "Ballroom" stage, and we'd congratulate each other for once again tempting fate and getting away with it. We never missed once.

The CKEY staff had several hang-outs. One was the beverage room of an old hotel on Elm Street, just on the edge of Chinatown. Another was an apartment rented by The Flame. She was a hooker, an accommodating young lady just beginning to show signs of wear and tear, and she enjoyed having "celebrities" around the place. I think she must have missed a lot of tricks entertaining the boys from 'EY.

There were groupies in unending succession. It's a little sad to remember how they were used and then discarded, though I suppose they expected nothing more. The same thing happens today, more openly, with rock groups and singing stars. The radio stars of the early Fifties weren't in the same league in terms of mass adulation, of course, but the process was the same—the cycle of idol-building, fantasizing, and exploitation—and where it operates, morality acquires a low priority.

Any excuse was used for a stag—birthdays, Victoria Day, name it. We'd take a suite of rooms in a downtown hotel, usually a different hotel each time: once we'd held a party in one of those respectable establishments, we were unlikely to be welcomed back. As soon as the bar had been set up, it was time to drink yourself silly, gamble your salary away, and try your best to focus on grainy old stag films. We were on pretty good terms with the police, so we'd invite a few of them and they'd provide the movies from confiscated stock. They were awful old things, scratched and worn so badly you could scarcely make out the images, drunk or sober—a far cry from the slick, technicolour epics of today. That, too, is progress I suppose.

The furry tongues and throbbing heads—the inevitable result of all the rough, rowdy living—were rarely perceptible on the air. CKEY rolled on, waking up Ontario, keeping the Ballroom's stage revolving . . . and Johnny Williams kept playing that terrible old jingle:

"For the best used car buy in the town,
Try Ted Davy, Ted Davy, Ted Davy."

* * *

The time came when I was faced with another serious career decision. For several months, I'd been doing some work with advertising agencies. Recording commercials was an extremely lucrative part of the business, and not something that could be ignored easily. I valued those jobs, not just because they paid well, but because they gave me an opportunity to work with all kinds of producers on a wide variety of material. There was the alluring prospect of getting good enough at it to make a living on a strictly freelance basis. If you could do that in Toronto, you could do it anywhere. The problem was my staff job was taking up too much of my time, what with running around with a tape recorder for news, filling in for other announcers, and doing staff chores as well. Or maybe, on reflection, it was just the old ambition bug biting again.

I talked with Don Insley.

"Harvey," he said, "you can be the biggest commercial announcer in Canada on any given day, and six months later, nobody will know you. Stay with the staff job, Harv. Do the other things as a nice sideline."

It was sound advice but I didn't listen.

Chapter 9

In the early 50s, CHUM radio was a poorly managed daytime station, signing on at sunrise and off at sunset. It had had a few years of success, but had slowly slipped in popularity and the station now languished in the doldrums. In an effort to capture some sort of an audience, Manager Bob Lee had embarked on a format of "quality" music: soft, homogenized, eviscerated stuff you hear today on background-only FM stations. Meanwhile, his wife Leigh, the station's program director, was searching for a morning man. She offered reasonable money, and there would be little disc-jockeying involved, since most of the music wasn't worth introducing and was simply rolled in. From sign-on until nine, there would be a few commercials, then there were hourly newscasts until one p.m. That was it. Lots of time to freelance.

I didn't really want to leave CKEY, but then I didn't want my career to come to a dead stop, either. I could see no chance of being assigned a regular show since none of the established performers seemed ready to leave. As far as news was concerned, Cooney and Armstrong had that sewn up.

I talked it over with Insley. "I have to take a shot at this," I told him. He understood, of course—he'd seen a lot of young bucks like me come and go, looking for bigger and better things. He wished me luck, as though he knew I was going to need it where I was going.

* * *

The CHUM studios were only a few blocks away from CKEY, but in terms of atmosphere and on-air presence, the stations were worlds apart. CKEY exuded a raucous, rowdy kind of confidence, the kind that goes with success. CHUM, on the other hand, had a muted, wall-flowerish feel . . . in the studios and on the air.

It's hard to say what makes a radio station go downhill. It's not like an ordinary business, where people either buy goods or services, or they don't. A radio station is a living entity, with a distinctive personality, defined in large measure by an on-air staff of living, breathing human beings. Its ties with the audience are thus mainly emotional. Perhaps, when a radio station starts to lose heart, its "sound" becomes dispirited and confused, and the audience looks to other, more self-assured sources of information and entertainment.

CHUM's owner Jack Q'Part (I never learned what the "Q" meant) seemed to have lost interest in the radio business: he spent less and less time on CHUM business, and put less and less money into the station. Bob Lee's "quality music" format didn't wash with the advertisers or the audience. Then, too, CHUM was saddled with a monstrous disadvantage in being stuck with a frequency which overlapped an American station. That meant it could only operate in the daylight hours, while all the other stations in the area rocketed on 'round the clock.

I'm sure I was insufferably smug, walking into the CHUM studios for the first time. Here I was, coming to this broken-down radio station from Number One. If it were possible to become a media star at CHUM, I'd do it. On top of that, I was in some demand in the freelance world: I wouldn't be around for long . . . I'd be making bags of money from commercials and in no time at all I'd be ready to take on the real big-time. New York.

It didn't quite work out that way.

My shift lived up to expectations—it was a breeze. As soon as I'd arrived at the station, I'd put together a newscast from wire copy, then roll records for a couple of hours, with a few commercials interpersed. At nine o'clock, I'd begin doing hourly newscasts of five minutes each, with a ten-minuter at 12:30. Another at one, and I was finished.

The new bosses seemed satisfied after a couple of weeks of this, so I embarked on my quest for freelance work. I made the rounds of the advertising agencies, getting to know those in charge of producing radio commercials. I went to auditions, I made audition tapes, I went to cocktail parties, and I hung out at the right bars. Nothing happened. I did a few small jobs, but certainly not enough to provide much encouragement. I persisted, and persisted some more. Still, there was only a dribble of outside work: CHUM was still paying the rent. I began to think perhaps I'd better pay a little more attention to my staff job. So for the next couple of years I did just that. Or tried to.

In my zeal to break into the freelance world and get rich quick, I'd let my interest in news fall off, and at CHUM it was not easy to fan the embers of latent enthusiasm. Our news resources consisted of a single wire service, and the daily papers. There were only two of us working in the newsroom: I covered the morning shift; Larry Martin, an old veteran, worked from two until sign-off. Larry had been working in radio news for years, through the heady days when CHUM was a force to be reckoned with in Toronto radio. He'd seen it all, and he accepted with equanimity the fact that the station was going to hell in a handbasket. Since he had no help, he did what he could, and that was it. I felt about the same way.

I guess . . . and I blush to say this . . . that's how we missed Hurricane Hazel, the biggest news event of 1954, and for a good many years to come.

In the east end of Toronto, Hurricane Hazel was nothing more than a heavy rainstorm. I found myself stepping over puddles as I left my apartment in the morning, but there was no hint of the severity of the storm that had savaged the other half of the city, taking lives and causing nearly a hundred million dollars damage. It was my habit each morning while driving to work to switch around the radio dial, listening to the competition, considering what I would put into my first newscast. On this day, I was astounded by what I heard. I pulled the car in to the curb and listened, stunned, to the reports of death and destruction throughout the city's west end and along the Humber River. Then came the blind rush to get to the newsroom. As I raced to the station, I asked myself over and over how it was possible for all this to have taken place while I, a would-be news reporter, had remained blissfully asleep.

For the next several days, everyone at CHUM was pressed into the service of the newsroom, as we played catch-up. We interviewed survivors and relatives of victims. We talked to fire-fighters and policemen and volunteer relief workers. I flew over the city in a light aircraft, and while a *Telegram* photographer shot pictures, I recorded a description of the awful devastation below. CHUM did a creditable job, after the fact. But, "better late than never" doesn't count for much in the news business.

It seems clear to me now that my experiences during those few days marked a turning point in my career. It was during my wild ride to the station the morning after, that, for the first time, I had begun to think of myself as a newsman—if only in criticizing myself for being derelict in my reporter's duties. It was somewhere in the aftermath of Hurricane Hazel that I shook off the terrible urge to become a commercial announcer and make bags of money.

Around this time, along with the rest of the staff at CHUM, I first became aware of a man called Allan Waters. He would appear occasionally in the CHUM studios, observing, asking questions, charming even the old vets with a warm, modest smile and a quiet intelligence. We decided he was a pretty nice guy, and word went round the station that he was the advertising manager for Jack Q'Part's pharmaceutical business.

The facts were that Waters owned a small part of the pharmaceutical company, and was about to trade those shares off in a deal to buy CHUM.

In December, 1954, Waters made his move. He gave his drug company stock to Q'Part as a downpayment, and agreed to pay $500 a month for sole ownership of the station. From that humble beginning rose an empire that was to have a profound and lasting impact on the country's entire communications industry . . . but that was later.

The change of ownership was duly announced to the staff at CHUM, and, at first, it had little effect on us. I still worked the mornings and did my newscasts. Larry Martin carried on with the afternoon news. Peter Nordheimer continued his mid-morning show. Court Johnston still bought his half-hour of air time and parceled it out to his own advertisers.

Then came a whirlwind of activity. Waters succeeded in having CHUM's licence amended to provide for 'round-the-clock broadcasting. There were staff changes, mainly on the management side. The studios were moved out of the tidy but expensive Mutual Street building, into an old warehouse on Adelaide Street, an area of grimy old factories. The building's second floor was renovated into a radio station. At its core were a control room, a studio, and a small, microphone-equipped newsroom from which the newscasts would originate. Ranged around this hub were production offices, the library, sales offices, and the engineering lab where smiling George Jones toiled to keep his new baby on the air. Morale at the station soared: we became fiercely loyal, not as much to CHUM as to Allan Waters himself.

The changes came at a time when radio all over North America was embarking on new directions, seeking new audiences. The big band era was coming to a close, and *Billboard* magazine was losing its taste-making influence over the popular music industry. Kids were buying the cheap, new 45 rpm discs by the millions, and their tastes were beginning to shape the hit parade charts. The smooth and effortless singers their parents admired were being replaced by Buddy Holly and Chubby Checker, Fats Domino and Bill Haley. It was the advent of rock 'n' roll. Of course, it didn't take the marketing men long to see the profit potential latent in this affluent younger generation, and they took dead aim with something called "top 40 radio." All over the United States, there were now stations that played nothing but the best-selling 40 records, plus a few they considered up-and-comers.

CHUM joined that band wagon. Phil Ladd, a bald-headed Texan from Lubbock, was brought in by management to be program director. He was supposed to be an expert on top 40 radio, and I suppose he was, but it was the wrong time and the wrong place for an outsider. He never had a chance. The station functioned much like the slick and smooth top 40 stations in the States, but our sound was raucous and uneven. I think we all felt we could do better for Allan Waters ourselves, given the chance, and so Ladd began running into roadblocks and dead ends. Eventually, he left.

In his place, Waters hired a young man who'd earned a reputation as a hot-shot program director in Edmonton. Allan Slaight was possessed of phenomenal energy and enthusiasm, and his brain seemed to be bubbling constantly with ideas, schemes, and gimmicks. He was, I think, the catalyst that pulled all the elements at CHUM together and put the station on a roll that has never stopped.

CHUM quickly built a fanatical following among teenagers. It was the only station in town catering to their tastes, and their loyalty knew no bounds. I continued to disc-jockey the morning show, with a couple of newscasts squeezed in between the records. Pete Nordheimer toiled through mid-morning, trying desperately to adapt to the fast pace and frantic music. I think both of us realized that our disc-jockey days were numbered.

An early casualty of the new format was Josh King's "Country Jamboree." Josh was in his twenties then, a long drink of water in a Stetson hat and a carefully cultivated cowpuncher's swagger. His noon-hour program had elements of a recreated sports event, with recorded crowd noise and sound effects mixed in with the music: if you closed your eyes, you could easily imagine you were listening to a live concert. Ronnie Hawkins, on his first forays into Toronto, was a frequent guest, as was Tommy Hunter. Having grown up on country music, I loved the program, and was sorry when Josh quit and headed off to California.

Slaight, in the meantime, was generating an unending stream of contests and promotions, designed to build our audience. Most of them did just that, though not always in the ways he'd intended. One of them, in fact, almost broke Waters. It was common knowledge among the staff that the station was desperately short of money, so there were some raised eyebrows when, in the spring of 1955, Al Slaight decided to put $5,000 in a safe in the window of a downtown store. There was a barrage of promotion. "Open the safe and claim the $5000"—the on-air staff repeated the challenge *ad nauseam* for days before the contest opened.

Not many knew it, but Waters had borrowed the $5,000 from the bank, on the strength of Slaight's assurances that there was no way anybody was going to open that safe.

Day one of the contest: a long line of people were waiting to spin the safe's dial, but there was no winner. A sigh of relief.

Day two. Mid-morning: a young man, 18 or 19, in working clothes, stepped up and expertly began to twirl the dial. He grabbed the door handle confidently and pulled.

The damn door opened!

The sound on CHUM that day was jubilant. We had a winner! But behind the mikes, we were stunned. Slaight was white. There was a long meeting in Waters' office. How could it have happened?

The explanation proved simple enough. The young man who had cracked the combination worked for a company that manufactured and serviced safes. Obviously he must have been very good at his job.

The newsroom rolled on: much of the time as just another arm of the boisterous promotional apparatus that was CHUM radio. An example: there was a newspaper story about a little girl who lived in lower Cabbagetown. She was suffering from leukemia, and her one wish was to have a white puppy. Al Slaight was not a cynical man, but neither was he one to overlook an opportunity to promote the station. He brought the newspaper to me.

"Look," he said. "Get on the air. Find a dog."

It took a few broadcasts, but we found a white puppy. I was detailed to deliver it. I objected.

"This is not a news story," I said. But Slaight prevailed. I did the job, and a more beautiful little girl I have never seen, nor a more shining happiness. We talked and I recorded the conversation, unable to see the controls on the tape machine for the tears in my eyes.

I knew that to capitalize on the tragic plight of the child would be an unconscionable act. Yet, when I saw her joy as the little dog leaped into her arms, any qualms I'd had about what I was doing vanished. Was Slaight using the girl to promote the station? Or was he using his job as station promoter as an excuse to get a dog for the girl? I knew which side I was on. I've learned over the years that the legendary cynicism of news people is often just a cover-up for a big, marshmallow heart.

My career was going better than I'd had any right to expect, given the leap into the void I'd taken in leaving CKEY. I was an integral part of the growth at CHUM: my newscasts were good, and while my abilities as a DJ were questionable, they were adequate for the moment.

The trouble was my personal life. It was a mess. Maggie was moving into newspaper and magazine writing, and since our working hours rarely corresponded, we seldom saw one another. I had my friends, mostly people with whom I worked, and she had hers. It was becoming a case of two voracious careers and an undernourished marriage. It wasn't long before we'd let it starve to death.

* * *

About 1955, CHUM initiated an arrangement with the *Toronto Telegram* that was to have a fundamental effect on my career. It was common then, and still is, for radio stations and newspapers to combine resources for special events like elections, or for coverage of major news stories. CHUM took the idea a bit farther—we began originating our newscasts from the editorial room of the *Tely*.

It was a new world. Suddenly, this facilities-starved little radio station had access to all the news-gathering resources of one of the continent's biggest and best newspapers. We had free use of all the *Tely*'s editorial copy, and the run of the wire room, with its many news services. Each morning Pat Bennett, a young Ryerson graduate, and I would put together the major noon-hour newscast. We could sometimes even cajole a *Tely* reporter into re-writing his story for radio and doing an on-air report. Working in that heady environment, I was more convinced than ever that my future lay with the professionals I was meeting in the grubby old Melinda St. city room of the *Tely*.

My career as a disc-jockey was about to end in any case, but not before I'd written a footnote to the chronicles of pop music in Toronto. I earned the distinction of being the first DJ in Toronto to play an Elvis Presley record on the air. When the 45 arrived in our library, I listened to both sides. One was an old blue grass tune, "Blue Moon of Kentucky," which appealed to my bucolic background. It was the first Elvis tune heard on Toronto radio. Within a few days, all of North America was clamouring to hear Elvis. Unfortunately for my reputation as a hit-picker, it was the other side of the record they wanted . . . something called "Blue Suede Shoes."

When I did get on track, I became an overnight celebrity with our young teenaged audience. They jammed the switchboard, night and day, wanting to come to the studio—anything to get them closer to this new singing idol. I made the near-fatal mistake of issuing an open invitation to kids to drop in during my Saturday morning show. When I arrived, there was a mob of mostly female teenyboppers, breathlessly waiting to jam themselves into the little studio to watch the record turn while Elvis warbled. This eerie scene was repeated every Saturday for several weeks, and then they just stopped coming.

That's about when my disc-jockeying days ended. Al Boliska, one of the best morning men ever to spill coffee on his commercials, joined CHUM as the official wake-up show host. I moved into the newsroom full-time, as news director.

The *Telegram* in the Fifties had some of the best writing and editing talents in Canada. Frank Tumpane, Wes Hicks, Alan Kent, Dorothy Howarth, Phyllis Griffiths, Ron Poulton, Peter Dempson, and Harry Halliwell were all household names in their day. Doug Creighton (now the upwardly mobile publisher of the *Toronto Sun*) was a police reporter, and later assistant to the legendary city editor, Art Cole. There was natty Norm Johnson, with his endless schemes to beat the stock market, Helen Allen, Mike Carmichael, and Gerry Toner, who delivered his occasional radio news reports in the monotone of Sgt. Joe Friday: "Dragnet" was big then. Dick Hayward, Art Holland, and dozens of others all helped to shape my interests and hone my abilities.

The sights and sounds and smells of news seeped into my bones, and I've never been the same since. I learned what a real news story was, and how it should be written. I learned to recognize the lead to a story—that catchy or significant tidbit that will grab a reader's or listener's attention, and hold him for what follows. I took to hanging around the city room long after my shift had ended, occasionally going out on a story with another reporter. City editor Art Cole would assign me stories to do in my off-hours, and then take the time to go over the finished product with me, helping me to polish it. I can say now, without equivocation, that I had the best apprenticeship the news business had to offer at that time, or perhaps any other time.

It was a revelation to watch some of those old *Tely* hands at work. Phyllis Griffiths was unsurpassed at human interest stories. One day, when a child had been found murdered in the Scarborough countryside and the newsroom had shifted into high gear, I tagged along with her. Phyl was in her thirties, I guess, but she looked older. Her close-cropped hair was pure white. Her clothes were tweedy and bulky, and when she put on her glasses, she looked like everybody's idea of a grandmother.

While all the other reporters were making tracks for the murder scene, Phyl was heading straight for the parents' house, where she proceeded to take over the kitchen, making tea and doing anything else she could to ease the pain for the distressed family. She asked a lot of questions; she asked for pictures—all the while hovering over everyone like a solicitous nanny.

I watched, and understood something basic to being a good reporter. Phyl, this tough old lady who'd been in news for years, was feeling the same pain the family was feeling. Because of that genuine empathy, she was trusted.

The arrangement between CHUM and the *Tely* gave me my first overseas assignment. It was not a shining success from a journalistic point of view, but it had its moments.

It was 1956, and Russian tanks and troops were mopping up the last resistance in Budapest, after having brutally crushed the Hungarian revolution. A flood of refugees crossed into Austria, and they were being housed in camps around Vienna. Their sheer numbers sorely taxed both the Red Cross and the Austrian government. There were international appeals for food and clothing.

It was nearing Christmas, and CHUM and the *Tely* launched a campaign to collect toys for the children in the camps in Austria. Maritime Central Airways agreed to fly the cargo there—they had the contract to bring over the thousands of Hungarian refugees Ottawa had accepted, and their flights east across the Atlantic were mostly empty anyway.

At CHUM, it was decided I should go along on this Christmas air-lift. The round-trip normally took three or four days, depending on the turn-around time in Vienna. My job would be to grab what I could in the way of interviews and actuality at the refugee camps. Alan Kent was already in Vienna for the *Tely*—he'd been dispatched soon after the crisis developed, and was to help me out with logistics once I arrived.

I boarded a venerable Maritime Central DC-6 in Toronto, and flew to Moncton, my trusty tape recorder clutched under my arm. The plane was chock full of cartons of toys donated by the people of Toronto. There was space for only a few seats for passengers, right behind the flight deck. In fact, there were only three other passengers besides myself; one of them was a United Nations man who was mortally terrified of flying. At Moncton, we took a fresh crew including pilot Max Campbell and co-pilot Ray Gingles.

It was an uneventful, if not exactly comfortable flight. The DC-6 had a well-known but nonetheless disquieting tendency to creak and groan a lot in the air, and the heating system never seemed able to keep ahead of the drafts. From time to time, the ice collecting on the fuselage would break away with a sharp crack, and our United Nations man would come close to passing dead away.

The first blow to my plan came when we arrived at Vienna. Red Cross officials had decided our lay-over there would be shorter than usual. There would be no time for me to visit the refugee camps. Damn!

Alan Kent was there to greet me. We tried our best to get a delay, but it was no use. I had to settle for a long interview with Alan, and a couple of shorter ones with harried Red Cross people. All was not lost though. I'd have plenty of time to interview some of the 70-odd refugees we were taking back on the plane.

So my first overseas assignment had amounted to about three hours at the Vienna Airport. There was worse to come.

The flight home had been routed through Shannon, Ireland; Keflavik, Iceland; Gander, Newfoundland; Moncton, New Brunswick, and then on to Toronto. We had a fresh crew for the flight, but Max and his people were aboard too, deadheading back to be home for Christmas. At Shannon, the two crews and I loaded up on duty-free Christmas liquor and then it was on to Keflavik, fighting severe head winds all the way. When we landed at the U.S. air base there, the pilot came back from the flight deck to tell us we were going to have to stay put for at least 24 hours because there were strong winds and storms between Iceland and Newfoundland. The DC-6 couldn't carry enough fuel to make the hop under those conditions. I didn't like the look of it—we were cutting it pretty close for a pre-Christmas homecoming.

Our refugees were settled in comfortably for the night at an American barracks, while the MCA crews and I were assigned rooms in the hotel that occupied part of the terminal building.

Next morning, December 23rd, in a howler of a wind storm, we all boarded the plane once again. Our captain informed us we were going to make a try for Gander, but that unless the head winds abated we'd probably have to turn back. It was an horrendous flight. The plane bucked and rocked and there were times I was sure the wings would be torn off. Everybody aboard was terrified, and many were sick. Finally, we turned back.

The refugees were installed once again in their barracks, glad, I'm sure, to be safely on the ground. The crews and I returned to our hotel rooms, resigned to spending Christmas in Iceland. On Christmas Eve, about a dozen of us gathered in Max Campbell's room, bringing with us the bottles we'd bought in Shannon. We were a pretty forlorn bunch, stranded in a remote airport with nothing around us but a few American Air Force buildings. Still, the booze was flowing freely. In a couple of hours, the two stewardesses had an inspired suggestion. We'd heard there was a party at the U.S. Air Force officers' club and their plan was to get themselves picked up and then to wrangle invitations for the rest of us . . . and they did just that.

Ray Gingles and Max and I were the last to leave the hotel room. Once outside in the frigid night air we realized that we didn't know where the party was. We had no transport to get us there. Then we noticed two big U.S. Air Force buses pulled up beside a snowbank, one of them running.

"Come on," Max said, and we climbed aboard the idling vehicle, Max slipping into the driver's seat. There was a harsh clashing of gears, and we were off. Max was wearing his pilot's cap, and he looked enough like a bus driver to fool the passerby we flagged down to ask directions to the officers' club. When we finally arrived, we cached the commandeered bus behind a building and went inside to join what had become one helluva party.

The last time I saw Max Campbell and Ray Gingles on that trip was in the corridor of a Moncton motel. I was due to embark for Toronto and we said our goodbyes. They turned, and the last I saw of them, Max was casually tossing something in the air as he walked. They were the Keflavik bus keys.

Chapter 10

Television was just beginning to hit its stride. True to form, we were watching a lot of American product—Uncle Miltie, Sid Caesar and Imogene Coca, Lucy and Desi, those great Hitchcock mysteries. Jackie Gleason made "How sweet it is!" a part of the vernacular. Ed Sullivan ruptured everybody's ratings when Elvis made his first TV appearance, even though the cameras shot him coyly from the waist up, leaving what went on from there down to the fertile imaginations of millions of intensely interested women. The names to be reckoned with in news were NBC and CBS smoothies John Cameron Swayze and Douglas Edwards.

In Canada, Larry Henderson, stiff and starched, delivered the CBC news, and the Corporation mounted an ambitious drama series called "General Motors Presents." Dick McDougal, Elaine Grand, Gil Christie, and Percy Saltzman became instant celebrities in Toronto when Ross McLean invented "Tabloid," and Uncle Chichimus squeaked along, with Larry Mann as his straight man.

My initial involvement in the medium was limited to doing the occasional voice-over track for a TV commercial. I had no great ambition to appear on camera—in fact the idea scared the hell out of me. I equated it with those bad dreams where you're in a crowded room and suddenly discover you're not wearing any pants.

The local CBC station had a program in which guest hosts took viewers to interesting locations around the city and described what happened there. Out of the blue, they called me, and asked if I'd appear as a host. Oh, God. I wrestled with that one for quite a while. Finally, I accepted. I shouldn't have.

I was given some research material on how trains are controlled in the huge rail yards on the Toronto waterfront, told when and where to meet the production crew, and assured it would be a cinch.

First, I couldn't find the crew or the building where they were supposed to be set up and waiting. When I finally did, I walked into the damnedest maze of lights, cables, microphones, tape recorders, cameras, and boxes with buttons and lights and switches I'd ever seen. It was like sending a cave man into an airport control tower.

Well, there was nothing for it but to forge ahead. On the air, I made a stumbling stab at trying to explain how little lights, moving along a line on a control panel, represented trains in the yard. I was so nervous, I couldn't remember any of the questions I'd planned to ask the railway men I interviewed, nor could I concentrate on their answers. It was sheer, blind panic. All I wanted to do was get off the air. We finally did, though I was only dimly aware of the director's frantic wrap-up signals. I was not asked for a return engagement.

My television career ought to have ended then and there but fate gave me another kick at the cat. This time I was more successful. One of the most popular dramatic series of the day was "Studio One," produced in New York and carried by CBC. Its sponsor in this country was Canadian Westinghouse. Like most television at that time, it was done live, commercials and all. While American audiences were watching Betty Furness sell the American sponsor's products, Canadians were treated to a commercial pitch shared by Joel Aldred, probably the most successful commercial announcer ever produced in this country, and Laddie Dennis, a vivacious, dark-haired young woman whose talent for selling refrigerators was at least the equal of her American counterpart's. The Canadian Westinghouse account was handled by wily old Spence Caldwell, a veteran broadcaster who operated several businesses out of an old mansion on Jarvis Street, across from the CBC studios. My call came from his assistant, Gordon Keeble. Aldred, he said, was leaving to be the spokesman for Chevrolet on "The Dinah Shore Show," and would have to be replaced on "Studio One." He invited me to audition, and I astonished myself by getting the job.

I was turned over to producer John Heaton, who informed me I'd be earning $75 a week, that I'd introduce the program, and that I'd be doing a few commercials, some with Laddie, some on my own. The bulk of the selling, though, would be left to Laddie, and that was fine with me. I was in 'way over my head, and scared stiff.

Heaton was also to be my coach. He handed me a sheaf of old commercial scripts:

"Memorize these," he said, "then call me in a couple of days. We'll go over them together."

"Memor . . . ? Ah, sure, okay."

There must have been seven or eight minutes of copy there, and I had a memory like a sieve. I worked away at it, and finally called Heaton. We had a number of training sessions, and then I started on the air. For 18 months, every Monday night, I walked into the CBC studios, knees trembling, palms sweating, stark terror chilling my heart. Strangely, though, I had few problems when it came to getting the job done. Laddie encouraged me, taught me little memory tricks, and propped me up on air when I needed it. Everyone bore with me as I learned—among other things: that I didn't have to shout to be heard by the camera 'way over there; that the microphone suspended out of my line of vision would pick me up just fine. Nonetheless, I decided I'd better not give up my staff job at CHUM. Don Insley had been right all along: best to keep the outside stuff as a nice sideline.

CHUM moved into new quarters at that now-famous address—1331 Yonge Street. It was a long, low building that had been built as a store, and had display windows all along its Yonge Street frontage. Slaight, ever the promoter, wanted the newsroom set up right there in those windows. We were due to end our arrangement with the *Telegram*, confident now that we could fly on our own, but none of us in the department liked the idea of working in a fish bowl. There was a fight. The outcome was never in any doubt: Slaight won, though he did agree to provide us with Venetian blinds, which we'd be able to close when we got tired of our audience on the street. As it turned out, we closed the blinds occasionally to keep the sun out, but never to block the view.

Our staff was growing: Larry Solway and Gary Ferrier were hired as copywriters, and Earl Bradford and Peter Dickens, one of the finest newscasters I've heard, were added to the newsroom. We started a phone-in show, and I was briefly its moderator, before being replaced by Dr. Marcus Long of the University of Toronto. The show ran for many years, but never so successfully or amid such controversy as when it was hosted by Larry Solway.

Weekend radio was a wasteland, and CHUM decided to do something to make it more relevant to its audience. The idea was to jam the airwaves with as much information as possible on things to do in and around Toronto. The project was handed over to the newsroom. We hired two brand new Ryerson graduates—John Spragge and Derek Lind—to help with the legwork. (Both went on to bigger and better things in the business. Spragge was, until recently, at CFRB radio in Toronto, and Lind is a newsman at CFCF radio in Montreal.) We organized a recording schedule and invited a parade of people to tape their messages: the Conservation Authority people plugged their parks, Red Cross and St. John's Ambulance spokesmen provided safety tips, city parks officials listed inner-city activities, the police and the Highways Department provided driving information, and we compiled an exhaustive calendar of sports and recreation activities. On Friday and Sunday evenings, I provided a traffic watch from the air.

By now, we had about ten people in the newsroom. While we were never going to beat CFRB and its stable of news institutions—Wally Crouter, Jack Dennett, Gordon Sinclair, and others—we were hammering every other station in town. For the first time, we had the staff to cover Toronto news completely and authoritatively. Where there was news, you'd find a red and white CHUM station wagon, and a reporter toting a tape recorder. The ear-splitting "whoop, whoop, whoop" that identified CHUM news on the air was no longer taken lightly.

As CHUM continued to grow and flex its muscles, CKEY went into a sad decline. Jack Kent Cooke pulled the plug by selling the station and moving south of the border.

Many of my old colleagues either quit, or were fired. The station moved from University Avenue to new studios in suburban Don Mills, and tried, without much success, to adapt to the top 40 format. It fell on hard times, and it was years before it regained even a small part of the stature it had enjoyed in the late Forties and early Fifties.

I suppose everyone reaches a stage where life becomes less a matter of unalloyed highs and lows than ironic combinations of the two—more complicated to deal with emotionally, but at the same time richer in meaning and opportunity for learning. It seems to be an inevitable by-product of the accumulation of experiences and human contacts. At some stage, they all begin to interact in unpredictable ways. The mid-Fifties were such a time for me.

* * *

Maggie and I were divorced in 1956. We'd been going our separate ways for months, but the final split was nonetheless traumatic for both of us. Divorce was by no means the simple, no-fault arrangement it can be today, and the rigidity of the law forced many people into an ugly morass of lies and hypocrisy. Adultery was about the only practicable grounds, and so incriminating scenes of unfaithfulness were sometimes staged for the benefit of the court. A typical scenario might involve hiring a loose lady for a few hours, renting a hotel room, and having a friend "catch" you together. The friend would then act as a witness for the party suing for divorce. The depth of the stupidity of such a system can only truly be understood by those who had the misfortune to have been dragged through it.

While the divorce process was grinding along, I was approaching my tenth anniversary as a broadcaster, a fact I found difficult to believe. The time seemed to have flown by. I'd changed directions several times, and my ambitions had been transformed until, here I was, news director of the hottest radio station in town. I was a member of the Canadian Radio and Television News Directors Association, and had attended a conference of the international association, the RTNDA, in New Orleans. Along the way, I'd obtained my pilot's licence, and occasionally would fly

101

to the scene of news events in a rented plane. CHUM was now paying well, and had instituted a profit-sharing plan which provided a healthy year-end bonus. I figured I was set for the long-term.

Then came a series of disturbing events at the station. Bill Drylie, a pugnacious, opinionated little newspaperman, was brought in from the *Star*. He was to do some commentaries and a personalized newscast. Soon, though, he was encroaching on what I thought was my territory—the running of the newsroom itself. He made no bones about the fact he thought we were a bunch of amateurs, and the two of us got into some dandy shouting matches.

At the same time, there was a subtle, and I suppose inevitable, change in atmosphere. CHUM had rocketed from obscurity to the top of the heap in less than five years. The challenge now was to stay there, and that required tighter direction, firmer management, and more careful planning. Hard work and enthusiasm were no longer enough. For a staff of energetic, young self-starters who had been used to a great deal of freedom, this was not a welcome development. It caused more than a little resentment.

So it was that early in 1960, when Dave Rogers called, I was ready to listen to his offer.

Dave was an old friend, and news director at CHCH, the television station in Hamilton. CHCH had been on the air since the mid-50s as a CBC affiliate. It had quickly established itself as the maverick in the Corporation's stable, eyeing with unseemly lust the big, hungry Toronto market so close by. It had expanded its coverage over the years to take in almost all of the so-called "Golden Horseshoe" from Niagara Falls to Toronto. Now it was gearing itself up for a complete break from the CBC, and an assault on the market the Corporation had ceded to its wholly-owned Toronto affiliate, CBLT.

Part of this plan was an overhauling and expansion of the under-budgeted, under-staffed news department. There would be more money for more reporters and camera crews, a new, more up-to-date look to the newscasts, and for the first time, a permanent, identifiable anchor.

Rogers wanted me to be that anchorman. He was offering $10,000 a year, which was a little more than I'd been making at CHUM, plus an opportunity to get into television news on the ground floor—at a time when just about everyone was predicting (incorrectly, as it turned out) that TV would make all other information media obsolete.

I had a couple of reservations: television still terrified me, and I was uncertain whether I'd ever be able to shake my fear of the camera. The second concern had to do with the station's management. It was owned by Ken Soble, and though he was a well-seasoned veteran of the business, he had a reputation for ruthlessness where his staff was concerned. Every year or so there would be stories of purges in which a lot of people would be unceremoniously dumped to make way for new talent. I didn't want to become one of Soble's victims.

"Not a chance," Rogers assured me. I guess I must have wanted the job pretty badly, because on the strength of that commitment, I accepted.

It was a perfect summer's day when I drove to Hamilton to tie up the deal. I was early, so I took time for a look around the city that would be my new home. Hamilton has always impressed me as having the potential to be one of the world's most beautiful cities: climbing from the crescent-shaped flatlands, along a beautiful bay at the west end of Lake Ontario, to its dramatic mountain backdrop. But Hamilton has had to make some sad compromises with the industries that provide its livelihood. The city lives on the steel mills, Stelco and Dofasco, and all the ancillary industries they support. The east end of Hamilton is a nightmare of industrial blight, and the bay is polluted by the effluence of the mills. A lot has been done to minimize the impact of heavy industry—they don't call it a lunch-bucket town anymore—but despite its reborn downtown core and its beautiful parks, Hamilton must still suffer its steelmakers.

CHCH's business offices were housed in a beautiful old gabled mansion a few blocks from the newly-rising City Hall. Production facilities were in a low building across a courtyard to the rear. The newsroom was in another house, a few doors down and across the street. I found Dave

Rogers, and his assistant, Ron Ellis, in an office there, overlooking the street. Behind that, in what must have been the parlour or sitting-room, was the newsroom itself, with a few desks, chairs, and typewriters. Down the hall, there were teletype and facsimile machines, a room for photographers and their equipment, two film-editing suites, and a lab for processing film. Compared to the big, new newsroom at CHUM, it was pretty primitive, though it seemed functional enough. I knew very little about television generally, and even less about the requirements of television news, so I wasn't about to make any strong judgements.

At the big house across the street, I was duly introduced to the big wheels: Ken Soble, the owner; general manager Sid Bibby (tall, craggy-faced, brush cut—I thought: not a man to cross); production manager Jack Burghardt (a smallish man with a big voice and serious demeanour), the person to whom Rogers and I reported. In those days, the news department was considered part of the programming or production area at most television stations. Since then, news directors have gained a great deal of autonomy and are generally included in station management.

The production centre consisted of one, big studio and a small booth with a fixed camera that could be turned on and off by the announcer. The main studio contained three of four permanent sets for regularly scheduled programs and, I believe, three cameras. The control room was a compact affair set up so that the director could double as switcher, operating the board that controlled picture sources—the cameras, telecine film projectors, slides, and so on. It was not fancy, but, like the newsroom, it was functional . . . or so it seemed to my inexperienced eye.

Nick Olchowy was assigned to direct my newscasts—a fortunate choice for me, because we hit it off immediately. Good rapport with the production staff was important, especially for an inexperienced newcomer like me. He was about 25, and had a homely kind of face that would naturally default to a smile when no particular expression was called for.

I moved into a comfortable apartment halfway up the mountain, with a gorgeous view across the city and out over the Burlington Skyway spanning the harbour. At night, the cars on the bridge seemed to be coursing their way through thin air in a graceful arc.

In the couple of weeks before I was to start on the air, we spent a lot of time practising. Whenever we could get studio time, Nick, Dave, and I would rehearse a newscast. It was to be an informal presentation, with the only props being a stool for me and a lectern on which I could place the script. I began to feel quite comfortable in that setting . . . began to think that looking into the camera wasn't going to strike me dead.

Then, debut time. I listened to the recorded introduction on the studio full-back and looked up in time to see the red camera light blink on. In that instant, all the confidence I'd gained in the rehearsals left me. Panic had me by the throat. I took a ragged breath, and plunged into the script.

Well, we got through it, after a fashion. I say "we," because everyone in the control room had been sweating along with me. It went on that way for the next two or three weeks. Each newscast was an ordeal. When we reviewed the recorded airchecks, it showed. I was thoroughly disgusted. I was making a fool of myself on the air. I was letting down the station and my friends and colleagues—all because of this irrational fear of the studio camera. I could do filmed interviews and reports, write copy—I even learned to edit film and, in a rudimentary way, use a film camera—but I could not master the live stuff in the studio.

I held post-mortems at my apartment, and talked with the other on-air people, even old Captain Bill, who did the kids' show. They all offered kind, reassuring words and compliments on my progress, but the fear remained.

One evening, I finished the late newscast, went home, cracked a bottle of Walker's Imperial, and sagged into a chair on my balcony overlooking the city. I liked this place, and I didn't want to blow my chances here. I didn't want to be a failure. I couldn't let that happen. Again and again I went over the problem, rattling the bars of the fear that caged me, trying to find a way out. Why? Why?

The fat bottle of Imperial was starting to thin out some.

Suddenly, I had a novel thought:

105

"Look," I said to myself, "that city down there is populated by a bunch of ordinary Joes, right?"

"Right."

"And you're Harvey Kirck, the big TV performer, right?"

"Right."

"Okay then, *be* that."

Performer? Maybe that was the clue. You can get away with being yourself on radio. But on television, where it's all hanging out, where what you see is what you get, you have to be a performer . . . an extension of the true self, an enlargement of the real person. You have to develop a bullet-proof persona, and send *him* out to face the damnable, merciless camera.

In my whiskey-soaked state, that all seemed to make sense. I went to bed.

Next day, before air time, I reviewed the conversation I'd had with myself. I thought, "Dammit, that's it."

When the newscast opened that evening, I seemed to be standing outside myself, an impartial observer. The tight, frightened voice had given way to a strong and confident delivery. I watched a cool, relaxed performer deliver a flawless newscast.

In my drunken state at three o'clock in the morning, I had found the key. Perhaps it was an arrogant solution, but it worked, and that was the main thing. From now on, I'd be able to concentrate on the job of providing reliable information for my audience, fulfilling the trust they increasingly placed in me in this highly personal medium.

Chapter 11

The personal nature of the relationship between a television newscaster and his audience was never better illustrated to me than by a polite but forceful letter I received from a professor of English at McMaster University. It could have been Polonius writing to his son. He told me, more in sorrow than in anger, that I had committed the grievous sin of referring to a man of the cloth as "Reverend John Smith," instead of "The Reverend John Smith." There were many others like that not always as polite, and not always dealing with matters of professional competence. I resolved at the time, and have held to it all through my years in television, that I'd accept advice on language and grammar and ties and suits, but that my *performance* would be governed by my judgement and instincts alone. I would not be directed into a pose that was uncomfortable, or unlike me. It was a good decision. Though it may have caused headaches for producers and directors from time to time, it allowed me to evolve a style—or perhaps, an absence of style—that turned out to be satisfactory for me and my audience.

For the moment, I had an idea of the kind of image I wanted to project, but, being new to the game, no clear idea of how to achieve it. I watched others, notably Chet Huntley and David Brinkley on NBC, discovering, for one thing, that Brinkley's choppy delivery was a simple way to overcome fluffs and tongue troubles. It also allowed for a kind of emphasis on words or phrases that was difficult to achieve in a smooth, flowing read.

I got a second shot at a foreign assignment when Dave Rogers came into the newsroom one day, grinning from ear to ear, to ask me if I'd like to spend ten days in Germany. The Adenauer government in Bonn had a program that involved sending selected journalists to West Germany for an expense-paid, guided tour. You could work if you wanted, or you could simply go as a tourist. It was a very good public relations gimmick for its time, but one that would not work today, as journalists, even in small operations, are much more scrupulous about accepting freebies.

Any scruples Dave and I may have had were easily overcome by our desire to take the trip. We decided we'd work while we were there, and the consulate arranged for us to hire camera crews whenever we'd need them. Neither of us had any experience in shooting documentaries, so we were going to have to wing it, making it up as we went along.

We spent several days in Berlin, and hit most of the country's other major cities as well, filming and doing interviews as we went along. We drank beer in the Hofbrauhaus, rode a sightseeing boat in Hamburg harbour, and soaked up the night life on the Reeperbahn. We talked to politicians in Bonn, and we visited Dachau. On May Day, we watched thousands upon thousands of marchers turn the streets of Berlin into rivers of colour with their banners and flags as they converged on a monster park near the East German border for a day of speeches. The oppressive heat, the intense colours, the masses of people, and the constant verbal assault from the PA system all contributed to a mildly hypnotic effect. I found it was not a difficult feat of imagination to transfer the whole scene back a generation to 1938 or '39.

We arrived home full of enthusiasm and profoundly impressed with the miraculous recovery Germany had made in just 15 years—from the near-total devastation it had brought upon itself in the war. We put together our little documentary as honestly as we could, and it duly went to air: our hosts reported that while they'd been unhappy with some of our observations, they were generally satisfied that we'd done fairly by them.

The Hamilton municipal elections of 1960 provided a challenge of a different kind. CHCH's coverage was to be anchored by Jack Burghardt, who, along with his management position, held the post of heavy-duty announcer at the station, to be called in whenever something special was happening. That meant I was relegated to the position of second banana, which was fine with me; I was still feeling my way along in television, and an election telecast can get very complicated.

There were meetings and more meetings: we were to do the telecast from City Hall. Results would be displayed by a clutch of young women writing with grease pencils on paper pads fastened to a large flat. There would be an anchor desk, an area where interviews would be conducted, and banks of telephones for receiving the latest results from stringers manning the polls.

Election day dawned, and with it came word that Burghardt was too ill to work. I would have to fill in as anchor. Mercifully, most of what transpired that night is gone from my memory: I recall that the mayor was re-elected as expected, and I remember interviewing John Munro (who later became a federal cabinet minister), and congratulating him on his election as alderman. But the rest is vague impressions of struggling to maintain some kind of order amid what I was sure was utter chaos. If there is an ultimate "ordeal by fire" for television newscasters, it's got to be their first election broadcast.

* * *

Hamilton was growing on me. It was a bit rough around the edges, but it was just the right size for a city—small enough to get around in quickly, and big enough to be interesting. I was still close to Toronto and my old friends. My family, in Ajax, was nearby for regular visits.

Among Hamilton's amenities were some good restaurants—one, a Chinese place that was an after-hours hangout for the CHCH staff. Angelo Mosca, the . . . um . . . burly defensive lineman for the Hamilton Tiger-Cats, sometimes dropped in. That often made for an interesting evening. Somebody always had to take a shot at Angelo, and Angelo was not a man to turn the other cheek. Damage to furniture and other appointments was often quite extensive.

My colleagues at the station were an interesting and lively group, and the standard of work they turned out was remarkably high. To top it all off, I had a very satisfactory affair going with a young lady in the copy department, and I was on good terms with her family. The universe seemed once again to be unfolding as it should. That should have been a warning to me.

It was within days of my first anniversary at CHCH. My phone rang around mid-morning. Jack Burghardt was on the line.

"Harvey," he said, "you won't have to come in anymore."

I didn't understand.

Burghardt explained that the station had decided it didn't need a separate anchorman anymore. My job had been eliminated.

"Don't bother to come in," he said. "I'll have a cheque made up for two month's salary and send it out to your home."

I was flabbergasted. I called Dave.

"What the hell is going on?" I yelled at him.

"Harv, there's a cutback in the whole department." He sounded about as upset as I was. "I don't know what's happening."

I sat down and tried to think rationally. Damn! I'd been caught in one of CHCH's bloody purges, despite the promises it would never happen to me. I'd never been dumped from a job in my life! It was time for kicking things, and I did some of that while I cursed the bastards at CHCH who'd screwed up my career just when everything seemed to be going right. So they were going to pay me two month's salary, were they? I considered telling Jack Burghardt what he could do with his conscience money, but reason prevailed: who knew how long it might be before I had another pay cheque? I thought: "I'll sue the sons-of-bitches." In the 1980's, that would have been feasible. Not so in 1961.

That afternoon, I began making telephone calls. I'd met a lot of people in radio and television across the country, and through my membership in the News Directors' Association I knew many of the department heads. I had some solid experience behind me, and I believed I was reasonably well-regarded in the business.

I called a friend in Halifax.

I called Winnipeg, and Edmonton.

Then I remembered that an old acquaintance, a man I'd done some work for when he was at McLaren Advertising, was now general-manager at CFTO-TV, in Toronto. CFTO had gone on the air on New Year's Day, 1960. John Bassett, Joel Aldred, Ted Rogers , and several others had won a licence from the federal government and had put together a Cadillac of a station. However, while the technical facilities were state-of-the-art, the operation was fat with staff and overburdened with debt. Then, in a series of lightning moves, John Bassett, the swashbuckling publisher of the *Telegram*, and the Eaton family of department store fame (hence the corporate name, Baton Broadcasting Ltd.), bought out the founding management and took direct control. W.O. Crampton was installed as station manager, Murray Chercover continued as program manager and E.J. Delaney became manager of sales. Together, they were given the job of making CFTO into a paying proposition.

Bill Crampton had been involved with television for several years. He'd been a studio lighting man in New York, and a producer of commercials for McLaren Advertising in Toronto. Despite his sympathetic countenance and a genuinely warm-hearted nature, he was to become known at CFTO as the hatchet man. The staff had to be pared down to realistic proportions. There was fear and loathing in the studio, as each payday brought more pink slips from Crampton's office.

Over in Hamilton, I'd heard all the horror stories about CFTO, and had commiserated with those employees I knew. Now I was facing what seemed to me to be a desperate situation: I was unemployed. I called Bill Crampton. He listened to my tale of woe, then suggested I come to see him.

Next day, I was there, and for the first time I walked into the sprawling, new, red-brick building that was CFTO. A uniformed guard took down my name at the security desk at the employees' entrance and then passed me on through a windowless, cement-block corridor to a bright, broad, marble-floored lobby. In one corner there was a window opening into a telephone switchboard room. An attractive little woman in a beehive hairdo took my name and directed me to Crampton's office.

For a man of his reputation, Bill Crampton proved unexpectedly affable and outgoing. Nervous energy showed in the movement of his hands, the constant shifting of position in the chair, the quick, clipped phrases. He knew all about me, he claimed—followed my career since the days at CHUM, when I'd done some commercial work for him; watched my work in Hamilton; liked what he saw. He explained that a lot of changes were in progress at the station, changes that could mean important opportunities in the near future. In the meantime, he thought there might be a position for me on the newsroom desk. Would I be interested in that?

A desk job was not exactly what I was looking for—I was more accustomed to running the department. I guess I hesitated a little.

"Then, maybe a little work filling in on the air. You'd get extra pay for that, of course."

A little voice somewhere in the back of my head said: "Take it, idiot!"

"Yes sir," I said. "I'd like it."

He said he'd talk with news director Ron Poulton, then get back to me in a day or two. In the meantime, would I like a tour of the place?

We stopped at an office next door first. There, I met a tall, gaunt young man with black, wavy hair and a pencil-thin moustache (the kind that Boston Blackie had). He spoke in the deep, rich, velvet tones of a matinee idol, and had a little of Ronald Colman about him. This was Murray Chercover, then program manager at CFTO, later to become president of the CTV network, and a man who would be a fundamental influence in my life, both professionally and personally. I met E.J. (Ted) Delaney. Ted had come to CFTO from Barrie, where he'd started out selling cars. He was short and stocky, and his hair was already thinning a little on top. One eye was a little out of line—not crossed, but off just enough to make talking with him slightly disconcerting: you could almost see the wheels turning in Delaney's head, but because of his eyes, you were never quite sure in what direction they were taking him.

I walked down the long, hospital-green corridors, through Studio 1, Studio 2, Studio 3, the rehearsal hall, the back shop with its busy carpenters and painters, and the wire-caged prop room, where you might find anything from a stuffed moose head to a portrait of Queen Victoria. There must have been a dozen studio cameras in the place, scores of flats and sets, and equipment for both film and video-tape editing and playback. And people! Young women hurrying here and there, carrying clipboards: young men, neatly dressed, looking purposeful; other men and women in jeans, casual, unhurried, obviously technicians.

I went up some stairs to master control, a big, window-less room, darkened, with monitors everywhere. Behind it, racks and racks of cable—the wiring for the place—and more control rooms, each with its own monitors, switching board, and audio booth. I was overwhelmed.

Finally, we reached the newsroom. It was a long, narrow room, near the middle of the complex, with a spartan, no-nonsense feel about it. There were some green, steel desks, wire and wirephoto machines, typewriters, and a big as-signment board which, it appeared, nobody used.

Ron Poulton sat in an office that walled off one end of the room. I'd known him as a feature writer and columnist for the *Telegram*. When Baton Broadcasting took over CFTO, John Bassett asked him to set up the newsroom. The ru-mour was that Poulton had accepted the job reluctantly, that his heart was still with the paper. During our brief encounter, I got the impression that he took his work, and himself, very seriously.

I left CFTO utterly agog. It was easy to see how the finan-cial problems had come about: there was enough equipment and studio space in the building to set up three television stations like CHCH in Hamilton—and enough people to staff them, too. It was magnificent: everything about it looked and smelled . . . professional. As I drove past the security gate and its guardhouse and out to Highway 401, I slowed down to look back at this imposing complex rising out of what was still undeveloped countryside: its sky-high transmitting tower, the acres of paved parking lot, all completely fenced with eight-foot-high chain link. I drove back to Hamilton elated by the possibility that I might work there—pleased, in fact, by the simple prospect of a job.

Two days later, Bill Crampton called back to formally offer me the writing/editing position, and I jumped at it. By then, the idea had developed in my mind that if Ron Poulton was truly unhappy in the job, maybe he'd want to go back to the *Telegram* some day. As far as I could tell, that would leave me as the only person in the operation with experience running a newsroom. Maybe I could be at the right place at the right time, once again.

* * *

It didn't take long for me to discover that, despite the outward appearance of professionalism at CFTO, there was a numbing lack of incentive to perform well. Morale was somewhere well down into the minus figures. Some groups of people gathered in hallways, talking in low, bitter voices. Crowds in the cafeteria at lunchtime looked up sharply whenever anyone new walked into the room. No one looked forward to payday: that's when the pink slips were issued. It was as though half the station staff was standing on the edge of a cliff, waiting for the push.

Oddly enough, the cutbacks barely touched the news department—perhaps because it was a union operation, affiliated with the Newspaper Guild, or maybe because the news was close to John Bassett's heart. Nonetheless, when I walked in on my first day, the suspicion in the air was almost palpable. How come, with more people getting axed every day, this new guy was getting hired? How many were going to get chopped to make way for him? It was quite some time before the idea that I was a threat disappeared. In the meantime, I concentrated on demonstrating my competence in writing and reporting.

Many of the people I met in those first days on the job was to become long-time friends and associates. There was Jeff Fry, the dour and taciturn line-up editor, head of the Guild local, quick and capable, and dedicated to "the news;" Gordon Penny, one of the best writers I've ever worked with, who could put words in your mouth you'd swear were your own; Mike Finlan, a writer with a black Irish sense of humour and a temper of awesome proportions; and Morley Safer, who was just on his way out to take up a new job at CBS, where he would become a top correspondent in Vietnam, and later a regular on "60 Minutes." There was reporter Doug Johnston, a big, bluff guy from Manitoba, now the top correspondent for WABC in New York; and Bob Evans, our second reporter, tall and dapper, who was a master of deadpan humour. His abilities were to make him a top correspondent first with CBC and later with CTV.

The department also had two news readers. I don't like that term, but that's what Don Parrish and Roger Goodrich were. They had virtually no role in the operations of the newsroom. Don was a big, smiling man, a *basso profundo* and professional singer. His beautifully modulated voice gave him an authority on the air that belied his lack of knowledge of the stories he was relating. Roger Goodrich had come to CFTO from Boston, where he'd spent some years as an anchorman. It seemed to me that he read copy with his eyes, and the words came out of his mouth, while his brain was thinking about something else. Despite that, he had a solid, clean presentation.

The bothersome morale problem manifested itself in many ways, principally in the notion that the best way to survive was to do your job, nothing more and nothing less, and to keep your nose clean. I simply could not work that way. I was too eager to learn, to gain experience. As a result, I wound up taking responsibility for things that were not within the purview of a junior writer. When an announcer failed to show up for booth duty, I'd do the station breaks. I read occasional newscasts, and if a bulletin had to go on the air, I'd do it myself. It soon became evident that I was prepared to make decisions in problem situations, and that I had no compunction about calling Chercover or Crampton at home to help find a solution.

Before I'd been at the station six months, I was summoned to Bill Crampton's office. With him were Murray Chercover and Ray Arsenault, the executive producer, another CHCH alumnus.

The conversation went something like this:

"Poulton has decided he wants to go back to writing at the *Tely*. We need a news director. Would you like to take it on?"

I didn't want to sound overly eager: "Well," I said, "I don't know if I'm ready."

That was true. CFTO was the biggest television station in the biggest market in the country. It was clearly destined to become even more important once the financial troubles had been cleared away. Directing its news operation was no small responsibility.

It was agreed that Poulton would brief me for a few days before leaving. Then I'd take on the job on a trial basis, to see how it worked out. If it didn't . . . no hard feelings, and I'd go back to my job on the desk. I thought back to my first visit to the station, and my hopes of being in the right place at the right time: that's pretty well how it had worked out.

There was a stinger: as I left his office, Crampton said, "We'd also like you to read the early evening newscast."

I thought about that for a minute.

"Let me get the office part straight first, and then we can move into that." They all agreed.

The jungle telegraph works fast in a television station.

"Congratulations," I heard. I tried to ignore the unmistakable sarcasm.

Another voice: "Lamb to the slaughter . . . ."

None of that helped my composure of course, but I had expected some resentment. I was determined to make CFTO's a first-rate newsroom and a satisfying place for any reporter or writer to work in.

Poulton was anxious to be on his way. It was only a few days until I took over the office at the end of the newsroom. Furnishings consisted of a green metal desk, identical to those in the newsroom itself, some filing cabinets, and a couple of chairs. It was a small room, and the cream-coloured cement block walls were stark and bare. . . but it was mine, and I was damned well going to keep it!

Chapter 12

It didn't take too many days for me to realize that commuting from Hamilton to the eastern fringes of Toronto was going to be both tiring and dangerous. Even in those days, negotiating the Queen Elizabeth Way between the two cities was a lot like flying combat: there were homicidal maniacs driving big semi's, lunatic teenagers blazing by in hot-rods, doddering octagenarians cruising the passing lane, and the usual collection of drunks, hang-over victims, and child-thwacking parents—all of whom had to be avoided if one were to make it home alive. I was working long hours, and a couple of hours of dodge-'em at each end of the day was no fun. So with great reluctance, I decided to give up my comfortable apartment on Hamilton Mountain, and move to Toronto. On Victoria Park Avenue, in the city's east end, I found a mile-long strip of undistinguished, but roomy and inexpensive apartments in blocks of five and six storeys. I hung my hat in one of those. My relationship with the copywriter in Hamilton continued, in fact had become quite serious. I was having second thoughts, though. I was not ready to once again complicate my life with a permanent commitment, so I decided to cool it for a while.

I got the complications in another way.

The apartment next to mine was occupied by the Luke family: Hans and Renate, and their daughter Gudrun. Gudrun and I became fast friends from the time we first exchanged greetings from one balcony to the other. She was about three at the time, small-faced and skinny. I became "Uncle Harvey," and she became a regular visitor to my place. Hans and Renate were recent immigrants from Germany, he from the north, she from farther south— and they were a study in contrasts. Hans was slight and hard, crisp and proper. Renate was pleasantly *zaftig*, though she usually kept her long red hair tied up for efficiency. She was the motherly type, and took that kind of an interest in me, making sure I ate properly and that my apartment was in a reasonable state of cleanliness.

Through Hansie and Renate, I met many members of the German community in Toronto, among them Raimund and Ilona Bock. Raimund was tall and scholarly, fluent in several languages, and the editor of a German-language newspaper in Toronto. His red hair was thinning a little, and he walked with a limp, a souvenir of his days as a Wehrmacht soldier in the snows of Russia.

His wife, Ilona, was a short, plump, blonde and unmistakably cultured woman whose interests ran to opera and the classics. Her English was correct but stilted—she spoke German to her husband and most of her friends, so her only use of English was through her job as a saleslady at Eaton's.

If Ilona had one passion, it was for her daughter, Renate, who still lived in their hometown of Hamburg. As a bachelor, I was regaled with tales of her beauty and charm, and was often told how unhappy she was with her husband, and how desperately she wanted to come to Canada. I was shown pictures of Renate at the beach. Renate dancing. Renate at a party . . . before very long I'd had Renate up to here. Nonetheless, when I received an invitation to a party in celebration of her arrival in Canada, I decided to attend.

It was a small affair, easily dominated by this stunning young woman with long, brilliantly blonde hair, a compact, curving body, and slim, well-shaped legs. She had a pretty face: her teeth were too big, but that didn't detract—in fact, it enhanced her sensuality. She looked the very model of young German womanhood. She was to give me some of the best, and some of the worst years of my life.

We spent most of her holiday together, each of us finding ways to overcome the language barrier, and I learned a little about her. She'd been born in Hamburg early in the war and had survived the fire-bombings of that port city, though her family home had been destroyed. Following the war, her mother and father had divorced, and she was sent to live with her father and step-mother, outside the city. Renate was strong and willful, and could not get along with her father's new wife, so she took off, finding her way back to Hamburg to live with her mother. She worked in her mother's dress shop on the edge of San Pauli, the city's red-light district, where many of her customers were prostitutes. She married a childhood sweetheart and had a son, Bernd, before learning that her husband had been carrying on with her best girlfriend. She eventually threw him out, and came to Canada for a holiday with her mother. That's where I entered the picture.

I learned that she could be warm and soft, but that she also possessed a temper worthy of Lady Macbeth. There was a moodiness about her that came and went like a summer squall.

I was bedazzled.

Renate returned to Hamburg: her intention was to get a divorce, and then move back to Canada. For four months, we exchanged impassioned letters, she composing hers with the help of an aunt who was fluent in English. I arranged to rent a new apartment, a small, two-bedroom townhouse with a tiny front yard. I moved in, and spent most of my savings on furniture.

In November, 1962, Renate arrived at the Toronto airport with a mountain of luggage, and a pudgy, red-headed baby who was grouchy after his long trip. We went straight to the townhouse, with Renate's mother and step-father tagging along. There was a short celebration, with baby Bernd already sound asleep in his bed, and Renate half-dozing through the many *prosits*. Living together without the benefit of clergy was not as acceptable then as it is now, so we set about planning our wedding almost immediately. That happened in Agincourt, in December.

It had been a hectic six months. Now, here I was, newly-married, again, with a built-in family. The future looked bright. Work was going well, and Bernie was a wonderful kid, fat and jolly, with a big, round face and bright red hair. I enjoyed him, but as the first few weeks went by I began to see that the beautiful and vibrant young woman I'd married so impulsively was not going to be easy to get to know. She was a woman of many parts, by turns soft and gentle, or stubborn and arrogant: on the one hand, kind and considerate, on the other, cold and unthinking. Her temper could explode at the slightest provocation, and an unkind word could reduce her to tears, instantly.

In a brief encounter, language differences can be interesting. On an everyday basis, they became a serious challenge. Renate strove mightily to get a handle on English, and I tried to learn a little German. Progress was slow and frustration at times led to strong words—words which, of course, only one of us could understand. We usually ended up looking at each other in helpless frustration and then bursting into fits of laughter.

One such flare-up took place one night when we'd just finished dressing to go out for dinner. After a few sharp words, I stormed out of the house and strode angrily across the street into a construction site. In the dark, I didn't see the drainage ditch. One moment, I was muttering about damn stubborn Germans: the next, I was rolling down a muddy embankment in my nifty new suit. I walked back to the house, stood in the patio doorway, and asked sheepishly if I could come in. Language didn't matter then . . . we spent the night at home, convulsed in giggles every time we looked at one another.

Renate's limited vocabulary seldom kept her from offering advice, whether it was wanted or not. One day when I felt she was getting a little too pushy, I took off my pants and threw them at her, yelling:

"If you want to wear the pants in this family, here they are."

She quietly picked up the trousers and went off upstairs. A few minutes later, she returned, wearing a puzzled frown.

"There is nothing wrong with these," she said.

It took a while, but I figured out eventually that she'd thought I wanted her to mend them.

* * *

The worst of the surgery was over at CFTO: the staff had been slashed by almost 40 percent, and it was now a lean and efficient operation. I'd been ordered to trim the newsroom back by one person. It was a part of my job that I didn't relish at all. Union rules said it had to be the person with least seniority, and so, much against my better judgement, I gave the heave-ho to George McKenzie, a diminutive deskman who did good, solid work. Before I gave him the bad news, I called all my contacts. Finally, the *Telegram* came up with a job. The paper wanted a regional correspondent to cover the Oshawa-Whitby area. I put it to George: he was glad to have anything. It made me feel a little better.

Don Parrish left. It wasn't his choice either, but he wouldn't suffer like George would have. Don was a fine musician. He had a solid side-line in choral singing, and in lucrative commercial jingles. To my knowledge, his stint at CFTO was his only foray into news. He has since had a long and successful career as host of a music program on a Toronto radio station.

I had added a daily newscast to my duties. It was good for me: I enjoyed performing the anchorman's role, and it gave me a chance to work on-camera in this huge station.

The news operation was split between two bases—the newsroom itself, and the CFTO desk in the city room of the *Telegram*. The reporters were based at the newspaper, closer to where the action was likely to be, and we had a teletype system linking the two offices. Reporters came out to the station to edit their reports, but film for "voice-over" items could be sent out by messenger, and a rough script delivered by teletype. A writer would then supervise the film editing and script the final piece, which would be voiced by the anchor during the newscast.

I hired Pat Bennett away from CHUM to work with Bob Evans and Doug Johnston and the other reporters down at the *Tely*. She functioned as assignment editor, and because she'd worked with me during CHUM's news sojourn at the *Tely*, she knew most of the paper's editorial staff. As a result, she was able to maintain good relations between the two news operations, whose interests were sometimes quite different—occasionally even directly competitive.

I also hired a secretary. Sheila Courrier had an insatiable curiosity about everything. She held a pilot's licence, rode motorcycles, and, when I met her, was involved in scuba diving. She possessed a bountiful supply of good humour—also an asset—and had a pretty good Irish temper as well: her maiden name was Hogan. Sheila became the newsroom organizer. She not only kept my office orderly, she did the same for the whole unit.

Many of us in the news operation were still learning about television, having come from radio or newspapers or magazines. So when a municipal election loomed, there was a certain air of unreality about our planning. We were assigned a director, David Cooke, and we held some meetings. David was a quiet, Oxonian Englishman, soft-spoken and impeccably mannered. When we presented him with the plans we'd worked out in the newsroom, he blanched a little.

"But you can't do that, " he said. "It just won't work."

"Why not?" we asked.

It went on like that for weeks, as frustrating, I'm sure, for David, as it was for us.

But we pulled it off. The Melinda Street city room of the *Tely* made an ideal set for the telecast. It had the grimy, gritty feel of "The Front Page." A camera was mounted on a platform several feet above floor level, and it had a clear shot straight across the room to our scratch pads, where pretty girls in skimpy clothes tabulated results. My anchor desk was at floor level, so that I had to look up high and to the left to work the camera. Bob Evans and Doug Johnston had a position for interviewing politicians, *Tely* staffers, and whoever else might happen by. It was a sweaty, dirty night, but what came out on the tube was pure showbusiness: entertaining and informative at the same time. When we'd packed it in for the night, we had one helluva party.

CFTO was a place where many aspiring TV journalists wanted to work. When we needed a new reporter, there was no need to advertise. On one occasion, Doug Johnston suggested a friend of his who was working as a weatherman, staff announcer, and sometime singer at a station in Cornwall, Ontario. Doug insisted he was quick and intelligent, and promised that what he lacked in experience he'd make up in hard work. The young man's name was Barrie Dunsmore. He came 'round to my office, tall, serious, baby-faced, voice a little on the high side. He wore his clothes as if they were tailor-made. I had him do an audition, which I showed around to Ray Arsenault, Murray Chercover, and Bill Crampton. Barrie passed with flying colours.

Harvey Krick of Uno Park

Me with my maw

Striking a serious pose with my dad

My brother, Rod, in front of the sometimes
faithful family Whippet (car)

EARLY RADIO DAZE

Look out, Walter Winchell!

The Errol Flynn (?) of broadcasting

Above: On air with Jim Ward in Barrie, Ontario

Right: My first radio boss and golf partner, Bas Scully, with his "important" look

On location with CKEY at junior police games, Cobourg, Ontario, 1953

I found out that commercials weren't my bag, but oh boy, was I sincere!

Pete Griffin preparing to unleash "goolies" on unsuspecting Calgarians

My first overseas assignment, Vienna, 1956,
with *Tely* reporter, Alan Kent and Red Cross worker

The talented CJOH newsroom: Larry Henderson, Ab Douglas
and myself, conferring with a youthful Peter Jennings

An intense but skeptical Charles Templeton
at the '67 Tory convention

The Apollo 8 Moonshot: one of the most moving
moments in my broadcasting career

The view from the desk

On set with Tom Gould during the '72 federal election

Political conventions can be breathtaking in more than one sense. Here I am wrestling with a dead mike at the '83 PC convention.

Celebrants at my 20th Anniversary Party: (left to right) Lloyd Robertson, Chief Anchorman and Senior News Editor for cτv News: Murray Chercover, President and Managing Director for cτv, and his wife Barbara.

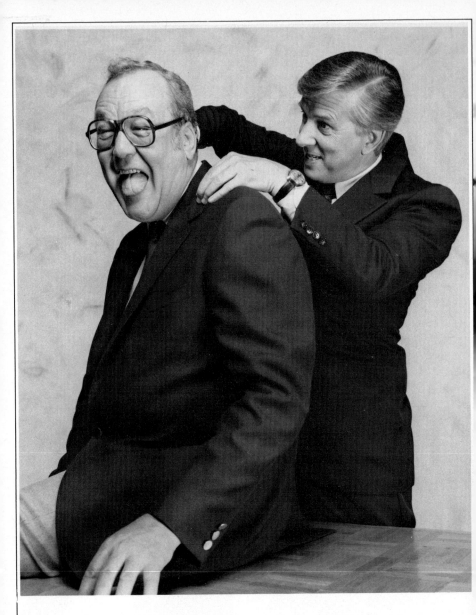

Lloyd receives news of my impending retirement
with customary calm and aplomb

Doug had been right: Barrie plunged into his duties with amazing energy and picked up the tricks of the reporting and writing trades with alacrity. So we now had three top-notch reporters—Dunsmore, Evans, and Johnston.

It was becoming a pleasure to work in the newsroom. Despite a small, and strict, budget, we were doing good newscasts. I had a virtual free hand, with very little interference from management—though Bill Crampton, ever the fire-engine chaser, made frequent, urgent telephone calls:

"You got the fire at Queen and Sherbourne?"

"Yeah, Bill, the crew's on its way now."

That didn't qualify as editorial interference in my opinion.

There was one occasion on which I was ordered to run a story that was a blatant promotion for Coca Cola. I resisted, initially, but finally gave in in the face of dire threats from on high. Then, I met the same resistance from the desk: "No way," they said.

We finally reached a compromise. I ran the story at the tail-end of the newcast, cut so short it was barely intelligible. I never had that problem again.

John Bassett called occasionally, his voice, booming through the receiver, loud enough to be heard at the end of the newsroom. He would ask questions and demand explanations, and occasionally suggest a story in the *Tely* that might be worth our attention, but that was all. He never once directed us to cover an event or slant a story in any way.

I instigated a newsroom hassle on my own one day. General Motors had a practice of shooting film of their new model cars each year, and shipping the clips out to various television stations across the country, to be used at their discretion. I received one such batch, and upon screening it, it seemed to me that just about everyone would be interested in seeing the new cars. I decided to run some of it in the newscast.

There was the predictable outcry from the purists: "All it is is free advertising for GM!"

I didn't think so. In any case, I didn't care. I was only interested in serving the audience. So the clips ran—tightly edited, but long enough to give the viewers a glimpse of what was coming. While the film was running, I glanced up from my script to see the entire studio crew gathered around the floor monitor. Upstairs in the newsroom, the same thing was happening.

After the newscast, I returned to the newsroom wearing a smirk. "Don't argue with Gunga Din anymore," I said.

I've never believed that audience interest alone is adequate justification for calling something "news." But then, there's a lot that isn't news that goes into TV newscasts. Cars are pretty harmless as non-news goes.

The management side of my job was another, less satisfying, story. I learned to dictate nasty memos when I was unhappy. George McKenzie came back to work for us and saved some of the more egregious examples, among them one about saving money by "severely restricting" the use of pencils and notepads. Bob Evans has two examples framed in his home: one contains fulsome praise for everyone on staff for the handling of a particular story. The second, dated one week later, severely reprimands everyone for persistently sloppy work. Nobody's perfect . . . .

Although management, which included me, generally tried to pay more than lip service to the rules and regulations of the Newspaper Guild, there were problems. I believe the trouble was that the local was so small no one took it very seriously . . . no one except its members. Everybody knew that a small local in a television station wasn't going to get a lot of support from the branches at the metropolitan papers. So the union's teeth were dulled. Jeff Fry, who could be a difficult man when he chose to be, was the Guild steward, and we had some pretty good shouting matches when contract rules were bent, as they often were. I remember once threatening to fire him on the spot if he didn't back down.

When you're under the kind of pressure I was feeling, you sometimes find peculiar ways to unwind. With Ray Arsenault, our executive producer, I developed a daily ritual around a CFTO children's show called "Kiddo the Clown." Kiddo was really Trevor Evans, a talented entertainer who later turned to directing high-profile television specials. While he was Kiddo, I'd stroll over to Ray's office each afternoon at five and the two of us would sit there drinking coffee, watching "Kiddo the Clown." It was "down time" in the newsroom—the time when most of the work for the 6:30 newscast was finished—except for the final burst of activity leading up to air time. Kiddo's humour was definitely juvenile, but there were occasional flashes which, I'm sure, were aimed directly at Ray and me. Kiddo could have said just about anything and he still would have been management's darling. His show had two very important assets in their view: it was cheap, and it was Canadian content.

Perhaps it was that show's success which inspired me to dream up a program on my own. I took my idea to Arsenault.

"Ray," I said, "I have an idea. I want to do a news department show, record it ahead of time, and run it on the weekend. And I can do it real cheap."

That last bit caught his attention.

"It'll be called FYI—as in "For Your Information"—and we'll use it to go into the week's news stories in depth. Maybe hire a commentator."

Ray took the idea to Murray Chercover, who bought it. So the newsroom came to produce its first regular program outside the newscasts. We kept the title "FYI" and we hired a curmudgeonly old commentator named John Collingwood Reade to work with me. There was no set to speak of: we cadged two steel desks, set them up in Studio Two, painted the floor, and made judicious use of Peter Edwards' lighting talents. The opening of the show had a wide shot across the floor to the two desks, each spotted in a pool of light. There was some taped electronic wizardry for the letters FYI, a bit of music, and then I would launch into the show.

The program didn't survive very long, but while it was on, I thoroughly enjoyed working with Reade. He took me back to my Calgary days and Guy Vaughan. They sounded exactly alike.

Chapter 13

No comprehensive history has yet been written on the beginnings of private commercial television in Canada. Yet it is a confusing, fascinating story, peopled by mavericks and buccaneers, big businessmen and entrepreneurs, who saw the glitter of gold fields on the horizon, and were prepared to stake them.

In the late 1950's and early 60s, second stations—CBC outlets being the first—were licensed in eight of the major Canadian cities. They were true independents, with no formal links between them. They formed a loose coalition, the Independent Television Organization, to share the cost of producing and buying programs.

In the meantime, one of the unsuccessful bidders for the Toronto station, Spence Caldwell, soothed his disappointment by tendering another application to the broadcasting authority, the Board of Broadcast Governors, this time to form a private television network. Lo and behold, it was granted!

Caldwell was, however, left in a room without a door. He had a licence to form a network, but no stations. Furthermore, the new independent stations, suffering growing pains of their own, had no wish to add to their burdens through affiliation with the new network.

Strange but true . . . the Canadian Football League played a major role in creating the CTV network as it is today. In 1961, John Bassett, operating CFTO-TV in Toronto, acquired the television rights to CFL games. To exploit these properly, Bassett needed national exposure to exercise his rights to this national game.

Again, not being privy to events in the boardroom, I can only guess at the wheeling and dealing that went on at that time, but John Bassett's football games went across the country, CFTO became a CTV network affiliate, and the remaining stations soon followed suit.

The second key event for CTV also came in 1961, when the stations took the decision to finance and produce a daily national newscast. The newsroom and production centre was at CJOH-TV, in Ottawa, and the "CTV National News" soon became a nightly feature at 10:30 in Halifax, Montreal, Ottawa, Toronto, Winnipeg, Calgary, Edmonton, and Vancouver.

So while it still had little identity of its own, CTV was beginning to spread its wings a little, providing ten hours of programming a week, then twenty, to its affiliates. It still remained dependent on the goodwill of the stations, however. (As a footnote in the future, it was not until 1965, when the stations bought out the Caldwell interests, that CTV became a viable organization. In the fall of 1966, CTV began its first season as a co-operatively-owned, independent television network, the first of its kind in the world.)

My own interest in the CTV network was, at the time, minimal; it seemed such a shoestring operation. When Michael Hind Smith, CTV's manager of day-to-day operations, called, asking if I'd like a job there, I told him no thanks. I was happy where I was.

*   *   *

The fledgling newscast at 10:30 soon died for lack of audience. It was woefully underfinanced, it was on at the wrong time, and while the two anchormen, Charles Lynch and Peter Stursberg, were knowledgeable newspapermen, they were less than charismatic television personalities. So CTV moved the newscast to the traditional 11 o'clock time slot, and launched an impressive on-air team.

This was to be Peter Jennings' introduction to network television. To offset his youthfulness and relative inexperience, the network teamed him with Baden Langton, a swarthy basso who'd been a fixture in Hamilton radio for years. Baden, or Buzz as we knew him, had a farm at Brantford, and his forays into media-land generally lasted just long enough for him to finance another project on his place. He was, nonetheless, a major asset for CTV. Then came Ab Douglas, a dour German-Canadian from the West, who had a strong background as a Parliament Hill reporter. He possessed a cool, no-nonsense presence on television. Charles Lynch stayed on as the fourth man, paired with Douglas. Each team would appear on the air three days one week, four the next and all four men worked as reporters in the Parliamentary Press Gallery (and as writers and editors as well). The unusual system had real potential for both editorial strength and on-air interest, but it was handicapped from the beginning by the program's inadequate technical facilities. The network had contracted with CJOH, the Ottawa affiliate, to produce the newscast, but neither the physical plant nor the production staff were up to the job. Worse, the network had to rely completely on a diverse batch of local newsrooms from Halifax to Vancouver for its coverage of events outside Ottawa, and these were almost all understaffed, underbudgeted, and busy—too busy to give priority to servicing the network's needs. The national newscast had no budget for microwave feeds, and that meant news film had to be shipped by air to Ottawa, often getting delayed or lost in the process. It was a pretty primitive operation, particularly when compared with the CBC's well-staffed and solidly financed production. Still, to the credit of all concerned, the network persisted. What the CTV news lacked in substance, it made up, at least in part, in presentation. Jennings and Langton in particular made an imposing team—Peter, young and dashing, and Buzz, the dark, sombre authority figure.

It was a thin, but not altogether inauspicious beginning for what came later.

*　　*　　*

By 1963, Ray Arsenault had left his job at CFTO to strike out on his own as an independent producer and director, making commercials and documentaries. In November of that year, he called and asked if I would do some commercial voice-over tracks for four Dow Breweries spots which were to be run in Quebec. (CFTO management at that time had no objection to news people doing commercials—they reasoned that it was, after all, a commercial station.) A few days later, I found myself sitting in a big studio in the Yorkville district of Toronto, facing a microphone, with Ray peering down at me from the glassed-off second-floor control room.

Cut one. Two or three takes.

"Would you do that again for me, Harvey?" Ray was being picky this morning.

Cut two. Cut three. We were eating up the time: I had to be in the newsroom before long. I glanced at my watch impatiently, and then something made me look up at the control-room window. Ray was staring down at me, his face suddenly grey and expressionless. I heard the little click as he opened the intercom key:

"Harvey, Kennedy's been shot."

"Very funny. Let's get this over with, okay?"

"Harv, I mean it. President Kennedy's been shot in Dallas."

I raced upstairs. A radio was going. I picked out the phrases . . . "Shot by marksman . . . Texas School Book Depository . . . rushed to hospital . . . condition unknown . . . ."

"Ray, I'm gone," I said.

Fifteen minutes later, I abandoned my car at the side door of CFTO, yelling to a security man to park it as I sprinted for the newsroom. I ran past crying secretaries and white-faced technicians: the place was in a state of barely controlled hysteria. The station had already plugged into the CBS coverage and was feeding the network live, while a small set was being thrown together in a studio not much bigger than an announcer's booth. I straightened my tie and stepped into that set to anchor the network's coverage of one of the most gripping stories of the century. The next few days fled past in a collage of horrific images: the pictures of the secret serviceman trying to climb into the back seat of the limousine with the Kennedys . . . the bursting silence outside the hospital, and the tears . . . the sombre music while we waited for word . . . the raw jangle of the Oswald arrest . . . the tiny sound of Jack Ruby's pistol and the rearing up of a burly, stetsoned sheriff . . .

and finally, the funeral . . . boots backward in stirrups, Jackie stiff and unseeing, little John-John saluting . . . .

CTV's coverage of the assassination marked the first time all the stations in the network had come together in a joint effort to cover a major event. The backbone of our coverage was provided by the American networks, and fed to the affiliates through the facilities at CFTO, where I was providing continuity. The CTV newsroom in Ottawa provided its archive material on Kennedy and interviews with VIP's; stations in Montreal, Vancouver, and across the Prairies shipped us whatever they could to provide a Canadian perspective on the tragedy. The result was a series of broadcasts that contained all the important elements of the American coverage, plus a strong representation of Canadian views and reactions. Though far from perfect, it was an effort the fledgling network could be proud of.

My thinking about CTV changed during that traumatic week. Until then, I had been content with my lot—controlling a big, professional newsroom and anchoring a daily newscast in the largest market in the country were things I had worked toward for years. Now there was the lure of national exposure, of being able—potentially at least—to speak to the entire country. Blind luck had put me in the right place at the right time to anchor national coverage of a complex and all-absorbing story of enormous impact. The idea of being in that position on a regular basis held a strong appeal.

When I received a third offer to join the network a few days after the assassination, I decided I'd better grab the opportunity while it was there.

Michael Hind Smith and I sat down to bargain. I'd join Jennings, Langton, and Douglas in Ottawa: we'd work in teams, four days on the newscast and three days on Parliament Hill as reporters. Like the others, I'd work whatever hours were required to get the show together on my on-air days, and squeeze in time off when I could. I'd have a couple of weeks annual vacation, and my salary would be $11,000 a year.

"Whoa," I said. "Stop right there. I'm damned if I'm going to take a pay cut to work for CTV."

It was a complicated situation. The CTV newscast was produced in Ottawa by CJOH, under contract to the network. That contract provided for CJOH to produce a newscast everyday to the network's specifications and standards, using personnel approved by CTV. So while in principle I was going to work for CTV, in fact I would be working for CJOH. That's how I first met Stuart Griffiths, and how he came to be involved in my salary negotiations.

Griffiths was a rotund, balding, little man with buck teeth and pebble glasses, who was so filled with energy that he bounced like India rubber when he walked. He was a brilliant broadcaster and knew as much about television as anyone in the country. He had spent several years at CBC during the beginnings of TV in this country, and then in England, where he was deeply involved in the setting up of an independent British television network.

As my salary negotiations dragged on, Griffiths and Hind Smith suggested that I take the $11,000, and they would give me a cash payment of $2,000 to bring me up to what I'd been earning at CFTO.

"What about next year?" I inquired.

"Oh, we'll work that out when the time comes. Don't worry."

I should have known better.

It has never been easy for me to leave a job. I had a special feeling for CFTO and the people there. I was proud of the newsroom and the way it was functioning: our newscasts had the respect of the community and I believe I had the respect of my peers. I also retained many reservations about CTV, chief among them the fact that the newscast originated in Ottawa. While Ottawa may be the focus of political news in the nation, that's about all it is. There's a lot more to news than politics. And, of course, the question of the level of technical competence at CJOH remained. It was not the place to be producing a network newscast. If that were not sufficient cause for caution, a look at the way the network itself was organized was enough to give anyone thinking of embarking on a career there the heebee jeebies. CTV was (and is) basically a co-operative wherein the network supplies the programs, but the stations control the budget. Each affiliate, according to its size and market, provides a percentage of the network budget, the size of those contributions being a matter for often bitter wrangling. It was not hard to see the potential for boardroom bloodletting when you looked at the line-up of independent-minded businessmen who were directors—men like John Bassett in Toronto, Ray Peters in Vancouver, Finley McDonald in Halifax, and Stu Griffiths and Ernie Bushnell in Ottawa. Clearly, CTV's growing-up would be long and painful.

All of this was on my mind as I discussed the move with Renate. We'd not been getting along very well. I believe she was frustrated with the language gap and with my long working hours, and was feeling generally lonely and isolated. She'd been back to Hamburg once, ostensibly for a visit, but I think, in her heart, to consider whether she should return home for good.

Renate agreed that I'd better take the opportunity while it was being offered . . . there might not be another chance. We both believed that this move to Ottawa would be temporary, that somewhere down the line the network newscast would certainly move to Toronto, where the network offices were located, and where the flagship affiliate could offer the best in technical support. So we plunged ahead.

Chapter 14

I hadn't spent a lot of time in Ottawa, and Renate had never been there. Before we began house-hunting, we took some time to look around. We drove by 24 Sussex Drive, peeking through the hedges and gates, half-expecting to catch a glimpse of Prime Minister Pearson: past Rideau Hall, Governor-General Vanier's official residence, with its vast gardens greying in the fall frost; then past the Chateau Laurier and around Parliament Hill. The city's beauty was undeniable, and we had almost begun to look forward to the move by the time we'd rented a small house on Cline Crescent. We had yet to discover that, despite the imposing architecture and the magnificent parks, this city of civil servants behaved like a small town, with small-town attitudes and prejudices.

We made the move in late November, and I began work immediately. I became a member of the Parliamentary Press Gallery, an exclusive little club only open to members of the media who cover, or have covered, Parliament. The gallery itself was a dusty, dingy place, cluttered with great stacks of newspapers and dozens of beat-up wooden desks that seemed to have been left over from the era of John A. Macdonald. There were bulletin boards that were liberally papered with flyblown news releases, and there was a small bar where drinks were cheap. The place was alive and bustling with people: bright-eyed, busy young reporters from newspapers and radio and TV stations across the country; middle-aged columnists and commentators moving slowly and sedately, running a little to fat; and tiny, grizzled gnomes barely visible behind mounds of paper and piles of government documents—old hands who gave the impression they'd been installed with the original fixtures. Here and there small groups of men and women huddled in quiet meetings—I presumed they were going over details of the latest news break; more likely they were settling a time for meeting on the first tee.

I made the rounds of the various office blocks, greeting some MP's I knew, introducing myself to civil servants I'd been in contact with. Langton, Jennings, and Douglas had all been in Ottawa for some time, and they were generous in guiding me through the maze of government. I made appointments with senior ministers for briefing sessions: Mitchell Sharp at External Affairs and Paul Hellyer at Defence turned out to be most forthcoming of the several I met, both providing frank answers to my off-the-record questioning. It was an interesting learning process, but one that I would not recommend now. Politicians are no longer frank, and Parliament Hill reporting is no longer gentlemanly. Too often, politicians make remarks that are not intended for attribution only to see those comments turn up on the front page of some newspaper along with the politician's photograph. That is probably where they belong, given that a reporter's first obligation is to the public: better a breach of trust with a politician than with the audience.

In any event, those briefings were an unsavoury business that could only add to the unhealthy clubbiness that, then, as now, tended to erode the essentially adversarial relationship between politicians and the news media.

The newsroom at CJOH, on which we relied for camera crews, film editors, writers, and reporters, was run by Joe Gibson, whom I'd known from the days when he'd been with a Hamilton radio station. Our line-up editor was Brian Nolan, a thin, dark specimen with a nose that could only be described as a beak. Brian had about as black a sense of humour as I've run across in a business notorious for sardonic wit, and he had an explosive temper. He was also a brilliant producer and editor. CTV News was operating on a shoestring, but Brian was able to scrape together film from Visnews and CBS Films, find still pictures, stitch them all together with clever writing, and make the show work, night after night. It was a discouraging, unsatisfying, often maddening task, and the pressures were great.

Recently Brian told me, with a long sigh, "It was hard." That seemed to say it all.

The man who held the real authority over the newscast was Stu Griffiths. Nothing, absolutely nothing, happened at CJOH without his knowing about it. He was liable to pop up anywhere, from the management offices upstairs, to the carpenter shops out back. He would often appear in the newsroom at 9:30 in the evening, just to have a look at what we were preparing for that night's broadcast. He'd been behind the forming of the station's in-house union, which had effectively blocked organizing efforts by NABET and the other professional unions. It was really Stu's station, a fact which is nicely illustrated by the tale of Marine Studio 3.

I'd heard about Marine Studio 3 on my first day in Ottawa, and eventually curiosity got the better of me. A little exploring led me to an addition built onto the back of the station. When I cracked open the door, I saw a magnificent sailboat hull that must have been 40 feet long. Stacked around it were piles of the finest teakwood stock I'd ever seen, plus an abundance of stainless steel and chromed bronze marine hardware, rigging and other paraphernalia. I found out that the boat was Stu's, and that the station carpenter was really a boatbuilder, who sometimes knocked together sets as a sideline. I never learned how Stu managed that, but I wish I had.

My network debut came on December 3rd, 1963. I sat down in the book-lined set with Ab Douglas, pondering my fate. This next 20 minutes could determine the course of my career for a long time to come. I had a pretty solid background in local radio and TV, but this time, I would be facing Canadians from coast to coast—a far wider audience, and a far less personal and forgiving one. Or so I had theorized. Local personalities gain a loyalty that extends through the station to those on the air. I wasn't sure that that sort of thing was possible on a national basis. I doubted whether I'd ever again feel that kind of acceptance.

A few minutes before eleven, Jim Shaw, our director, called on the studio intercom from the control room: "Good luck, Harv."

The studio crew chimed in with their own good wishes. I felt a pleasant warmth, as though I had the whole gang behind me. The red light came on and we were away.

There were no hitches: Douglas and I moved smoothly through the newscast, alternating stories, until finally, we reached the end and said our goodnights as we collected our scripts. I picked up my pipe and stuck it in my mouth.

Back in the newsroom, I was clapped on the back and told what a great premiere I'd had. Jim Shaw, a slightly built young man with a shock of sandy hair, sauntered over and said:

"I liked the bit with the pipe. You should use that all the time."

Strangely, I continued to hear comments about that pipe, day after day. I didn't smoke it much in reality, though I liked to chew on it now and then. Eventually, it became a regular fixture in the newscast, and a personal trademark during several of my early years at CTV News.

Not long after that first newscast, I had one of my most memorable experiences in Ottawa. A few of us were sitting around the newsroom on a dull weekend in the doldrums between Christmas and the New Year. Parliament was in recess. There were no natural or man-made disasters that we knew of, no fires or robberies or deaths or births of any consequence: in short, there was no news.

"So what the hell are we going to fill 20 minutes with tonight?" someone wanted to know.

I had an idea.

"Look," I said, "why don't we call Pearson and Diefenbaker and ask them if they have a holiday message for the country."

This was well before Christmas and New Year's messages from politicians came into vogue. It was a suggestion only somebody new to Ottawa would make.

"You'll never get 'em, and if you do, they won't say anything worth putting on the air anyway."

"Let's try," I persisted. "What have we got to lose?"

We started cranking the phones. Pearson was out of town—no chance there, but Dief was at home and would be glad to give us a few choice words.

I piled into a car with a skinny cameraman named Paul Eckland, and we headed for Stornoway.

We were met at the front door of the opposition leader's official residence by Olive Diefenbaker, and she took us to her husband's study. It was a small room filled with books, which on closer examination turned out to be mostly bound copies of Hansard, the official record of the debates of Parliament. The walls were hung with photos and other mementoes of the Chief's long career as a lawyer, politician, and prime minister.

Paul set up his camera and before I could ask a question, Dief was off and running, regaling the two of us with one fascinating story after another, each replete with the kind of detail that does not fit easily into a 45-second clip. Several times I tried to steer him back to our subject. When I sensed something was coming that might be of use for our newscast, I'd nod to Paul and he'd start the camera whirring. But John would ignore it, and sally off in some new and fascinating direction. Minutes later, I'd hear the whirring stop.

There was no real conversation: you listened to John Diefenbaker, perhaps contributing the occasional "uh-huh," or "my goodness."

Elmer, John's brother, appeared at the study door; we were introduced and John continued. Olive brought tea and cookies; we thanked her and John continued.

After nearly four hours, Paul and I were beginning to worry about getting back to work. It was clear we weren't going to get anything of substance for the newscast here, though I could have stayed and listened for many more hours. As we were packing up to leave, Dief hauled a volume of Hansard down from a shelf behind him and handed it to me.

"Read some of this," he ordered. He listed some page numbers. "John A. Macdonald. Greatest Canadian who ever lived."

I took it, touched by the gesture.

Back in the newsroom, when I confessed I had come up with almost nothing for the news, I endured a chorus of "I told you so's." Cynics said I'd witnessed a classic Diefenbaker performance, a carefully wrought technique he used to get new members of the Gallery on side. None of that did anything to dampen my delight in memories of that December afternoon.

At about the same time, I had begun to get to know another larger-than-life Canadian—Ernie Bushnell, in whose name CJOH had been founded. Bush was getting on, and no longer took much of an interest in the day-to-day management of the operation; but he was a wonderful old character. A small man, he'd been shrunken further by age when I knew him, but he managed to be an imposing presence nonetheless. He was one of the authentic pioneers of Canadian broadcasting: his career had begun in the days of Marconi, and he'd been a part of the founding of the Canadian Radio Broadcasting Commission (later, the CBC). His secretary, Miss Appleby, was not much off his age, and had been with Bush for more years than she cared to confess to. She still guarded his door with quiet, prim efficiency, sorting his mail and bringing his coffee. I made many visits to that office, just to hear Bush spin yarns about the early days. He seemed to enjoy my company, too, perhaps because I was a good listener.

Aside from Bushnell and some of the studio crew, I made few friends in Ottawa. The camaraderie I'd experienced at most other places where I'd worked did not seem to exist at CJOH. Nor did I make any close friends in the Press Gallery. I found it a stuffy and self-important place whose members tended to consider themselves an arm of government, albeit in opposition. I could never take seriously the carryings-on in the Gallery—the race to get to freshly posted news conferences, the breathless wait for a ministerial pronouncement that, in many cases, would mean nothing beyond Smiths Falls, 40 miles away, but which would nonetheless be treated by the Gallery as if the future of the nation hinged on it. The fact that I aired those views in the Gallery from time to time did nothing to endear me to my colleagues there.

I was still a freshman on Parliament Hill when I was sent to London with a few of my Gallery cohorts to cover a Commonwealth Conference. These meetings of Commonwealth heads of state are held in camera, and the only meat a reporter is likely to latch onto comes from briefings at the end of each session. For the life of me, I couldn't find anything worth reporting. After two days, I got a call from Ottawa telling me in no uncertain terms to get something on the plane for use that night. So, at the end of the day's session, I made a list of what was said at the briefing, then stood in front of the camera and read this list, wrapping up with " . . . as I said, not much news from today's meeting." I didn't attend a Commonwealth Conference again for a good many years, and that was fine with me.

I did have a memorable experience in London that trip, but it was not the sort of thing I could file for the news. The fact was, I wasn't the only Gallery reporter who was finding the Conference a deadly bore. One night, a group of us got together to seek some diversion. We wound up in Shepherd's Market, where the ladies of the night had apartments, each with a name on a doorbell at street level. On a dare, I rang one of the bells, opened the door, and ventured up a creaky, poorly lit stairway. At a landing, I looked up and saw what at first I took to be a witch. She was 60 if she was a day: her teeth were bad, her hair looked like stooked straw, and she was wearing a filthy housecoat. I turned, raced down the stairs, and shot out into the street, right into the arms of my colleagues. They assured me, between fits of laughter, that the person I'd seen was a housekeeper. That may have been the case—I never returned to investigate—but I had a strong suspicion that the whole thing had been a set-up for the new boy in the Gallery.

I didn't know it then, but my career as a Parliamentary reporter was mercifully coming to a close. This was not so much in answer to my wishes as because of a series of changes at CTV News. These had begun about the same time as my debut, and were eventually to effect a switch in format from rotating teams of anchormen to a single anchor. It started with the departure for greener pastures of Baden Langton. He was approached by ABC News in New York, and although Buzz never liked to stray too far from his farm in Brantford, he decided the opportunity was too good to pass up. That left three of us to share the anchoring chores. The team arrangement pretty much fell apart, with each of us working when we could, and Charlie

Lynch coming in now and then to plug the gaps. Then we learned that Peter Jennings was also dickering with ABC. Over a period of a few months, Peter spent much of his time in New York, disappearing each weekend, sometimes missing a Monday broadcast.

His manner of leaving CTV is, I think, a story not widely known. He came back to Ottawa from New York one morning, two days overdue this time, just as Stu Griffiths was launching the boat that had been a-building for so long in Marine Studio 3. Some of us had gone down to the marina to watch.

Peter approached the boat.

"Stu, can I talk to you?" he asked.

"No, Peter. You're fired," was Griffiths' carefully modulated reply. We all heard it, and there was a stunned silence. Stu turned his attention back to the boat, and Peter departed.

Those of us who'd come down for the launching felt obliged to hang around for a ride on the yacht (which, it turned out, was so over-built it handled like a coal scow). None of us had the nerve to ask about Peter. We knew he was close to something big in New York, but it wasn't until we got back to the station that we learned he'd landed the plum. ABC wanted to revamp its newscast to present a younger image, in hopes of yanking the program up from it's third-place ratings. Peter had been offered the anchor desk. It was a stunning coup: he was going to a job coveted by every TV newsman on the continent. We were all quick to offer our heartiest congratulations, of course, but there was no denying the touch of envy they held. In the end, I don't think Peter was ever really fired from CTV—the differences with Stu Griffiths were cleared away and he left with a clean slate, and the network's best wishes.

Although Peter didn't last very long in his first go-round as anchorman for ABC, he went on to become one of the most respected correspondents in U.S. television, travelling the world for years, then heading up the London bureau before returning to New York and the anchor desk. He now has the stature, confidence, and experience for the role.

Larry Henderson was hired to join Ab and me. Larry had been the first newsreader on CBC television. Although he'd been out of network television for some years, there was no doubt among us that he would be a definite asset to our telecasts. He was tall and thin, and dapper as a silent-screen Lothario, with slicked-back hair and a thin, carefully manicured moustache. I was surprised at his lack of self-confidence, almost a timidity: he seemed to want very badly to be one of the boys, but didn't quite know how.

Soon after, Michael Hind Smith paid a visit to Ottawa, and the anchor people were called to a meeting. There was to be a change in format. Henceforth, I was to be the general anchorman, Larry would specialize in foreign affairs, and Ab would be the senior correspondent on Parliament Hill. The description sounded a little fishy to me: I was to anchor the entire show, calling on Larry and Ab in their areas of expertise, and yet I was to be given no special recognition. I decided to wait a while, before raising any objections; but sure enough, that's the way it worked out: the other two dealt with their specialties, while I was stuck with everything else. It meant a heavier writing load in the newsroom, and a heavier responsibility on the telecast.

I phoned Michael Hind Smith in Toronto. I was angry.

"Look," I said, "I'm carrying this whole newscast, writing most of it, and I'm still considered one among three equals."

Michael, the consummate salesman, assured me that the whole matter would be cleared up in a short time, but for a variety of undefined reasons, it was necessary for things to stay the way they were for the time being.

"How about money, Michael," I said. "You know I took a loss to come here."

"Harvey, that, I assure you, will be looked into." He could be as persuasive as a snake-oil peddler.

In the end, I continued to operate as the whole anchorman in all but title for several years, until the program moved to Toronto—and it wasn't until that move that I finally got the money business straightened out.

* * *

In 1964, there were no satellites whisking pictures and voices around the world at the speed of light: stories were filmed on location, then shipped by air to wherever the broadcast was to originate. When Winston Churchill died, there was a scurrying around in North America to find the nearest substitute for live coverage of his funeral. CTV joined in the general frenzy, with the newsroom pulling together every scrap of archive film we could lay our hands on. Being a relatively new organization, we didn't have much of a library. We were faced with going to air with really nothing more than a verbal description of what was happening in London, based on wire-service reports and telephone calls to observers there.

On the day before the funeral, Stu Griffiths raced around CJOH in apparent panic, before suddenly closeting himself in his office. His line on the telephone switchboard lit up and stayed that way.

We were too busy putting the finishing touches on our telecast plans, such as they were, to wonder what he was up to. I was to anchor the coverage, and Jim Shaw would direct. We had scripted our scanty archive material, and it was ready to roll. Newsroom staff had been assigned to run wire copy from the teletypes to my desk in the studio. We expected the wirephoto machines to be of some help in providing still pictures. It was a hopelessly inadequate plan, and we knew we were in for a drubbing from the CBC, to say nothing of the American networks.

As we left the studio after the newscast that night, we could hear Stu, still in his office, talking fast into his telephone.

After a couple of hours of troubled sleep, I returned to the station where I met Jim Shaw just outside the front door. It was four a.m. and the funeral was about to begin in London.

"Here goes nothing," I said. We were in for a 12-hour "wing-it" session.

In the lobby, we were accosted by a haggard Stu Griffiths. He was hoarse, his clothes were a wrinkled mess, but his eyes were burning like coals.

"Here's what's happening," he said. "The RAF is going to fly BBC videotapes from London to Halifax in their Vulcan bombers. They'll be copied *en route*, then distributed to each of the five North American networks. They'll be an hour long and you'll get them at intervals of an hour and a half or two hours, so you'll have to fill that time. Then you'll have another hour of tape to go with."

Jim looked at me. I looked at him. Our mouths fell open.

"How the hell . . . ?" I started.

"Never mind. You'd better get to the studio. The first tape will be in Halifax before long."

I was never able to confirm what had gone on in Stu's office during that long night. I believe, however, that he singlehandedly changed North America's coverage of the Churchill funeral, using his connections with Granada television in London to arrange for the Vulcan airlift. Coups like this one were part of the reason I had to admire Griffiths, even though I was finding it increasingly difficult to work with him.

* * *

At home, my life with Renate had reached another crisis point. We couldn't seem to avoid those mean and vicious arguments that would leave us both hurt and despairing. I was proud of her—proud of the way she looked and proud of her efforts to fit into the Canadian scheme of things. Her poise and confidence in public were something to behold: once, I did a studio interview with Prime Minister Pearson, and Renate and Mrs. Pearson were left alone in a viewing room to watch. Later, Renate told me:

"Mrs. Pearson said she thought her husband looked good."

"Yes," I replied, "and what did you say?"

"I said, 'And so does mine.' " she replied.

I thought, though, that she was a victim to a deep sense of insecurity; I often wondered what effort it took her to assume her self-assured role. She seemed to have an anger in her that would not be assuaged.

I wasn't surprised when Renate announced one day that she was leaving . . . going back to Hamburg and taking young Bernie with her. I watched glumly as she packed some of the furniture and other effects she'd brought with her, called in a mover, and ordered the stuff shipped home. Then she bought plane tickets, and in a few days she was gone.

Rattling around that half-empty house, I couldn't make up my mind whether this was right or wrong. I spent long, agonizing hours alternating between gloomy self-recrimination and self-righteous anger. I tried and tried to understand this woman who made me so happy one moment, and utterly miserable the next. In the end, I decided to leave the initiative to her . . . and wait.

A week later, she telephoned from Hamburg. She'd been wrong, she said. Could she come back?

"Yes," I said.

Then I got on the phone and stopped her shipment of furniture and personal effects, catching it as it was about to be loaded onto a ship in Halifax.

Renate stayed on in Germany for another week, visiting friends and relatives, then returned to Ottawa. We moved to a different house, outside the city in a small subdivision near the Rideau. I thought the change of scenery would be good for us both, and there was more room for Bernie to roam. I looked forward to a new relationship with my family.

Chapter 15

CTV News covered its first general election in 1965. There was little money, so we scrounged and cajoled up and down the network as the campaign began. With the help of our affiliates, we were able to scrape through, one day at a time. Meanwhile, a set was being built in the back shop at CJOH, and Bell installation men were busy wiring dozens of telephones in the studio. A print shop was preparing slips of paper with candidates' name, party, and riding, to record poll-by-poll results, as our stringers called them in from across the nation on election night. I was to anchor the election telecast with veteran Parliamentary reporter Charlie Lynch. There would be panelists and experts and all the talking-head stuff that makes up election coverage.

We were halfway through the process of preparing for election night in the studio, when Stu Griffiths and Michael Hind Smith announced we would have a computer to tabulate results, project trends, call "electeds," and do all the lovely things an election computer is supposed to do. If our coverage of the campaign had been a bit spotty, the election show itself was to be first-class all the way.

Election night came and a crush of eager, excited people crowded into a studio ablaze with lights, rehearsed and ready to tackle their appointed jobs. Charlie and I climbed to our perch above the rest, expecting an easy night of discussion and rumination, with the computer doing all the drudgery of assembling and assessing results. For about the first 30 minutes into the telecast, that is what it was like. Then the damned computer quit!

Charlie and I watched first with concern, then with growing alarm as the back-up paper brigade on the studio floor stumbled into action, and almost immediately began to crumble in confusion and panic. Orders were shouted back and forth across the studio. Wild-eyed men and women ran hither and yon. Perspiring computer technicians in white coats worked frantically on their cables and couplings and electronic gadgets. Within minutes, the information flow to Charlie and me had dried up completely, and we were left groping in the cameras' baleful glare for something, anything, to talk about. Then, runners started handing us the printed slips of paper with the individual polling-station results recorded on them. A slip for every poll in the country. There were thousands of them!

After a while, we realized it was no use. We grew nonchalant and detached—as I have read men do in the final stages of drowning, or death by exposure. Charlie would pick up one of the little slips of paper that by now covered our desk to a depth of perhaps six inches: "Oh, here's something interesting," he would say, and he'd go on to relate the numbers and perhaps give a little information about the riding or the candidates. Then it would be my turn. I'd dig into the pile and reel off some completely unrelated bits of information. It was like trying to assemble a script by picking sentences and paragraphs out of a hat: it made no sense whatever.

Though you might not have known it from our broadcast that night, Prime Minister Lester Pearson and his Liberals were re-elected. The stage was thus set for the bloody regicide of the Tory leadership convention two years later in which a battered and humiliated John Diefenbaker was replaced by laconic Bob Stanfield: poor, decent Bob Stanfield, who sauntered onto the federal political scene just in time to be pulverized by the Trudeau juggernaut.

The logistical challenges of election-campaign coverage provide about as thorough a test of a news operation as can be imagined. This one had mercilessly exposed CTV News' inadequacies: our lack of national correspondents outside Ottawa; the weakness of our support staff and the lack of technical facilities at CJOH; our tiny budget. There was an upsetting feeling that CJOH was subsidizing its local newsroom with the money paid to the station to produce the network newscast. While that may have been a perfectly permissible business arrangement, it rankled those of us in the newsroom who felt we should be doing more than we were. Brian Nolan had left us for ABC, following in the footsteps of Langton and Jennings. We seemed unable to find anyone with the experience or imagination to replace him. Jack Van Dusen, a former United Press reporter, joined us. But Jack, ever smiling and accommodating, was new to television, and was thrown into the breech without any apprenticeship. He made a mighty effort, then finally left for the civil service. Bert Marsh, another wire-service man, was hired. Bert weighed close to 300 pounds and drank prodigious quantities of beer. He had bad teeth and a squeaky voice, and he could pound out pretty good copy faster than anyone I've ever seen, his two index fingers flying over the keyboard and creating a deafening clatter. Unfortunately, we needed a line-up editor—a producer—and not a speedwriter; Bert, too, was out of his element. We struggled along.

I made a nasty vow to myself: henceforth I would do everything in my power to help get the newscast back to Toronto, under the direct control of the network. I had a willing ally in Don Cumming, number-two man to Joe Gibson in the newsroom. Gibson himself was dissatisfied, but his representations to Stu Griffiths were easily brushed aside—Joe had fallen into a little trap Griffiths sometimes prepared for valued employees, by borrowing money from the station to buy a house.

Prospects for a move to Toronto improved dramatically with the news that Murray Chercover had become the new general-manager of CTV. The old guard—the founders—Spence Caldwell, Gordon Keeble, Caldwell's chief lieutenant, and Michael Hind Smith were soon gone. Chercover brought with him a new and progressive approach to management, and a more constructive relationship with the board of directors.

The announcement we'd all been waiting for came in the middle of 1966. Beginning in September, CTV News would no longer be contracted out, but would become a staff operation run by network employees working out of studio and office space leased from CFTO in Toronto. So that there would continue to be a strong representation from Ottawa, the anchor desk was to be split between me in Toronto and Ab Douglas in the capital. The plan brought sighs of relief in the newsroom, the loudest from me.

Peter Reilly was appointed head of news and public affairs programming. Reilly was a hot-headed Irishman who'd been around the business most of his working life. Hard-nosed and aggressive, he'd brook no interference, real or imagined, and he was one of those people who manage to come up smelling like a rose, no matter what they fall into. Reilly came to Ottawa to look at the news set-up and meet the people involved. He asked me if I'd like to take on the job of setting up the newsroom in Toronto and then managing its day-to-day operations, while continuing to anchor the newscast.

"How much?" I asked.

"$17,500," he said.

That was a big jump for me. There was going to be a lot of work involved, and long hours.

"What about the newsroom?" I asked. "You've got some money to spend there?"

He said he had plenty.

I said: "I want Cumming with me. And we'll have to take two or three weeks off to get things organized."

He agreed.

With that, Don and I packed up our wives and kids and moved for two peaceful and productive weeks into his family cottage at North Bay, where we planned out a newsroom and began the search for people to staff it. We lured Brian Nolan back from New York to be our line-up editor, and hired Gordon Penny and Mike Finlan to assist him on the desk. They were both former colleagues of mine from CFTO, two of the best writers I knew, and both uncontrollable hellraisers. CFTO assigned Ralph Abraham, a stocky, swarthy Arab, and a cousin of Paul Anka, to be our director. Ralph was full of energy and bounced a huge mane of black hair around when he became excited. He was excited now, working with Brian Nolan to shape a news program that would be fast-paced, informative, and designed to rivet the viewer from start to finish. We planned to be as different as possible from our competition—the CBC National News—which we deemed to be dull, stodgy, and long-winded. Their one great asset, in our view, was Earl Cameron, who was rock-steady, straight, and believable.

Finally, in mid-September, it was time for us to put our ideas to the test. We'd rehearsed for days, and we all knew what we wanted to accomplish and how we wanted to go about it. Now, there was nothing left but to do it.

Our first newscast as a network operation was better than anything we'd hoped for. The pace was brisk, with short voice-over film clips, brief talking-head sequences, and reports compressed to about a minute in length. Ab, in Ottawa, came through with the same style—though, fittingly, a little less breezy and irreverent.

We were also in colour for the first time. That is, the studio segments were in colour. Anything we had to shoot on film—and that included virtually all non-studio content, including all the reports and film clips—was still black and white. That didn't stop us from opening the show with: "In colour! The CTV National News."

After the newscast, there was one helluva party. It was just as well we celebrated right away, because for the next six weeks, we had nothing but disasters. Everything we touched seemed to fall apart. Film did not appear when it was supposed to, or the wrong film came up. Videotape playback went haywire and broke up. We lost our microwave line to Ottawa in mid-show. Studio lights exploded on air. Pages of script went missing. Film broke in the telecine projectors. Graphic cards were pulled on-air. At first, head office called nightly to rant about incompetence, and CFTO people sniggered behind our backs. Then, as things continued to deteriorate, everyone began to feel sorry for us. That was even worse. Brian Nolan went into a deep depression; Mike Finlan and Gord Penny got drunk; Ralph Abraham, I'm sure, grew some grey hairs in his black mop; and I wanted to cut my wrists.

Finally, though, we began to get a grip on the program. We loosened our pace a little, and that gave a bit of breathing space to the people running the various technical aspects of the newscast. Telecine began getting film straight; videotape was there when called for. Studio technicians began to feel more at ease, and more sympathetic to our interests.

It was during this period of intense pressure on the newsroom that Vic Phillips became a victim of some ill-considered decisions—most of them by me. We desperately needed an anchorman to take over the weekends, as I was working seven days a week, and rapidly wearing myself out. Several applicants were considered, but none quite fit the bill. Vic was a young newsman working in Kingston at the time and when I looked at his audition tape, I decided he had the kind of potential we were looking for. He was younger than I would have liked, with big glasses obscuring his moon face, but he had warmth and friendliness on the screen, and I thought his delivery could be developed. I asked for other opinions, and got a good response. Vic was brought to Toronto. Then his trials began. Someone didn't like his glasses, so Vic gamely wrestled contact lenses onto his eyeballs while the tears streamed. Someone else thought he looked too young: "Put some lines in his face," make-up was told.

Vic did his best to meet each complaint head-on, eager to provide whatever it was the powers-that-be were looking for. Trouble was, nobody seemed to know what that was. It was obvious almost from the start that Vic wasn't going to make it: we found him another job, and he went on to have a long career as a TV news reporter with CFTO and, more recently, with Global Television. (He's also become a promising author.) Nonetheless, I'm sure there is still some disappointment in his heart, and I can't escape the feeling I did him a grave injustice.

Our staff of correspondents was rapidly expanding. Wally Macht became CTV's first bureau chief in Canada, hired away from the network affiliate in Moose Jaw, Saskatchewan, to cover Western Canada and the Arctic. All two million square miles! Wally set up his bureau in Winnipeg. His mandate called for him to provide CTV News with a presence everywhere north and west of Kenora. During the next two years, he and his cameraman logged tens of thousands of miles from the Arctic tundra to the drylands of southern Alberta, and from the Rocky Mountains to Lake Superior. After that, Wally came to Toronto to anchor the weekend newscasts, a job he held for the next eight years.

Henry Champ was plucked out of a radio station in Ottawa and made head of a new bureau in Montreal. He was an exceptional reporter who had an instinct for being in the right place at the right time. He was also the most undisciplined and disorganized correspondent on staff, and the business side of the Montreal bureau was a book-keeper's nightmare. His skills as a reporter, however, kept the sharp pencils at bay, and Henry went on to staff the network's Washington and London bureaus before moving to *W-5*, and then to NBC News.

Max Keeping, too, came out of Ottawa radio and, for my money, was one of the best Parliamentary reporters CTV News ever had. Max was a hustler: as a radio reporter, he had raced around with a tape recorder working on half a dozen or more stories at once. It took him months to slow down to the more relaxed pace of providing material for just one newscast a day. He had an on-camera presence that was superb; Max was one of those people who jump right out of the tube at you. For many years now, he's anchored the evening news on CJOH in Ottawa, where his fans are legion.

We were becoming more and more a force to be reckoned with. Some of the papers picked up on us, calling the newscast fresh and slick and interesting. I was becoming pretty well known across the country, though not yet what might be termed a media personality. Nevertheless, we were still far from being a serious threat to the CBC and Earl Cameron, the rock.

Then, Peter Reilly left the network in spectacular style, paving the way for further change. Reilly publicly accused John Bassett of interfering in the operations of CTV news. His charges came as a surprise to me—I'd been in control of the daily operations for some time, and I'd never heard a word about our telecasts from John Bassett. The story hit the papers, and Reilly made a weak attempt to substantiate his accusations before finally backing off and resigning.

The stage was now set for the Charles Templeton era at CTV News.

* * *

What we lacked most in those days was prestige and credibility as an news organization. It was in part to provide those elusive qualities that Charles Templeton was brought into the organization. The right man for the right time. Charles the Renaissance man and media star: writer, broadcaster, inventor, former evangelist, former newspaper editor, former cartoonist, and former God knows what-all else. It was a measure of his enormous self-confidence—some would say ego—that he took on the job of managing the network's news and public affairs department without a scrap of television administration experience. But Murray Chercover had lured Charles to CTV, so Charles could count on Murray's support and advice. We were soon to learn that Charles had some pretty firm ideas of his own.

In the newsroom, there were mixed feelings about Charles' arrival. I think we were all a little skeptical, some of us more than others. Don Cumming, who'd been my assistant since the move from Ottawa, was not a Templeton fan, a fact he made clear to anyone who cared to listen. He felt Templeton was not a newsman, and argued that since he had no experience in day-to-day news, he should keep his nose out of the newsroom. It was obvious to me that a clash was building, but Don would not listen to warnings. When it finally came, it was over a few frames of film of a nude woman that we'd aired in a newscast—but that was only a pretext. Behind the confrontation was Don's ill-concealed contempt for Charles, and Templeton's readiness to return the sentiment. Don left for the CBC.

The loss of Don Cumming was a blow. He'd been instrumental in setting up the newsroom, and was a key man in the day-to-day operations of the department. He was on good terms with contact people at our affiliates, and had a fine rapport with our staff correspondents. The fact was, he knew the operation's routines much better than I did, and I felt lost without him.

About this time, Templeton suggested that my own work load was too great, and that I should confine my activities to anchoring and assisting in the production of the newscast. On the face of it, it was an attractive idea: it meant shorter hours, less responsibility, fewer tiresome administrative duties, and a chance to concentrate all my energies on the presentation of the news. When I heard who Charles had in mind to replace me, however, I dug in my heels. He had nominated John Must, an affable young Australian who was a fine producer, but who had had no previous contact with CTV News. I had the impression, in fact, that he had never worked in a newsroom. Charles and I had a number of "discussions" on the question, but digging in your heels with Charles Templeton is like trying to get a grip on wet clay. In due course, John Must was placed in charge of the day-to-day operations of CTV News.

In retrospect, it was a good move for me. As I had expected, I was able to devote more of my energy to production and presentation of the newscast, and that showed on the air. For John Must, it was not as satisfactory. He was out of his element, did not receive the support and respect of his staff, and thus was not effective. He didn't stay long, but went on to produce a brilliant and long-running wildlife series for the network.

John Must was succeeded by Jeff Fry, who was as dour and undiplomatic as he'd been when we worked together for CFTO. He, too, moved on before long. It was not until Charles Yellowley arrived on the scene from Montreal that our newsroom achieved a degree of stability. Charlie was a lean, soft-spoken young man who'd paid his dues in both radio and television news in Montreal, and who had done work for our newscast while he was employed by CFCF-TV, the CTV affiliate in that city. His appointment was greeted with enthusiasm all round, and, for several years, Charlie laboured to gain a bigger national audience for CTV News.

*   *   *

Ab Douglas quit after a long series of disputes over his autonomy as Ottawa bureau chief. It has always been my belief that any reporter, no matter what his seniority or assignment, must be answerable to the main desk, where the newscast is actually assembled under the direction of the assignment and line-up editors and, ultimately, the executive producer. Unfortunately, when Ab was put in charge of the Ottawa bureau, the network led him to understand that he would not be answerable to me or anyone else in Toronto . . . that he would have complete autonomy to cover the news as he saw fit. A newsroom can't operate that way—the tail can't be allowed to wag the dog. With so much news from so many places competing for attention each day, it is unwise to give first dibs on precious air time to any bureau, capital city or not, if for no other reason that it gives unmerited editorial weight to that bureau's file. In packaging a daily summary of national and world news, judgements as to any story's merit ultimately have to be made at the centre, where all the competing elements can be given a fair hearing and be judged on their intrinsic merits. Ab could not accept that, and so made his departure.

Tom Gould became our new Ottawa Bureau Chief, hired on the rebound after he'd ended a long association with CBC, where he'd quit over a matter of principle. We were to learn that such disputes were part of his stock-in-trade. He was a big man—big shoulders, big hands, big face, and he was blunt and aggressive—given sometimes to overblown rhetoric and explosive, often misplaced anger. Later on, when he became vice-president of the department, our VP for sales, Ray Junkin, dubbed him "Mr. Integrity." It fit.

Tom was given the same autonomy in Ottawa as had been granted Ab Douglas, much against my better judgement. Fortunately, he seemed to have a deeper understanding of the problems of producing a daily newscast. We quickly reached a *modus vivendi* that saved us all a lot of aggravation. He would discuss with the desk what might be covered on a given day, and if he could convince Toronto that all his material was vital, then it went to air. If he couldn't, then he had to get along with whatever time was available. That usually worked reasonably well.

At about the same time as Gould was hired, another CBC refugee, Don McPherson, was brought into CTV as Templeton's assistant. An easy-going production wizard, McPherson's first assignment was to plan CTV's coverage of the 1967 Conservative Party leadership convention. Given the dramatic events that had preceded it—John Diefenbaker's bitter, often pathetic struggle to maintain control over a party that no longer wanted him—the convention promised to be a spectacular event in itself. At CTV, we saw it as our chance to establish CTV News in the hearts and minds of Canadians once and for all as a credible alternative to the CBC. All the troops were to be called in from the far-flung bureaus, and we would blanket the convention with reporters. Pierre Berton—already a national institution—was hired as a special floor reporter, as was columnist and former NDP MP Doug Fisher. Tom Gould, Charles Templeton, and I were to share the anchor desk. No expense would be spared to give us the best technical facilities available: we were to have as many cameras as we could conceivably use. We'd have a fancy new electronic process called Chroma-key, which could project or "key" a picture shot by one camera, as a backdrop for the picture of another. Thus, in the same shot as our anchor desk, high in the stands at Maple Leaf Gardens, would be the crush of delegates on the convention floor. Best of all, our coverage would be entirely in colour.

McPherson proved his worth to CTV during that one event. Calling the shots from a small, glassed-in control booth next to the anchor desk, he orchestrated television coverage that was fresh and exciting. The program was a *tour de force*.

Nevertheless, there had been serious problems with our coverage, and those problems brought me as close to resigning from CTV as I have ever come. This kind of telecast was new to Templeton. When the red tally light came on, Charles began talking, and he talked, and talked, and talked. Tom Gould, on one side, occasionally managed to squeeze in a word or two, but I was relegated to making station breaks. Worse, our floor reporters were either ignored, or their information was not believed.

I was furious! From my perspective, what was happenning was a serious embarrassment for the daily news operation and its major players—me,and the staff of bureau reporters from across the country. They were being systematically kept off the air, and I was being left to say little more than: "We'll be back in a moment"—all in the context of a program that was perceived by viewers and critics alike to have been sensationally good.

Next morning, I was in Murray Chercover's office bright and early.

"You saw what happened, Murray. I'm finished. I quit. I will not be put in that position. What the hell does that man think he's doing?"

Chercover was conciliatory. He agreed with me that Charles had dominated the telecast more than was necessary, but he argued that his behaviour was unlikely to have harmed the daily program: we had come out of the convention with a clear win over CBC, and that victory would do nothing but good in the long run.

It's not easy to argue with success, but I was firm on one point:

"Murray," I said, "I will never work another telecast like that with that man."

I expected that word of my visit to Chercover would get back to Charles, and, while we never discussed it, our working relationship was cool for some time after. A year later, when the Liberals met in Ottawa to choose Pierre Trudeau as their leader, I remained in Toronto. And therein lies another story.

Chapter 16

My marriage to Renate continued its stormy course. There would be periods of great joy, followed by episodes of dark depression, and though I know this is not what the textbooks say is supposed to happen, it seemed the more we talked about our problems, the more frequently they occurred. I believe Renate increasingly resented being an appendage to someone who had a degree of celebrity—I think that deepened the sense of insecurity she'd been afflicted with ever since I'd known her. If that was the case, however, she never confided in me. She still kept a wonderful home: her decorating skills made the ordinary seem different, and she was a good cook and a dedicated and loving mother to Bernie. Bernie did not do well in school in his early years, and Renate spent endless hours trying to help him with his studies. Then we learned he suffered from a mild form of dyslexia, and Renate spent more hours, and miles of driving, taking the boy to downtown Toronto for special schooling.

But dammit, we were constantly in confrontation, battling over insignificant issues on which neither of us would give an inch.

The fact that I had to organize my life around the unpredictable demands of the news made matters worse. Renate's health was not good, perhaps because of the deprivations of war-time in Germany. She suffered from ulcers, and once, when I had been assigned to cover a Royal visit to Quebec City, I received an urgent call from a neighbour: Renate had collapsed in a supermarket, and was in hospital. She needed surgery . . . now. She had the operation, the first of several for ulcers, but the fact that I was not with her, rankled. She was unhappy that I'd been away at a dangerous time for her, and I felt guilty for having been unable to help.

In 1967, we bought a house in a small subdivision close to the Rouge River area of Scarborough that we loved. Renate was a good money manager, and for the first time, I'd been able to accumulate enough cash for a down payment.

In October, 1967, Tina Marie was born. Again, I was working. Renate called: "It's time."

I raced home. Renate was packed and ready. We sped to Scarborough General Hospital, where Renate was taken to a delivery room, and I was left to do all those things I'd seen other expectant fathers do. Walk up and down. Smoke a cigarette. Call the office to warn them I wouldn't be in tonight. Walk up and down some more. More cigarettes.

Finally, Renate waddled into the little waiting room, accompanied by a nurse. It had been a false alarm. Back home we drove, and as we walked through the door, Renate crumpled a little: "Ooooooh."

Another race to the hospital. This time, it was the real thing, and after more pacing and smoking, a nurse appered before me carrying a wrinkled little person, all purple and squinty.

"Harvey, you have a beautiful girl," nurse said.

Having had little experience with newborns, I could not for the life of me see the beauty in this little bundle. Then she moved her head, waved a tiny hand, and squawked, and she *was* beautiful!

Tina grew into a fat, happy little baby, but she was plagued with bronchial and allergy problems. In her first two years, she suffered through 13 visits to hospital, each time for decongestion treatment, and a few days in a tent to help her breathe. Finally, with the help of those treatments, she grew out of the condition into a truly beautiful, bright little girl.

* * *

If 1967 marked a point of departure in my family life, it was also to usher in a period of important developments in my career.

CTV News was at last beginning to gain the recognition we had sought for so long. Our audience figures were still far behind those of the CBC, but that was in part due to the fact that we had far fewer stations along the network. We also had the disadvantage of getting on the air at midnight in the Maritimes, while CBC produced a newscast at eleven for the Atlantic audience. Even there, we had a large and loyal following: I was always amazed on visits to eastern cities to be recognized as often as I was. Our affiliates were rapidly setting up repeater stations throughout the country to enlarge our coverage. Where we were able to compete head-to-head with the CBC, we did extremely well, often topping them in the ratings. The sales department was happy with us: our program was sold out for years in advance, with a waiting list of advertisers to sign up if one of their number dropped out for any reason.

Despite our success, CTV News laboured away with a budget that was miniscule compared to our competition's. There was a perpetual lack of manpower, both in Toronto and in the few bureaus we'd established, and our reliance on affiliate newsrooms remained a hit-or-miss proposition. Happily, we had a gung-ho staff who made the best and most creative use of what we had. Our studio sets were models of simplicity, and economy. For several years, we were afflicted with a terrible backdrop—a map of Canada made from styrofoam blocks painted a bilious yellow beige. Government regulations forbade commercials for the first ten minutes of the newscast, but we managed to get around that by opening with a series of datelines.

"Good evening. Tonight's stories are from Toronto, Washington, and London."

As I spoke the words, one of the studio cameras would focus on a black board with slots cut in it. Good old George Beck, rest his soul, stood at one side of this board, and, as each dateline was mentioned, he'd slide back a black, cardboard mask to reveal the name of the city, which was keyed or superimposed on the styrofoam map. Today, of course, all of this is done electronically. But our home-made system worked well, except when George got a little shaky, and the card wobbled a bit as he pulled: viewers might then have been forgiven for thinking we had an earthquake story coming up.

Management, of course, could not be denied its perogative to manage, however successful we were becoming. These interventions were not always helpful.

Charles Templeton had a bright idea for showing the CTV flag across the country. We would close the bureau in Winnipeg, bring Wally Macht and his crew to Toronto, then use the bureau budget to pay local reporters and newsrooms to cover regional stories for us. To some of us, that sounded like a step backward to the system we'd had to put up with during the old days at CJOH in Ottawa. But Charles reasoned that the West was far too big an area to be covered effectively by a two-man bureau in Winnipeg.

The only good thing about that plan was that it brought Wally to Toronto. A big, rugged Westerner, he was good in the studio, and would be an important asset to us, taking over the weekend anchor position. As for closing the bureau and relying on the local stations for coverage of regional news, that part of the scheme was a disaster. All of us who'd been associated with daily news realized that the local newsrooms were hard-pressed to look after their own needs . . . that any work done for the network would come second to their own interests. We'd been that route before, and the few dollars Charles planned to distribute for work done would not make a whit of difference. After the initial honeymoon period in which there was some enthusiasm shown by the affiliates, the level of co-operation sank back to the absymal level we all knew so well.

*   *   *

When the time came for us to cover the 1968 Liberal leadership convention in Ottawa, I stuck to my word and stayed home: if memory serves, Charles avoided a confrontation by not even suggesting that I go. The network's convention coverage matched the success we'd had at the Tory convention a year earlier, but the CBC had sharpened up a great deal in the interim, and their programming improved markedly. This time, CTV did not have it all its own way.

If I felt the tiniest bit left out, watching at home, the sensation was to be quickly dispelled by the slip and slide of circumstance. On the final day of the convention, as delegates were sweating their way through the voting that would give the leadership to Trudeau, a rifle shot cracked over some run-down buildings in Memphis, Tennessee, and Martin Luther King staggered, then dropped to the floor of the balcony outside his motel room. He died in the arms of friends and aides. For several hours, there was an ominous quiet on the news wires. Then, in a paroxysm of anger and frustration, the black ghettoes erupted in a nation-wide orgy of arson, rioting, and looting.

Moments after the first bulletin from Memphis moved on the wires, I got a call from the news desk. Within minutes, I was in the newsroom, on the phone to Ottawa. The network would have to break away from the convention as often as possible, to allow us to keep up with the story unfolding south of the border. A studio crew was assembled, and a podium was set up for me in Studio 2 against a curtain backdrop. For the rest of the day and into the early evening, CTV cut between convention coverage in Ottawa and our little set-up in Toronto, where I kept up with events through wire copy, occasional reports from U.S. networks, and whatever else came to hand. The newsroom dug up a library biography of King, gave me a handful of notes, and I ad-libbed a commentary over the film. It was an incredible day, the kind when adrenalin flows freely, and fatigue and emotion are held at bay until it's all over.

It was to be a long time in ending for me.

When we'd wound up our special coverage in time to prepare for the newscast, I walked back slowly to the newsroom where I found a telephone call waiting for me.

"Mr. Kirck?" an unfamiliar voice asked.

"Yes."

"Mr. Kirck, this is the Durham Regional Police. I'm sorry, but I must inform you that your father has had an accident. Your father is dead."

There were no feelings. Just a sudden, heavy weight in my chest.

I called Renate, telling her only that we had to go out to my parents' home in Ajax right away. Then I told the newsroom I had a problem, and left.

On the way home, I tried to digest the news. My father had had a couple of heart attacks a few years earlier, but he'd been in relatively good health lately. There had been a time, years ago, when we had not been very close, but as my career had begun to grow, I had learned to lean on him for advice. Although he'd been a labourer all his life, his insight had been invaluable to me. He was just 63, and he'd been looking forward to his retirement. He had ordered a new car, one that would better pull his little house-trailer, and he and my mother had plans to do a lot of travelling in a couple of years.

Renate and Bernie burst into tears when I told them what had happened. We drove to the Ajax Hospital, and there I was directed to a small emergency room where I found my mother, her face streaked with tears, holding Dad's lifeless hand. She couldn't speak: her eyes had an anguished look I'd never seen in anyone before.

I looked at my father. He seemed to have been thrown onto the tiny steel bed. One leg hung over the side, his head was thrown back over the top, mouth open, false teeth removed. He looked awful.

"Come on, Maw," I said, and I led her from the room.

I found a supervisor, and angrily demanded that someone put my father's body in reasonable order. It was done, and my mother and I spent the next hour with him, sharing our grief.

Dad had been baby-sitting my brother's children that night, while Rod and his wife, Marg, visited the Home Show in Toronto. He had complained of not feeling well to one of the girls, and about 8:30 he said he'd better go home. He drove his car about two blocks, then was hit by a massive aneurysm—a bursting of one of the arteries to the heart. A doctor told me he was dead in that instant. His car continued down the street, broke off a lamp post, jumped a curb, and came to a stop against the front wall of a house. The residents rushed out and opened the car door. My father apparently tried to say something. It was unintelligible.

There were a dreadful few days to be lived through—funeral arrangements, visits to the mortuary, the forced small-talk among family and friends. Finally, the morning of the funeral, my brother and I went to the chapel to see that everything was in order.

Lying there in his open coffin, Dad didn't look right, Rod and I both agreed. We puzzled over that. Suddenly, it hit me: he wasn't wearing his glasses. For years, he'd never been without them. We hurried back to the funeral home and demanded the funeral director find them and put them on him. Now he looked like Dad.

I find funerals hard to take at the best of times, but I was coping well enough with this one. Dad had been an Oddfellow, and members of the Lodge performed their rite for departed brothers. Then came the regular funeral. I happened to turn to the door of the chapel and there, just arriving, were Charles Templeton and Murray Chercover. I suppose it was simply their unexpected gesture of kindness that affected me so profoundly, but I lost my grip completely and bawled like a baby into Templeton's chest. I cherish their thoughtfulness in that moment to this day.

* * *

The pressures of work helped to bring me out of my grief. With both major political parties sporting new leaders, a general election was in the offing, and when it finally came, CTV was fired with enthusiasm. With two successful convention telecasts behind us, the newsroom was on a roll, and looking forward to the really big show. The campaign promised to be the most exciting in years. The old warhorses Diefenbaker and Pearson were both gone, and the contrast between their respective successors was fascinating. Stanfield: older, staid, gaunt, a nice man whose personality withered and died when the television cameras turned on him. Trudeau: dynamic, aggressive, athletic, some said brilliant; a lean, saturnine face that could flash withering contempt and, almost instantly, irresistible charm. He was unconventional, pragmatic, and, in the hyperbole of the time, charismatic.

Trudeau owes an unpayable debt to whoever co-opted the word "Beatlemania" from the rock group and applied it to the intense national curiosity about the new Liberal leader. "Trudeaumania" became a self-actualizing media creation. Reporters covering his campaign loved him . . . he was good copy, great film. He had an instinct for what would make the front page, or become an unforgettable image in the lead item on the newscasts: kissing teenaged girls instead of babies, bouncing on a trampoline with the grace of a martial arts expert, clowning beside a swimming pool. He was so fresh and interesting, he was almost un-Canadian. The country had never seen a politician quite like him, and the idea that he could well become prime minister seemed to make us all a little giddy.

There were warnings about Trudeau, about his millionaire dilettante's background, his radical political leanings, his arrogance, his insistence on complete, unquestioning loyalty—but they were swept aside in the euphoria of Trudeaumania.

Bob Stanfield, on the other hand, seemed to possess nothing but the best human qualities. His misfortune lay in the fact that he'd been born into the television age. Stanfield would have made a fine campaigner in the days of the railroad whistle-stop and cracker-barrel political discussion. In the TV-saturated atmosphere of 1968, he was a non-starter. He walked with an old man's stoop, his long chin thrust forward, his eyes squinting behind hairbrush eyebrows. Who can forget his pathetically awkward attempt at the opening kick-off of a football game? Who can explain what it had to do with his merits as a politician? Stanfield was unwary enough to get caught eating a banana by a cameraman, and the *Toronto Star*'s brilliant cartoonist, Duncan Macpherson, lampooned him mercilessly in a devastating series of cartoons in which the banana became a permanent fixture. Stanfield's thoughtful speech, laced with "ahhhs" and "errrs," became a subject for parody by a nation of budding Rich Littles. Nobody seemed to care what he was trying to say.

CTV's plans for the election coverage were ambitious. The set containing the central command post for tabulating returns would take up a whole studio in the CFTO complex, with rows and rows of trestle tables, banks of telephones, computer terminals, and a large anchor desk. Tally boards, driven by computers, would display numbers throughout the night. Tom Gould and Charles Templeton would comment and interview, and my job, sitting at a desk across the set from Charles and Tom, would be to keep track of the arithmetic, with the tally displays visible behind my shoulder.

Election telecasts have an excitement all their own. They are also a pain in the neck. They are like an arithmetic exam . . . count the numbers, make the comparisons, and name the winner. Everything else is extraneous—interesting, but extraneous. Moreover, for anyone but a died-in-the-wool politics buff, trying to remember who is running where in the 280-odd ridings, is next to impossible. I have never been a politics buff, and so I was happy to simply look after the numbers for a change and let Charles and Tom do the punditry. In fact, I was entertaining a sly and nasty thought that tonight might provide me with some comeuppance for the Tory convention fiasco in which Charles had reduced me to the role of booth announcer.

Charles, erudite and knowledgeable, experienced with his personal forays into the world of politics, had prepared a thick briefing book of notes to work from. Tom and I both tried to tell him what was going to happen in this election telecast.

"Charles," we said, "forget the book until late in the program. You won't have a chance to talk when Ontario and Quebec results start to pour in. Believe us, Charles, it's like an avalanche that continues until we're across the Prairies and into B.C. It's hard enough just to keep track of the numbers."

Charles Templeton was never one to be intimidated by what he didn't know. He felt his expertise would be invaluable throughout the evening—and for a while, it was. Election telecasts begin when the polls close in each time zone. So when the program started, results from Newfoundland were the only information we had. Then the tempo began to pick up, as the Maritimes opened up half an hour later. Charles' comments were cogent and interesting.

On the eight o'clock station break, Tom and I looked at each other, and at Charles' big briefing book. We knew what was coming. For ten or fifteen minutes after we returned to the air, the flow was normal. Then came the deluge: results from almost 200 ridings in Ontario and Quebec pouring into our election central; every phone line in use; the numbers changing every second; and no time to do anything except try to keep the figures up to date on the tally boards behind me, as I provided the barest sketch of what was happening where. It was a straight reporting job, with no room for comment.

By nine o'clock, many of the Quebec and Ontario ridings had been decided: the flood began to ebb. Then, results from the next time zone came on stream and, once again, we were riding the crest of the wave.

From the corner of my eye, I noticed Charles leave the set. He had said nothing for some time, leaving occasional brief interpretative comments to Tom and the bulk of the telecast to me. It didn't take a great deal of talent to do my job in the telecast, but it did take a knowledge of how the whole process worked, a cool head, and an ability to keep the telecast under control—to know when to throw in a comment and when to concentrate on the results. It also took a bit of moxie to know how to fake it when the computer fouled up, as ours did from time to time.

After the wrap-up, Charles was visibly shaken. He vowed he'd never take on a similar role in an election telecast again. Like the time he'd attended my father's funeral, I caught a glimpse of a Charles Templeton I hadn't known existed. I found him a more interesting human being for it.

Charles left CTV soon after that, off on another facet of his fascinating career. He was, and remains, a unique and amazing man—sometimes hard to like, but always worthy of respect. If I state that I am one who both likes and respects Charles Templeton, it should not be thought that I am biased merely because, in one of his novels, he created a very interesting character, a newsman, whose name is Robertson Kirk . . . .

1967 . . . 1968 . . . they now seem like watershed years for CTV News, and for me. The daily newscast was gaining acceptance with every broadcast, our ratings slowly and painfully creeping up each month. Tom Gould was moved to network headquarters in Toronto. To replace him in Ottawa, the network hired Bruce Phillips, a seasoned Parliament Hill reporter and former Washington correspondent for Southam Newspapers. Bruce has a reputation as a hard-nosed, serious journalist, with a spiky and penetrating wit—less pugnacious than Gould, but just as stubborn. He was a tall, slim man, with a mop of dark hair, and a luxuriant moustache that completely obscured his upper lip—which, as a result, appeared to be oddly immobile when he spoke. It was a long time before he could be talked into removing it. When he did, what was revealed by the razor was one of the more expressive and interesting faces on television. Bruce was to become a thorn in the side of a long string of line-up editors in Toronto, an often obdurate and always unrepentant champion of the prerogatives of the Ottawa bureau. He was also to become a mainstay of CTV News, a role he continued to occupy until his appointment in 1985 as press attaché to our embassy in Washington.

Don McPherson had succeeded Charles as CTV's Director of News and Public Affairs. Though not an experienced news executive, he was an authentic production genius. He loved specials, those ad-lib, "wing-it" situations that crop up when a story gets too big to hold back for the nightly newscast. When the order-takers in the sales department signed a deal with Texaco Canada Limited for what we called "instant specials," Don was elated, and his enthusiasm spread through the department. Now we could go on air with a big story without the network losing money from pre-empted commercials. Texaco had even agreed to pick up a portion of our production costs.

With Texaco's sponsorship, we became adept at mounting specials at a moment's notice. What we were really building toward, however, was Apollo 8 and the NASA moon missions.

Chapter 17

CTV News had followed the progress of the American space program in our daily newscasts, but had not, to this point, done much in the way of special coverage. Apollo 8 would be different. Scheduled for 1968, it was to be the first manned moon shot: Frank Borman and his crew would fly to the moon, circle it, and return to Earth. We were going to cover it from lift-off to splashdown.

The question was: How? We certainly didn't have either the manpower or the technical resources to mount coverage of this scale on our own. The cost of microwave lines from Houston to Toronto alone, would use up our budget for the next two years. So McPherson made a deal with NBC to carry some of their coverage, which would include the live pictures from space, and we planned to fill in with as much of our own material as we could pull together. NASA had a magnificent public-relations machine, and made available to the news media a vast library covering every aspect of the space program. Bob Conroy, an enormously talented young director with CFTO, was assigned to our project. He ordered several miles of film from NASA, screened it all, and edited it down into short clips that fit what we had planned to do in studio, when we were not carrying NASA material live through NBC.

Our affiliation with NBC did pose one serious problem. Their telecast, anchored by Frank McGee, would be sponsored by Gulf Oil. Ours would be sponsored by Texaco. We couldn't very well have Gulf logos popping up in our Texaco telecast. After much discussion, we settled on a plan: we would run whatever we took from NBC on a seven-second delay. That meant recording the material when it came into the building, running it through a tape loop that lasted seven seconds, and then playing it back on air. Mary Gorman, a wonderful, gifted woman who'd been production manager and assistant on a number of programs before joining CTV News, was designated our "Gulf-watcher." Her job, among others, would be to watch like a hawk for the Gulf logos that would pop up whenever NBC went from its Houston NASA pictures to its anchor desk, or to a commercial break. When one appeared she'd yell "GULF!" and we'd have five or six seconds to shift to our studio before the dreaded Gulf logo showed up on CTV.

We collected as many props as we could find: models and photos of the spacecraft and its components. I went on a research binge, spending every spare moment learning as much as I could about the space program, and the Apollo missions in particular. A couple of weeks before the launch, Bob Conroy and I flew to Houston, talked with information officers, went to news conferences, and absorbed the atmosphere at the Johnston Space Centre. Then we did the same thing at Cape Canaveral (called Cape Kennedy in those days). We talked with astronauts, and met Frank Borman and his crewmates, James Lovell and William Anders. We rode the elevator to the top of the Vehicle Assembly Building, reputedly the largest building in the United States at that time, and got a close look at the huge rocket that would lift men on their way to the moon. It was an exhausting trip, but Conroy and I soaked up information like a couple of sponges, enjoying every minute.

On the day of the launch, we were as ready as we'd ever be. I had a million facts in my head, Conroy had all the material cut and catalogued, McPherson had the production facilities rehearsed and ready, and Mary Gorman was practising shouting "GUUUULF!"

Our telecast went beautifully. It was loose, relaxed, and informal. Bob Conroy was able to second-guess my actions, and when we weren't entirely in synch, the comfortable atmosphere allowed us to recover gracefully from what minor errors we made. McPherson was delighted, his big face beaming behind heavy glasses. Mary Gorman caught every "Gulf," and the crew received congratulations all round. It was, for me, the highlight of the whole series of Apollo specials. There was an atmosphere on Apollo 8 that was never matched. It was the first lunar mission, and when the tiny, fragile space craft disappeared behind the moon, carrying men to the hidden dark side for the first time in history . . . when communications were lost while the capsule was out of sight of the Earth, it was a heart-stopping wait. Then we heard Frank Borman's voice cracking through space, and the elation was indescribable. Since it was just before Christmas, each crew member quoted a verse or two from Genesis. It ended with Frank Borman saying: "And from the crew of Apollo 8, we close with good night, good luck, a Merry Christmas, and God bless all of you on the good Earth." That moment had an impact that surpassed even Neil Armstrong's "giant step" when he became the first human to set foot on the moon's surface.

The success of our Apollo 8 telecasts led us into even more extensive coverage of later missions in the Apollo series, which reached its climax with Apollo 11 and the first moon landing. By now, we had become adept at on-air editing of NBC studio material, and our set in Studio 3 had expanded to include several different anchor areas, each devoted to a different aspect of the mission. We brought our own expert commentators in, some from NASA, and some from the University of Toronto, which had played a role in most of the moon missions. During our tours of Houston and Cape Kennedy, we had discovered Dr. David Strangway, a U. of T. geophysicist who was among those in charge of training astronauts for the moon exploration, and who would be in charge of examining moon soil brought back to Earth. (It was Strangway who had the bright, if controversial, idea of bringing the astronauts to the barren, rocky, sulphur dioxide-poisoned moonscape outside Sudbury, Ontario, for training sessions. The people of that city did not appreciate the publicity.) Dr. Strangway's contributions to our telecasts were invaluable, both in the understanding he had of the complexities of lunar exploration, and in the contacts he provided.

Apollo 11 was a marathon. We were on the air for more than 30 hours of broadcasts from space in the vicinity of, and on the surface of, the moon. It was a surreal experience just to watch the pictures as they were relayed back from so many thousands of miles away. On the studio floor, cameramen and lighting and props technicians clustered quietly around monitors. On-air people perched on the edges of desks, faces intent. In the control room, technicians hunched forward in their chairs, watching their wall of monitors—watching as Buzz Aldrin, Michael Collins, and Neil Armstrong made history. Armstrong's contrived statement: "That's one small step for man, one giant step for mankind," was, in my view, anything but poetic, but in the context of those incredible pictures of the lunar landing module and the white-suited creature climbing stiffly down its ladder to the powdery surface below, it seemed to fit.

The Apollo telecasts of 1968, 1969, and 1970 were the most demanding, and at the same time the most exciting and rewarding of my entire career. Technically, they were marvellously intricate, and the research was fascinating. Best of all, they dealt with positive stories, wherein a noble objective was being pursued by men displaying good, old-fashioned virtues like courage and selflessness. There was suspense and danger, comedy and bathos, all in larger-than-life proportions. It was a story to transport us away from the horrors of Vietnam and Biafra, away from the floods and earthquakes, the hijackings and bombings and kidnappings. The Apollo program was a high road, and it was good to walk it for a while.

* * *

My last contact with the space program came in 1974, when Apollo astronauts explored the surface of the moon for the last time. CTV had very little air time planned for this launch, so I begged off and took my son Bernie to Florida. I'd covered many a launch, but I'd never seen one with my own eyes. Since this one was to be the last for a while, I was determined to be there.

At Cape Kennedy, I was informed that I could have a pass for the press area near the launch site, but children were not allowed. That gave us pause for a few minutes, until we ran into a friend who was in the same boat . . . he wanted his son at the press site too. We decided there was nothing for it but to smuggle the kids in.

We put the two of them on the floor of the back seat of my friend's station wagon, warned them to silence, and threw a blanket over them. That got us through all the checkpoints, and into the press area, where we discovered we weren't the only smugglers; there were a lot of youngsters around. The next problem was keeping the boys awake until something like three in the morning: this was to be NASA's first night-time launch. By midnight, 12-year-old Bernie had had enough, and I agreed to wake him before the launch. He curled up, and was sound asleep in moments. When we were a few minutes from the launch, I shook him. No response. I shook him again:

"C'mon Bernie, you've only got a minute or so."

It was just a few seconds to the launch when he finally came fully awake. He held his camera ready, and I held mine.

Then it came. A great rumbling across the water, a flash of light, then a godalmighty roar unlike anything I'd ever heard or imagined. The ground shook . . . there were crackles and snaps in the air like monster Rice Krispies . . . great tongues of flame poured out in a liquid stream, then curled off in strange, flickering tails. Faces flooded with greenish-yellow light strained upward as the mammoth rocket lifted itself off the pad and into the atmosphere, the earth bright orange beneath it. A wave of cheers broke out in our grandstand and rolled outward to where it was picked up by the thousands of Apollo-watchers overflowing the camp-sites and lining the highways all around the Cape.

Then the ship was disappearing: an inch of fire visible in the ink-dark sky, then a pinpoint of light, then the darkness, undisturbed.

My son and I returned to our hotel exhilarated, still trying to absorb what we'd seen. For Bernie, it had been an awesome adventure, a chance to witness a bit of history. He went to sleep, finally, still chattering his excitement.

As for me . . . I'd grown pretty blasé about space shots over the years. I wasn't anymore.

Chapter 18

1969 had been a hard year. A little rest was called for. Some friends owned a cottage on a lake north of Kingston, Ontario, and we stayed there for a couple of idyllic weeks, with Bernie and Tina enjoying the sandy beach, and Renate, a natural swimmer, taking long sweeps through the blue water. We almost forgot about disagreeing.

In the next cottage, a friendly neighbour had a beat-up boat with a 35 hp motor hung on the transom. He guaranteed it would pull me on skis. I am no lightweight. I'd been on water skis before. I had my doubts about being pulled by that boat and motor, but after some urging from the kids, I bravely decided to give it a whirl.

It worked. I went gliding around the lake, waving as I passed the beach, cutting across wakes, and generally showing what an athletic fellow I was. It worked so well, I thought I'd try it on one ski. That was a mistake. I got up okay, but when I fell in the middle of the lake, I really tumbled. Then the little motor tugged and snorted, trying to get me back up again. It dragged me through the water, my arms feeling as though they were about to be yanked from their sockets. Eventually, I was dragged all the way back to shore.

That night, I felt a twinge of pain below my shoulder blades. Nothing serious. Next day, it was time to go home, and driving along Highway 401, I was aware of a dull ache in the middle of my back. At home, Renate and the kids unpacked the car, while I got out the mower and started on the lawn. Suddenly, there was a stabbing pain starting in my back and running down my leg. The leg buckled, and I couldn't make it work anymore. I crawled to the front door, and yelled to Renate. With her help, I stood up. The pain was excruciating, so I sat down, but that only made it worse. We staggered to the car, and headed for the closest hospital. There, in the midst of all the red tape, I began cursing:

"I'm in pain, dammit. Do something!"

Nobody in a hospital emergency ward listens to that kind of cry.

Finally, I got to a bed. A tall, thin, pale young man with a plummy British accent appeared at my side.

"We think you've slipped a disc," was the essence of what he said. This was Dr. Bernard Woolford, an orthopedic surgeon with a reputation that placed him among the best in Toronto.

"We'll have to do a myelogram before we can say for sure."

I had no idea what a myelogram was.

"Oh, it's not bad," he assured me.

My family doctor, Colin Kelly, walked in.

"Kelly," I asked, "what the hell is a myelogram?"

Kelly had a soft Irish accent. "Ooch, it's not so bad," he said. "They stick some dye into your spinal column so they can see what damage has been done. It's no big deal."

No big deal, the man said. It was without a doubt the most horrible torment I have ever experienced—lying on a steel bed with a monstrous needle stuck in my back, being tipped up and down so the dye would flow freely through my spinal column, and looking at a TV monitor that *showed* that damn needle in there. Then the warning: "Don't move your head around too much or you'll get a bad headache."

The upshot of this torture was that I needed an operation to clean up a ruptured disc, probably earned in my waterskiing escapade. The operation wasn't half so bad as the diagnostic procedure. Woolford prescribed a stretch of immobility after the surgery, and so for ten days I lay in bed, propped on one elbow so I could read. That elbow suffered some nerve damage as a result.

Finally, Woolford came in one day with some good news.

"Want to get up?" he asked.

I threw back the sheets and put out my feet . . . then sat up. Then I stood up. The world spun.

"Just go easy," Woolford said. "We'll get you up and out of here tonight."

That's what happened, but he didn't tell me until later in the day that I was in for another month of enforced rest.

Back at the office, poor Wally Macht was filling in for me during the week, while continuing to do his regular stint on the weekend, as well. It was an impossible grind, and when I got home I called Don McPherson.

"Find somebody to help Wally," I yelled into the phone. "I'm stuck here for another bloody month and Wally can't work seven days a week."

There weren't many people with studio experience at the network, and those who had it were too busy to help out. Jack McGaw, then at W-5, volunteered to work one weekend, but that was it.

So I had the first of two back operations, and Wally Macht was left to work the national newscast seven days a week for more than six exhausting weeks.

* * *

1970 began innocuously enough. The Biafra-Nigeria civil war ended, the first Jumbo jet flew from New York to London carrying 362 passengers and 19 crew members, Fort William and Port Arthur became Thunder Bay, Robert Bourassa became leader of the Quebec Liberal Party, and Prime Minister Trudeau took Barbra Streisand to a performance of the Royal Winnipeg Ballet in Ottawa. His knack for publicity was uncanny. So was hers.

Those were a few of the stories we chronicled nightly on the CTV newscasts in January. Before the end of the year, we were to experience the national trauma of the October crisis and the War Measures Act; and the flawless safety record of the Apollo missions was to be punctured by an oxygen tank exploding aboard Apollo 13, putting the astronauts' lives at risk for several excruciatingly anxious hours.

The biggest-ever world's fair was about to open in Osaka, Japan. CTV planned to make what it could of Expo 70, with live coverage of the opening ceremonies and a con-

175

tinuing series of specials over the life of the fair. Don McPherson had made several trips to Japan in preparation for the opening: I was to anchor the telecast, with a young Japanese employee of the Canadian embassy as my assistant and expert on things Japanese. We would be using pictures from Japanese television, with our own commentary—not an unusual arrangement for telecasts of this kind.

What was unusual was that our crew would consist of just three people: Don, his wife Barbara, who was a well-qualified production assistant, and me. Obviously, it was going to be left to me to provide research, write whatever script needed to be written, and generally look after myself for commentary in this Oriental extravaganza. I voiced my concerns about that to McPherson, and got the expected reply: "Don't worry, we'll be fine."

There were only a few passengers on the CP Air DC-8 that took off from Vancouver *en route* to Tokyo on March 7, 1970. Among them, the McPhersons and I were delighted to find Charlie Lynch, my old friend and colleague from Ottawa. Charlie introduced us to Ian Sinclair, president of Canadian Pacific.

It was an interesting flight. Charlie and Sinclair were old chums, and they soon began bargaining over the CP railway. Sinclair was going to sell Charlie all the rolling stock—though of course he would keep the track. That session took us through a drink or two and out somewhere over the northern Pacific. Then Sinclair, who'd been a bomber pilot in the war, decided he should fly the plane for a while. Ian Sinclair is a large economy-sized man, and I wondered how he'd ever fit into the flight deck, but he lumbered forward. A few minutes later, we felt the wings of the aircraft dip in turn, just slightly. Then Sinclair reappeared, a grin splitting his big face.

"Told you I could," he said.

We found out, though, that he hadn't flown the plane: the captain was an old war buddy, and had waggled the wings a little to give credence to Sinclair's bluff.

I spent four days on the Expo site, waiting for the Saturday opening. I talked with as many people as possible, trying to get something into my head that would serve me during the telecast. As our air date approached, I became more and more apprehensive. The young man who'd been assigned by the embassy to help me, gave me no indication that he knew what would be expected of him on air—nor that he was likely to learn in the time remaining.

Finally, I decided that since this was going to be a colourful, exciting ceremony, the less I said, the better. Let the pictures carry the telecast and speak only when you have to, I told myself. That way, nobody will discover how little you know.

With that philosophy firmly in place, I went to a reception at the Canadian pavilion. The bartender was a Montrealer, and had watched me for years, he said. I noticed when I handed him a highball glass that he disappeared into a room behind the bar, then returned with it nearly full. That happened a couple of times. Finally, I asked him.

"What've you got back there?"

"Just for you, Mr. Kirck," he whispered, "Crown Royal."

Then it hit me, in more ways than one. My Montreal friend had been pouring me straight belts of Crown Royal! I thought, "What the hell," and tossed back another. I left the pavilion quite late, in something of a fog, but for the first time since I'd arrived in Osaka, the cold didn't bother me a bit.

Our broadcast of the opening of Expo 70 went better than I'd expected. My plan to let the pictures carry the story worked out well, and my Japanese friend from the embassy turned out to be quite helpful, though his English deteriorated somewhat whenever the red tally light came on.

When it was over, I took advantage of a free afternoon to take some pictures and stroll around the fair. I dropped in at the German pavilion, a place we'd been favouring for its wonderful luncheon menu. Charlie, Don, and Barbara were there, but as I approached their table, only Barbara looked up. Charlie and Don were intent upon two objects before them on the table. I looked over their shoulders. They were staring at a pair of stopwatches, their noses almost on the watch faces.

"What the devil is going on?"

"Ssshhh," they said.

Suddenly, in unison, Don and Charlie bellowed incoherently.

A couple of dozen Japanese diners were looking our way, no doubt thinking dark thoughts about Western barbarians.

"What are you doing?" I asked again.

"We're having a stopwatch race," Don replied. I wasn't sure I was hearing right.

"Sure," Charlie drawled. "We both bought stopwatches in Tokyo and we're racing them to see which one is faster." There was a lot of guffawing. I took my schnitzel to another table.

We took the Bullet train from Osaka to Tokyo next morning. I'd never gone a hundred miles an hour on a train before, and I'm not sure I'd want to again—the landscape goes by awfully fast, and the carriages sway more than a little. We arrived at Tokyo station, and then went on to the airport to re-organize our flight home. We'd heard that Pan American would be flying a Boeing 747 to Los Angeles, and since none of us had ridden a Jumbo, McPherson changed our tickets. It was now Tokyo-Los Angeles-Toronto. We rode the monorail back to Tokyo, jammed together like sardines in a windowed can, and in the evening we visited the Ginza and had raw fish for dinner, my first shot at that. Back at the airport in time for our 10:30 flight, we boarded the 747 and waited for it to take off. And waited. And waited. The Jumbos had just begun to take to the air at that time, and we learned there was fierce competition among airlines to be first between any two points with the new aircraft. Japan Airlines was apparently using its leverage at the Tokyo airport to delay the Pan Am flight to California.

By midnight, it was obvious we were in for a long wait, so the crew opened the bar, turned on the music, and the grounded plane became the scene for a huge party The big seats were more than comfortable, and the wide aisles made walking around enjoyable. It wasn't until four a.m. that we left Tokyo—although by that time, the party had palled a little. It seemed an appropriate end to an assignment that had been a little unreal from the outset.

The Kirck family had fallen in love with the snowmobile. When I returned from Japan, we scrounged enough money to buy an old, disused farm near Marmora, in an area referred to by some residents as "the Ozarks of Ontario," because of its poverty and rough and unproductive land. For $9,000, we got 258 acres, most of which was swamp and heavy bushland. We also got a big barn, and the ruins of a long-forgotten schoolhouse. With the help of friends and neighbours, we built a 24-by-30-foot cabin on the school foundation, insulated it heavily, covered it with aluminum siding, and then waited for the first snowfall. The harsh countryside softened in winter, and a moonlit ride by snow machine was almost magical. I had been host for a number of company functions and in-house films for Bombardier, the inventor of the snowmobile, and in return I'd been given the use of two machines. I purchased a third tiny snowmobile for Bernie, and the little rascal soon became the best rider in the family. Tina rode with her mother or me, hanging onto a small set of handlebars, specially made to fit below the regular bars, just her height.

When spring came, weeds and scrub took over the cleared land around our cabin, and the young man on the next farm moved his Herefords onto our pasture. We'd discovered during the winter that the old schoolhouse well was not producing enough water to meet our needs. One weekend, I mentioned that to old Bob Bronson, a local handyman who'd helped us build the cottage. He had a look at the well, which had been drilled through solid granite about four feet from the cabin foundation, and, after some ruminative scratching at his whiskered chin and thoughtful tugging at the peak of his baseball cap, he allowed as how a friend of his had some "denamite" and that a little stuffed into the bottom of the well might just open up some new cracks and allow more water to seep in. I was willing to try anything that might work; the cost of drilling through that granite was horrendous. In due course, Bob reported that he'd talked to his friend and they were ready to proceed with the job during the week.

On Tuesday or Wednesday, I got a call in Toronto from Bob.

"Ahh, could you come up here, maybe tomorrow?"

"Is something wrong?" I wanted to know. I had visions of the cottage blown to smithereens.

"No, no, nothing's wrong. But maybe you should come up."

Next day, I found out what had happened. The two old coots had stuffed a load of dynamite down the four-inch steel casing at the top of the well, down through the granite to the bottom. They'd tamped it down, and then laid a couple of old mattresses over the opening.

The dynamite went off with a whoosh, tossing the mattresses about 40 feet through the air. The steel well casing came roaring out of the hole like a projectile fired from a cannon, and took some siding and shingles off one corner of the cabin. Worse of all, because the force of the blast had gone upward, there were no new cracks in the well to let water in—just a lot of rubble and sediment to foul what little water was already there.

I should have known better, but I used the "talents" of these two men again.

In the middle of the farm, there was a huge beaver pond, covering maybe 20 acres. The pond was growing and the water the dams backed up was causing the swamp to expand to a point where it had reached within 50 yards of the back of the cabin. I didn't want to kill the beavers, but something had to be done. I discussed the problem with Bob.

"I know whatcha mean," he said with a tug at the peak of his cap. It was his favourite expression. "Maybe if we could bust up the dam, them beavers would go away."

That seemed to be a reasonable idea: I couldn't see how he could do much damage way out in the bush by the beaver dams. Bob agreed to get his dynamite friend again, and do the job before the next weekend.

The following Saturday, as we were driving along the road leading from Highway 7 to the farm, I noticed a short detour built around a washed-out culvert. A little farther on, I noticed part of our neighbour's garden seemed to be missing, and there were deep water-erosion scars on his field. There seemed to have been a flood.

I looked at Renate. She looked at me.

"Oh, my God." It came from both of us at about the same time.

Through the day, we pieced the story together. Bob and his friend had slogged their way up to the beaver dams, placed their charges and then blown them. What no one had counted on was the tremendous volume of water backed up behind those dams. As the dirt and tree limbs and muck levitated with the blasts, millions of gallons of water burst through the gaps. Old Bob and his friend ran hell-bent for leather to get to high ground, and managed to escape the torrent in the nick of time. The water found a path into two tiny streams, which became roaring rivers, one headed for the culvert we'd passed, the other aimed at the gap between my neighbour's barn and house. After washing away his garden and a lot of good topsoil in an adjoining field, and after uprooting the culvert, the water rolled on down into some low ground and disappeared into another swamp, eventually finding its way into the Moira River.

It wasn't long before Bill Kelly was at our door. Bill, the father of our young neighbour, was a stern man, a life-long farmer, but also the man in charge of road mainte-nance for that part of Hastings County. I figured I was for it now.

He chastised me, but only gently, for he knew the beaver dams could have burst on their own without warning. So that was a plus. The neighbours hadn't lost anything of value in their garden. That was another. I learned never to trust anyone with dynamite. Still another.

About the only minus in the whole affair was that the bloody beaver dams were right back in place the next summer.

Chapter 19

The Expo 70 caper in Osaka turned out to be one of Don McPherson's last major productions for CTV. He was offered, and accepted, a senior executive position at CBC. Tom Gould took over the directorship of news and public affairs programming. Unlike the phlegmatic McPherson, Tom was a volatile hustler who sent off sparks in all directions. He hired Donald Cameron, an old buddy from his CBC reporting days, and gave him the task of revitalizing *W-5*, the network's long-running current affairs weekly. While we'd all become accustomed to Tom by now, there was a wariness in the newsroom about Cameron. He'd been preceded by his reputation for belligerence and harsh language, though we had to admit his journalistic credentials looked good; after training as a fighter pilot in World War Two, he'd worked for years as a correspondent, roving the world for CBC television. He'd covered the Biafran war, done time in Vietnam, interviewed Che Guevara, and had been one of the mainstays of the CBC's highly-respected *NewsMagazine* program. We wondered how he'd manage in a sedentary administrative job.

In the meantime, a whole new field of interest was opening up for me. News and public affairs at CTV in those days produced a good number of documentaries each year— something that has stopped happening in recent times, thanks to a tight-fisted board of directors, a shortage of sponsors and a perceived lack of audience interest. Susan Dexter, a bulky young woman with a wide, wonderful smile—at that time a staff producer with the network— called me one day to ask if I wanted to narrate an hourlong film she planned to produce on the subject of nationalism. It was a topic well worth addressing in that time of strife in Quebec, and I accepted at once. I looked forward to a new experience: while I had narrated many short news programs, I'd never before been involved in a full-length full-blown documentary.

I was parachuted into several different locations to meet Susan and the crew, and film on-camera bridges, or "stand-ups"—links between stretches of voice-over narration. As we moved into the studio for the voice-over, Susan made some suggestions.

"Harvey, don't shout at me. Be soft. Just talk to me."

I was learning something. This was a much more intimate kind of delivery than I'd been accustomed to.

"Lower your voice, Harvey. Soften your voice." Susan could be a real nag.

"Softer, Harvey," Susan coached, as I again attacked the script.

After a dozen or so takes on the first page, Susan had me speaking in a voice just above a whisper. I was surprised to discover a richness there, a modulation and tone that I'd never heard in my voice before. The finished film dealt with the excesses of nationalism, and the extremes to which the sentiment is sometimes carried. The incipient violence in the pictures, the strident voices, were counterpointed by this low-key narration, and the result was hypnotic. I never again questioned Susan Dexter's direction, and I credit her for providing me with a technique that I was able to use with some reasonable success in many future documentaries and documentary series.

One such series was called "Window on the World," which dealt in some depth with Canada's role in a changing international economy. It was produced, written, and directed by Richard Thomas, who looked and sounded like a typical English fop, wispy-haired, cherry-mouthed, and plump, and burdened with an effete, upper-crust accent. Only his eyes gave him away. They twinkled with mischief, and when he beamed a smile in your direction, they almost disappeared. In the course of travelling thousands of miles with him, shooting a lot of film, and sharing a lot of discomfort, I came to know him as one of the finest documentary producers in my experience. Though with a

183

lot of fussing and fretting, Richard could move a program from concept to completion with unerring instinct.

But working with him was not without its frustrations. Our first film together was about the effect multi-national corporations were having on world trade. Most of the film had been shot by the time I became involved. Richard decided that we should do my parts in Karlsruhe, West Germany, a town where almost every multi-national in the world has a plant or branch office. Richard had been in Karlsruhe for days, and he had maliciously passed the word to all the local dignitaries that a "big Canadian television personality" was on his way. So when I arrived, I had to attend a civic reception at the mayor's office and then appear at a local fair. Two businesses that were featured in the film held cocktail parties in my honour. I was also interviewed and photographed by the local newspaper. Through all of this, Richard made himself scarce, but I would catch occasional glimpses of him, his eyes almost invisible, his face sporting a devilish grin.

I swore I'd kill him, but I found a better way to get even.

Richard had made arrangements to shoot one of the stand-ups at the Singer sewing-machine plant, a difficult trucking shot, with me walking down one side of a production line while the camera followed from the other side. Richard was a fussy director, and he spent a lot of time making sure he was getting exactly what he wanted. We did the sequence, which seemed fine, and then waited while cameraman Randy Platt and soundman Francois Gabereau packed up their equipment. Outside the plant, I took Richard aside.

"Richard," I whispered, "I'm sure I saw camera wobble on just about every one of those takes. Maybe we should set up here and get some insurance."

"Oh God, no," Richard moaned. "You mean we've blown four hours of shooting?"

He questioned the crew, but they knew nothing about the camera shaking.

"Well, Richard, I probably imagined it, but . . . ."

"No, no, no godammit, we'll do another take right here with the Singer sign in the background. Hell's bloody bells, I don't know why you couldn't have told me sooner."

The crew was not delighted to have to unpack and assemble their equipment all over again, but they did, and we got another take. The first one was a good one. Richard didn't know he'd been had until he'd returned to Toronto and screened his film: there was no camera wobble.

Part of "Window on the World" was an ambitious program dealing with the Pacific rim, and Canada's place in that burgeoning trading basin. In Vancouver, Richard got the bright idea that we should have a couple of sequences with me on the deck of a coal transport. We spent an entire day at Roberts Bank, outside Vancouver, shooting with two crews in a giant coal yard. When we returned to our hotel, we looked like escapees from a black-face minstrel show. (It turned out later that not a foot of the film was usable—it had been damaged by the coal dust.) There was no time to clean up—we were leaving for Tokyo next morning. After a shower and a few hours sleep, we stuffed our grimy clothes in suitcases and caught our plane for Japan.

Tokyo is not my favourite city. There is too much smog, too many cars, too many people, and too much noise. I was in a foul mood when we arrived and that mood did not improve when I heard from Richard what he had planned for the first set-up.

"Let me see if I've got this straight, Richard," I said. "You want me on top of a water tower in a steel-mill yard at four a.m. Right?"

"Right."

I yelled at him. "Are you nuts?"

He wanted a shot with me in the foreground, and the sprawling yard of the steel plant behind me—behind that, dozens of huge freighters anchored in Tokyo Bay: all this as the sun rose in blazing glory out of the sea. Oh, the symbolism, the poetry of it!

Next morning at three o'clock, we were in a rented van heading for the steel plant. We went into the plant offices, had a ritual tea, and then climbed the tower. Everything was ready: Richard, I'm sure, was feeling like Cecil B. De Mille. We waited. And waited. Eventually, in the sulphurous gloom across Tokyo Bay, there appeared a faint

185

patch of grey. It was the sun, 'way back behind about a million tons of smog.

Richard could not be faulted for lack of persistence. We tried for three days to get that shot, but the smog blanket was a permanent fixture. We finally settled for a daytime shot that showed the steel yard, and, if you looked hard, a ship or two out behind it.

Next, it was a sunset Richard wanted, and he kept us out on a foul-smelling beach at a fishing village north of Tokyo for two days to get it. Then we were off to Yokohama, where I had one of the strangest experiences of my life. Richard had hired a researcher, a young Australian woman who stood six-foot-two inches. I'm six-foot-three. This young lady and I were to meet Richard and the crew in Yokohama early one morning, and to get there, we rode the train from Tokyo. As we disembarked, we stood aside, and watched as a torrent of humanity poured through the station gates and hurried on its way . . . thousands of little people: black hair, white shirts, and dark pants. Occasionally, one of them would cast a sidelong glance up at the two round-eyed giants watching from the sidelines, and then hurry on. I had the bizarre sensation of being an utterly alien being.

Our shooting schedule next took us to Hong Kong, a fascinating city with an ambience that felt soft and pliant after the harshness and bustle of Tokyo. We completed our work quickly, the formalities and permissions being much less rigid than they had been in Japan.

We were enjoying a celebratory end-of-shoot dinner with a newspaper friend of Richard's, when someone suggested we take a drive in the country and have a look at the Chinese border. The newspaperman volunteered that he knew of a spot where you could get within a 100 yards of the border and look right into the People's Republic. It was much superior, he said, to the regular tourist lookout which was at least a quarter of a mile from anything really Chinese. He volunteered his teenaged son to guide us there the next day.

Early next morning, we left Hong Kong, crossed into Kowloon, and began our adventure on the Chinese border.

After an hour or so of driving, we came to a small village where a country market was in progress. Richard thought that it would add colour to his documentary, so the camera was set up, and I was instructed to walk through the stalls, chatting to vendors . . . maybe buy something. It was a blistering day, and I was happy to get out of the car and stretch my legs. I walked through displays of freshly slaughtered pigs, vegetables I'd never seen before, mounds of grotesquely ugly fresh fish. Then I spotted a little girl—shy, pretty, in her best dress, obviously—selling some amber liquid by the glass. The camera was grinding away as I approached her, and I took a chance. I bought a glass of whatever it was, and mimed a question: "Should I drink it?" to which the little girl nodded her head. I drank it. It tasted good, like camomile tea. All of that went on film, but the aftermath did not.

Within minutes, my temperature had risen by what felt about 20 degrees, my knees were weak, and my head was swimming. The crew helped me to the air-conditioned car, where I collapsed into a seat, fearing the worst. Then, just as suddenly as they had come upon me, the strange symptoms vanished and I was well again. Evidently, I'd had some sort of herbal remedy, though I've no idea what it might have been.

We continued on our quest for the Chinese border with only slightly subdued enthusiasm. As we wandered over back roads and trails, up hill and down dale, it became quite clear that our young guide was not at all certain where he was going. We drove through the middle of a British Army compound. Nobody stopped us. Then, on a deserted stretch of road, there appeared a lone British Army Land Rover: it flagged us down, and a moustachioed sergeant-major demanded to know who we were and just where we thought we were going. We explained.

"Well, sirs," he said, "if you keep going another 200 yards, you'll be picked up by the bleedin' Chinese border guards. You're that close to the bleedin' boundary."

With appropriate thanks, we backed our car around and left as quickly as dignity would allow. Then we spent another hour finding the place where the tourists look at the Chinese border. That seemed close enough.

* * *

Our experience at the old farm near Marmora led Renate and I to decide that country life suited the family, and that we should consider moving out of the city. We began looking for a place that had a bit of land, a few trees, a house, maybe a barn or some other outbuildings, all within commuting distance of the TV studios. Finally, a real estate agent told us of a place between Oshawa and Brooklin, just east of Toronto—a marvellous old stone house on 12 acres, she said, that could be bought cheap.

When we saw it, it became obvious why. The land had been owned by an eccentric old man in Oshawa who had a penchant for collecting junk. There were junked cars, and trucks, and farm implements; stacks and stacks of drywall which had been left outside for the rain to ruin; bins of car parts and nails and mounds of used tires; and millions of feet of lumber, much of it in the form of hardwood pallets from Oshawa factories, all of it now weathered and useless. The junk yard covered perhaps eight of the twelve acres. The big stone house itself was in reasonable condition. The current owner had begun renovating before deciding to sell. The place clearly had potential, but I dismissed the whole notion of buying it when I learned that the asking price was over $100,000. I wasn't prepared to pay that, even if I'd had the money, because it was obvious there was a lot of expensive, back-breaking work to be done to put the place in shape. Renate was not so easily defeated. When I left town on an assignment, she decided there was nothing to be lost by putting in a ridiculously low bid, and did just that, offering $75,000. I arrived home to find the offer had been accepted!

We moved into the old house in January, 1971, in the middle of a snow storm, and quickly discovered that the wind whistled in through cracks around doors and windows. No matter how high we turned the thermostats on the electric heating, it was never warm. There was a monstrous steel staircase in the middle of the combined living-and dining-room, on which I constantly banged my head.

"I guess we'd better get rid of that," Renate said wisely.

"Amen," I answered.

188

We hired a contractor to handle the removal, and at the same time to rebuild the whole living-room. He sent us a remarkable carpenter.

Orville was perhaps 45 when we met him. He'd been unable to hear or speak since birth. He'd been educated in schools for the deaf and mute, where he'd met his wife who suffered the same disabilities. They'd had three normal children. Orville carried pads and pencils to communicate, and for several weeks our house was littered with little pieces of paper as we planned and re-built. If the place is ever torn down dozens of sketches will be found on the wallboard under the wallpaper and mouldings, where Renate and Orville decided on how a fireplace mantle should look, or what kind of window treatment would be installed. From sketches, Orville built a new central staircase that would do justice to the finest cabinetmaker. It was wide at the bottom and narrowed to fit the smaller opening to the upstairs floor. The thing took two or three tries to get right. But when it was finished, Orville wore a grin as wide as the stairway.

As soon as spring came, we got to work on the yard. A scrap dealer in Oshawa had agreed to buy the wrecked cars and trucks and implements. For two weeks, a crane was kept busy loading the scrap onto big trucks, which trundled through our property ripping up the grass and leaving foot-deep ruts. With the scrap machinery gone, I hired a huge bulldozer. The remnants of the barn foundation were buried, and then the tractor attacked the remaining junk, pushing it into great piles.

The Ministry of Environment people came out from Oshawa. They agreed with me that the only way to get rid of the mess was to burn it.

I went about getting rid of the wood in a reasonably systematic way—whenever the winds were right and a little rain was falling, I'd set a fire, and eventually it was all gone but one massive pile. That one worried me: it was huge, it was near the property line, and it was close to a stand of trees I didn't want damaged.

It happened that there were a couple of scruffy old men coming to the property almost every day, picking up bits of scrap metal the 'dozer and the scrap yard had missed.

They'd arrive each morning in their beat-up truck, and were usually three sheets to the wind by mid-afternoon. They loved watching my fires. I should have suspected something.

About this time, Renate, the kids, and I went on vacation. On our return, sure enough . . . the big pile was gone. I walked to where it had been, but all there was to see was a large area of scorched and blackened earth. My trees had survived, but they were charred a little near their crowns, which gave some indication of the fierce heat and the height of the flames. It must have been a hell of a fire.

Word started coming in. The fire had been first noticed in the early evening and it soon lit up the sky like a beacon, bringing spectators all the way from town. They watched as the flames ate their way through thousands of board feet of wooden junk. The fire brigade arrived, but their tanker truck was no match for this blaze, and since there was no hydrant within miles, they settled in to watch the fire and make sure it didn't spread. That led to another nasty surprise: looking through my back mail, I found a bill from the Oshawa Fire Department, charging me for the cost of keeping a crew and equipment on my property from eight in the evening until eight the next morning. It was a figure to make your hair stand on end. I was able to get it withdrawn eventually, by pointing out that I hadn't even been home when the fire started, and that all the other burning I'd done had been carefully controlled. (I didn't mention the scrap-pickers, and I never saw them again.)

After that, it was fairly easy to finish the clean-up. The bulldozer came back and pushed the remaining debris to the banks of a small creek that ran through the back of the property, and there it was buried. We had a nice high bank for the stream, and the Kirck estate, while looking a little scarred and blackened, was no longer a junk yard.

Sadly, any hope Renate and I had shared about the move helping our relationship soon proved to be illusory. The tension between us continued, and eventually our marriage failed, in a painful and bitter separation. It was an unhappy time for all of us—for my children and for Renate and me, and many of the scars remain just beneath the surface.

During the last years of our marriage, Renate and I had excused some of the bickering and fighting by saying it added zest to our marriage . . . that no relationship could move along on an even keel without becoming dull and stagnant. I know now that that was a specious rationalization; that no matter how forgiving an individual may be, there is a poisonous residue left with each dispute, and it slowly and steadily accumulates. Each ugly incident in a marriage builds on the last, and love and empathy become more and more submerged in darkness and confusion. Having had some experience with turbulent marriages, I know that however passionate a love may be, it can be dimmed and finally extinguished when lovers too often take too strong a stand.

The CFTO switchboard girl with the beehive hairdo—the one who'd greeted me when I first set foot in the station all those years ago—had become a make-up artist, the beehive replaced by a kind of brushcut. Brenda Brady was now divorced, raising her son, Michael, on her own. She was a tiny woman, in her early thirties, who had a motherly concern for all the young strays in the TV station. "Go talk to Brenda. She'll know what to do," was a commonly heard piece of advice. It was not unusual to see Brenda and one of the young crew members sitting in the make-up room, deep in conversation. She was Ann Landers and Big Sister combined.

In the miserable days when my marriage seemed to be falling to pieces, Brenda had become a confidante, listening patiently to my tales of woe, making no judgements, offering no advice. Eventually, we became lovers, and a few years ago, we were married.

There are ups and downs in our relationship—when there is a high, we are both there, and when there is a downer, we are both there. We don't argue—we accommodate. We don't oppose—we support. To disagree is not to confront—it's to discuss. I don't know if this is a unique arrangement or not. It sure is for both of us.

Chapter 20

The federal election of 1974 looked to be a significant one for CTV News. We'd managed a creditable job in the general election two years earlier, and it was expected that we'd do even better this time.

In '72 the computer had, to my surprise, worked relatively smoothly, but there had been other problems. Three days before the election, I lost my co-anchor, Bruce Phillips, when his father was stricken by a heart attack. Bruce left for the Lakehead to be with him. There was some frantic scrambling: I couldn't possibly carry the anchor desk alone, but who would replace Bruce? Tom Gould had been off the air for some time now, but he was always up-to-date on national politics . . . Tom was the obvious choice. With some reluctance and, I think, a little pride, Tom agreed to take the seat opposite me.

The minutes before an election telecast are pretty tense. Will that intricate reporting system we've devised really work? Will the intercoms and phones all function as they're supposed to? Is the decision desk fully prepared? And most important for me, will that infernal computer put out the way we've planned?

I could see Tom was tense: it was one thing to have a general knowledge of an election campaign, but quite another to appear on a major telecast as an expert commentator. He'd had only three days to prepare.

The broadcast began, and I did the usual introduction before throwing to Tom. He began talking, and he talked, and he talked, and talked.

I caught his eye, signalling him to throw back to me. He did. I went through my material, then asked him a question. He started, and was unable to stop again.

I believe there are people in the television business who cover their nervousness by talking, and although Tom denies it, I believe that is what happened to him that night. (In my case, when I get nervous, I freeze, and feel helpless.)

As the night wore on, Tom settled down, though not before being told off-camera a couple of times to: "for Christ's sake, shut up," by his anchor desk partner (and once being kicked in the shins under the table). On balance, he performed remarkably well, given how little preparation time he'd had.

In this 1974 election, we were to have everything going for us, and there were going to be no last-minute hitches. Once again, cost was no object when it came to getting the best facilities . . . that was always the case now at CTV where major specials were concerned. (Money for the daily news was another matter—it was perennially scarce.)

The set was arranged with a great computer-operated "flapper board" behind me. On it were to be displayed the popular vote tallies, percentages, seats elected for each party, and so on—the numbers changing on command from the main data processor.

By coincidence, CTV documentary producer Gerry Lawton was deeply involved at that time in a film about stress for his "Human Journey" series. Since there would obviously be a lot of stress for all of us during the election-night telecast, he wanted to know if he could wire me up to an electro-cardiograph, which would record the ups and downs in my system during the program, and thus illustrate the effects of stress on the body's physiology. I agreed to go along with the idea.

On election night, Bruce Phillips and I held down the anchor desk; Bob Conroy was directing, with Tom Gould and Don Cameron looking over his shoulder from the producers' dais behind him in the control room. Our national reporters were seated at a table on the studio floor, each ready to assess local results from his or her assigned region. During the sketchy rehearsal just prior to air time, the cardiograph made little hills and valleys just like it was supposed to, and the documentary-makers were overjoyed.

So confident were we that this would be our best election telecast ever, we'd put 120 bottles of champagne on ice for the "wrap" party. We should have remembered that in TV news as in show business, hubris invites retribution.

Our luck ran out about an hour into the telecast. Under the onslaught of results pouring in from Quebec and Ontario, the computer gave up. Panic swept the studio. While Conroy found a shot that did not include the unchanging numbers on the flapper board, Bruce and I chatted as easily as we could, trying not to let on we were in serious trouble. A few minutes later, the computer came back up as suddenly as it had gone down, and we got caught up on results. To be on the safe side, though, Ottawa reporter Craig Oliver was assigned to watch CBC's coverage and monitor some radio stations.

Then Conroy's voice came through in my ear-piece: "The damn thing's gone again." And sure enough, the numbers stopped changing on the display behind me. By now, though, someone had figured out how to move the flappers manually, and Craig Oliver began feeding us what numbers he could glean from CBC and the radio stations. It was agony, faking it like that, and the longer it continued, the less likely it was that we'd ever be able to get back on track even if the damned computer was repaired. Slowly and immutably, the program descended into total disaster. We signed off an hour earlier than we'd planned, out of sheer embarrassment.

Fate would not even allow us to drown our sorrows in all that iced champagne. CFTO had a rule that liquor could not be consumed in the station unless a vice-president was there. Because we'd signed off an hour early, the vice-president was nowhere to be found.

Even the cardiograph was a failure. While my heart rate had fluctuated somewhat during our rehearsal, when the broadcast began it went up about ten points and stayed there for the duration, just a monotonously uniform scribble on the chart.

The election night debacle hit newsroom morale hard, probably because it seemed to confirm our own sense that the news operation had been operating on inspiration and blind luck—running on "empty"—for too long. Ingenuity, creativity, hard work—all these are required in any television production effort—but money is the fuel, and manpower is the engine. For too long, CTV News had been short of both. Charlie Yellowley was working himself into a state of nervous collapse as line-up editor and newsroom manager, struggling against hopeless odds to try to match the CBC on the air each night. He was tired; so was I, and so was everybody else. The spark in the newsroom was dimming: tempers were short, mistakes were becoming more and more frequent. We were looking sloppy on the air.

Charlie and I would go at each other, accusing one another of failing to get us back on track. When we weren't doing that, we'd take turns going downtown to network headquarters to badger Don Cameron and Tom Gould and whoever else would listen to our concerns.

"We're collapsing," we'd rail. "Do we have to wait for the ratings to drop before you do anything about it?"

But Cameron and Gould were themselves overworked with W-5 and the new baby, *Canada AM*, plus the various other progrms the department was responsible for. Nor were they ignorant of the fact that the newscast was sold out: a long list of advertisers were lined up and waiting for time to become available. By the ultimate standard of commercial television, we were a success, but it was our "success" that was preventing us from getting what we needed to improve the newscast.

Later on during this long slump, I had one of the worst on-air experiences of my career, even worse than the election of '74. It became the subject of an article in the old *Weekend Magazine*, which by grotesque coincidence had assigned two writers to do a comparison between the CBC and CTV newscasts on the night of March 6th, 1975—the night of the newscast that died.

Norman Hartley was the writer assigned to cover CTV and I quote his opening paragraph: "It was to be one of the blacker days in the history of CTV News: a day that would see the unflappable Harvey Kirck sweating on camera; a day that would age Charlie Yellowley by a couple of years; a day that would bring writers and editors to their knees on the studio floor to produce a newscast that will become part of the lore of the craft."

It had been shaping up as a more or less routine news day: nothing particularly significant going on. Assignment editor Bob Dowling, a cheerful fellow the women in the office called "Bobby Dumpling," had pulled together a respectable run of material from the bureaus. Tom Gould popped in to record his "Backgrounder" at the usual time. Charlie was lining up; Al Parks and Gary Ralph, an ex-*Telegram* reporter, were on the desk as writers.

The only abnormal thing about that night was that, since CTV was carrying the world figure-skating championships from Colorado Springs, the newscast was to be delayed until about midnight.

At eleven, we ran through the rehearsal, everything working just right. In the control room, director Bernie Paizel, switcher Dick Young, and production assistant Bernice Gillies watched the minutes tick by until midnight, and then we were on the air.

The first two stories went fine. Then came my cue to Mike McCourt, standing by on videotape in Ottawa with a report about shipping contracts. Dick Young punched the Ottawa line, and up came . . . colour bars.

Bernie Paizel: "Ottawa, you're giving us bars! Ottawa!"

"No we're not," Ottawa replies, "we're rolling the item. It's leaving here fine."

The camera comes back to me, and I apologize for the technical troubles.

The cataclysmic thought hits everyone at about the same time: if we've lost Ottawa, we've lost more than six minutes of newscast content!

We shuffle stories, moving the Ottawa items down in the newscast, moving items available locally to the top, while Bernie and Dick and a growing number of technicians frantically try to sort out the problem with the Ottawa line. Back in the newsroom, someone is ripping wire copy off the teletype machines and racing it downstairs to the studio. To quote *Weekend*:

" . . . (they) creep in on all fours to Harvey Kirck. Gary Ralph has the scissors, and cuts the pieces of wire copy and hands it to (Al Parks), who slips it to Harvey Kirck. Harvey stares at an item in disbelief, then bravely reads it, strong, powerful, as though it were of earth-shaking importance." It's a story about a retraining program for unemployed teachers. Another appears on my desk: it concerns a couple of prisoners in the Prince George jail who wanted to get married, having already consummated their love during recreation periods.

By now, we've figured out what has happened. The Bell Telphone man in Ottawa had seen our rehearsal at eleven, figured that was the show, pulled all his patch cords, and set up for *Canada AM* the next morning . . . then gone home.

Weekend again: "Harvey Kirck is beginning to sweat. Then comes an item that nearly floors him. MP Flora MacDonald is up in arms about housing assistance to low-income groups. She's talking about something called AHOP, and Harvey Kirck has never heard of AHOP and doubts there is any such thing, so he calls it OHOP. Much more convincing."

When it was time, finally, to sign off, I said: "I'm Harvey Kirck, I think."

Norman Hartley had a kind comment for us, when it would have been easy to create blisters. He said: "The news has never been worse, and I doubt the team has ever been better."

I have had occasional nightmares about that broadcast. I have often wondered why I didn't just say something like, "Hey, folks, we have a problem here. Bear with us." On the other hand, it was pretty obvious we were having troubles—it really didn't need to be said.

The newscast continued to limp along night after night, the victim of continuing benign neglect from head office: we'd be there every night at eleven with a program our audience appeared to find acceptable, even if we knew it was often far from adequate.

Then, the ratings began to sag. That in turn brought about, in the summer of 1976, a magical transformation in the network's attitude. People at network headquarters began listening to our bitching and complaining. A designer was brought in to build a huge, new set, which would go into operation in the fall. I was called into Don Cameron's office to be told I was "colourless," and that I'd better go out and get new clothes that would do justice to the new set.

"For God sake," Cameron growled, "get yourself a red tie."

There was even a rumour that CTV had been talking to Lloyd Robertson, who'd been anchoring the CBC newscast for the past several years. I was asked how I'd feel about working with Lloyd, and I responded that I didn't care what was done to get the program back on the rails, so long as it was done quickly.

Lo and behold, another miracle: I was asked if I'd make a promotion tour across the country! The idea of the network spending that kind of money to promote the news was unheard of. A young lady in our tiny publicity department was assigned to organize the details, and she, Charlie Yellowley, and I set off on a round of newspaper interviews, radio talk shows, and television appearances.

I was holding court in Calgary—and enjoying it—when word came for me to return to Toronto immediately. I guessed what was coming.

After protracted negotiations, Lloyd Robertson had agreed to join CTV News as co-anchor—but only on condition that I accept the change. When all the parties had gathered in the CTV offices, I made my position clear: Lloyd would be a strong asset for us, and I felt that we could work well together. The two-anchor format would provide an opportunity for each of us to get out of the studio on assignment, while still maintaining the continuity in the daily broadcast which all of us knew was essential.

So the pact was sealed: the new set, already under construction, was altered slightly to accommodate two anchormen, and Lloyd and I became a team.

* * *

I can say without equivocation that I cannot imagine a finer partner than Lloyd Robertson. He is a generous and dedicated professional completely devoid of what the British call "side"—the egoism one so often sees in "celebrities." He's a nice man to boot. We have had a long and close relationship, virtually free of unhappy incident.

"We made it, Harvey."

"Welcome aboard."

That's the way the first CTV newscast with Lloyd Robertson and Harvey Kirck ended. Lloyd, after 22 years with CBC, was making his first regular appearance in private broadcasting, working in an atmosphere radically different from Mother Corporation, and with an unfamiliar format.

As for me, I was still on home turf, surrounded by people I knew well. My job was to learn how to work with another man on the newscast. We mastered that together, and by the end of the first week, I think we both realized we had a successful partnership going. There was an interesting contrast between us . . . Lloyd neat and trim, rather serious, and perfectly poised behind the desk; me, the rumpled one, slouching, sartorially less than elegant.

There was also a marked difference in the way we delivered the news. I tend to "tell" the news, to be conversational. Lloyd had a smooth, serious, more formal delivery, which had made him an early stand-out among announcers at the Corporation.

Having said all of that, I would be less than honest if I didn't confess that there are times when I ask myself a few questions: "What if" 's.

What if CTV had spent a lot of money beefing up the newsroom staff and production facilities? What if we'd had more money available to promote the newscast? What if we'd slicked up the set and the graphics and the rest of the show's visual elements, to make it more interesting to watch? And what if we'd done it all instead of hiring Lloyd? Could CTV News, with ol' Harv as the single anchorman, have taken over the top audience from CBC?

It's a question that will never be answered; but I spend a little time with it now and then. Not much.

The fact is that that first newscast in 1976 marked the beginning of the most successful two-man news combination in Canadian television history. Our professional association was to last almost a decade, and our friendship continues today. In the sweat and blood of live television news, that is a remarkable feat. It is also a tribute to Lloyd's forbearance and patience in the face of my occasional pig-headedness and sometimes outrageous, often loudly-proclaimed opinions. Never once were there serious differences between us: never once was there what might be termed an "ego problem." Working with Lloyd was always a pleasure.

Chapter 21

Soon after Lloyd joined CTV, a personal time-bomb of mine exploded. I have been a two-fisted drinker for most of my adult life; maybe it was inherited from hard-drinking uncles, or maybe it was just an acquired taste. I've had some good teachers—my "yacht club" pals at CKEY and all the others down the years. I can't blame them: I was an eager student. Moreover, I enjoyed it. I enjoyed the lift alcohol gave me, the feeling of well-being, the illusion of heightened awareness, of sharpened responses. It was all spurious, of course, but the fact is that for many years, alcohol was an integral part of my life. I was able to handle it well: it never seriously impaired my work, and rarely was there the deterring factor of a bad hangover. The idea that alcohol could be a problem in my life had never even occurred to me.

But it was.

In October, 1976, Brenda and I traded our 25-foot runabout on a 34-foot Chris Craft cabin cruiser. It was an older boat, a real beauty—and big enough for two people to live aboard all summer in complete comfort.

We drove to Crate's Yacht Basin, near Orillia, to sign the deal. Brian Crate and his father, Lloyd, were old friends, and after the business was done, we celebrated. When it was time to leave, I knew I'd had too much to drink, and so I asked Brenda to drive home. Our car was big, and Brenda was nervous—she'd only recently renewed her drivers' licence after years of not owning a car.

From Brian Crate's marina to the highway is about two miles, and there are two stop signs. At the first of these, Brenda stopped, then slowly began a left turn. At that moment, a car came barrelling over a small hill, right down the centre of the road. Instinctively, Brenda hauled the wheel to the right, and the car slipped into the ditch. The speeder passed and Brenda began pulling our car back onto the road. Frightened and confused, she stabbed a foot at the brake pedal, missed, and tramped the accelerator. In a flash we'd shot forward across the road through a fence and into a farmer's barnyard.

As I understand it, the farmer's wife was standing at her kitchen window, saw the car thunder into her yard, and called the police.

I climbed out the passenger side and walked around the car. It was hub-deep in mud, but I thought it could probably be eased out. The problem would be getting it back across the ditch and onto the road. I figured we'd need a tow truck or a tractor for that. Thoroughly sobered now, I decided I could move the car to the edge of the ditch, then walk back to Crate's for some help. That was my mistake. As the car reached the side of the ditch, an Ontario Provincial Police constable drove up.

The fact that I'd only driven the car 30 or 40 feet across a farmer's barnyard to the edge of an impassable ditch cut no ice with the constable. Brenda and I were invited into the back of his cruiser. He was gregarious and friendly, obviously proud of his new calling. Only a few months earlier, he told me, he'd been a salesman in the camera department of a Woolco store in Whitby, and had sold me a camera.

He drove us to the local O.P.P. headquarters, where I failed the breathalyzer test.

There was a legal controversy in Ontario then about the mandatory length of time between the two stages of breathalyzer tests. Mine were 15 minutes apart, but there was a new interpretation of the law that required the tests to be *more* than 15 minutes apart. On that slim peg, my lawyer hung my defence.

The Crown had a surprise witness—the driver of the car that had forced Brenda off the road in the first place. He didn't say that. Then they produced an expert on breathalyzers from the Forensic Centre in Toronto. It seemed to me that the government was going to a lot of trouble and expense to assure a conviction.

The judge dismissed the case on the grounds that the breathalyzer results were invalid, given the interval between the two tests. Then the Crown appealed. I was convicted, and my driver's licence was suspended for three months.

The second incident was much more serious.

It happened during a period of severe emotional stress for me. Renate and I were in the throes of divorce, and could not even speak civilly to one another on the telephone. My children blamed me for the marriage break-up and would have little to do with me. Revenue Canada had attacked my company in a "crackdown" on personal service corporations, and had re-assessed me for taxes going back four years—a sum which, if I'd been forced to pay, would have left me bankrupt. All these outside pressures were taking their toll on my work, and I was worried about that, too.

On one especially bad day, I ended up visiting my mother in Ajax, pouring out to her my anger and frustration. At the same time, I was pouring liberal belts from her "company" bottle of whiskey. On my way home, I realized Brenda was working, and I was heading for an empty apartment. I decided to pick up some dinner, and stopped at a Chinese take-out restaurant.

Cruising along on Highway 401 back to Toronto, I got hungry, so I pulled over to the shoulder and fished an egg roll out of the package, before driving on. As I moved back onto the highway, I noticed an O.P.P. cruiser in the mirror. He followed me for about a mile and then pulled up alongside, signalling me to stop. The officer, a big, dark-haired man, strolled back to my car and asked if anything was wrong. I said no. He told me he'd seen me stop on the shoulder, and thought I may have needed assistance. I explained what I'd been doing. Then he asked to see my licence, and took it back to his cruiser. When he returned, he had the black box with him, the roadside breathalyzer. I failed it. We then returned to the Whitby O.P.P. headquarters, where I failed the formal breathalyzer test as well. I was charged with driving with more than the legal limit of alcohol in my system, and this was my second offence.

A conviction on a second offence, I knew, carried a mandatory jail sentence.

I was scared stiff . . . and some of that came out as moral outrage. How can a policeman stop someone on the highway for no apparent reason? What right did he have to pull me over when, as he was to admit in court, my car was not weaving. I was not speeding, and the car was mechanically fit . . . what right did he have to flag me down merely because he thought I might need "assistance"?

I reported to CTV president Murray Chercover and vice-president Donald Cameron. Both were angry and severe in their reprimands, but with that over, they decided to wait to see what happened before taking any action. So far, there had been no publicity; it was to be almost a week before an enterprising reporter for a weekly paper in Whitby dug the facts of my arrest out of the police blotter.

I became news right across the country, and I continued to be news throughout my trial and conviction, which, on the advice of my lawyer, Bruce Affleck, I appealed. Bruce had been one of the country's more famous Crown Attorneys before going into private practice, and he felt there were grave errors in the case against me, notably in the judge's acceptance of the right of the officer to have stopped me in the first place.

Through it all, I had a constant case of butterflies. I was terrified for my job and my reputation. I worried about what it was doing to my family and close friends. Don Cameron, who had had his own troubles with alcohol in the past, assured me it would all turn out all right; but, at the same time, he sent me the obligatory letter pointing out that I might be in violation of my contract—that bringing the network into disrepute was cause for termination. Murray Chercover suggested that, if I were convicted, I should take a few months off, while we all thought things over.

On a day with particularly harsh headlines, the network had a lavish party for advertisers. Marge Anthony, that jewel of a lady who runs the promotion department, insisted I attend. I felt roughly six inches high walking into that hotel ballroom, facing all those elegant people, but

Marge came to my side, put an arm around me, and stayed by my side the whole evening. You remember a kindness like that for a long time.

On that same evening, a young man stuck his face against mine:

"I'm from the *Sun*," he said.

"I haven't anything to say to you." I pushed my way past.

He grabbed my shoulder: "I have a message from Doug MacFarlane. He wants to know if you'll do a series for the *Sun* from the inside."

Doug MacFarlane, one of my old mentors from the *Telegram*. God, I thought, he must be on hard times.

I lost the appeal. The newspapers, radio, and TV stations reported my conviction with what seemed to me vindictive relish, given that every headline was another potential blow to my chances of hanging on to my career.

My sentencing was delayed while the judge awaited the outcome of another case which might affect my own. It did not, however, and I was summoned to appear in court on a Monday in June. Cameron and Chercover had agreed with my plan to go to court, serve whatever jail term was imposed, then immediately disappear on my boat for an extended vacation in the wilds of Georgian Bay. That way, I'd be out of sight and thus, we hoped, out of mind as far as reporters were concerned.

Brenda and I spent the weekend before my court appearance on the boat. On Saturday, two of our best boating friends, Jack and Joy Sherritt, invited us aboard their yacht. As I stepped over the gunwale, I put a foot on a thick power cable, twisted my ankle, and went down hard. Later in the day, the ankle began to swell and grow painful. I didn't get much sleep that night, and in the morning it was worse than ever.

"Dammit," I said to Brenda, "I think it's broken. That's far too sore to just be a sprain."

We had another boat by now, one with a small aft cabin: I'd had a lot of trouble getting down the steps and through the narrow hatchway the previous night. Now the pain was so excruciating when I tried to put weight on my foot, or even jarred it, that I couldn't get back out. Lindsey

Williamson, a big Scotsman with an answer for everything, arrived and poked his head into the aft cabin.

"Linds," I said, "I can't damn well get out of bed."

"We'd better get you to a hospital and have that looked at," he said.

Then Jack arrived and stooped low to peer in at me, a cigar butt clamped between his teeth. He withdrew to the saloon to consult with Lindsey on how to get me out of bed, through a small hatchway, up a couple of stairs, across the saloon, up some more stairs to the deck, and from there onto the dock and into a car.

If it hadn't hurt so much, it would have been funny. Lindsey was almost my size, and Jack was not a small man either: they hoisted me off the bed, then pushed, pulled, wedged and levered me through the various obstacles. Finally, we were off the boat and onto the narrow dock. With Jack in front and Lindsey behind, we hopped and lurched to dry land, jarring my ankle with every move, and from there they half-carried me until I plopped, exhausted, onto the back seat of the waiting car.

The doctor at the local hospital diagnosed two broken bones in my ankle, and I went back to the boat later that morning wearing a cast that extended from the tips of my toes to just below the knee.

So it was that at ten o'clock the following morning I swung into the courtroom with crutches digging into my armpits. I considered working up a few grimaces and low moans of pain to wring what sympathy I could from the court, but then decided against it. My lawyer had already pointed out to the judge that my case was attracting national media attention, that my job was in jeopardy . . . he'd even called the whole business a case of cruel and unusual punishment. A sympathy play now would have been overkill.

I was sentenced to two weeks in jail, with an immediate referral to a halfway house where, if I chose, I could continue to work, returning to confinement only at night. I chose to stay there full-time, just to keep out of the limelight for a while. A car was sent for, and while we were waiting, I was lodged in a small cell beneath the courtroom. Then it was on to Whitby jail, where I was processed and given lunch in another holding cell, before being driven to the halfway house. My ankle hurt like hell, but not half so much as my pride.

Durhamcrest is an old house in the east end of Oshawa. At the time I arrived, there were about 20 inmates, most of them young men who worked in the daytime and stayed there at night. Those who did not have jobs were expected to do certain chores around the house: clean windows, paint, cut the grass, or assist the part-time cook in the kitchen. The inmates, who were a little better versed in the vernacular than I was, called it "good time."

My time, in fact, was "very good time." A 14-day sentence is really nine days: there is time off for good behaviour, and the day you arrive, usually late in the evening, and the day you leave, usually early in the morning, both count as full days. Our supervisor was a large, good-natured, but hard-edged woman who showed some sympathy for my broken ankle and exempted me from most of the work details. (I spent most of my time reading and watching television.) She even thought it a great joke when I unwrapped a package from Michael Harris, the CTV News line-up editor at the time, to find a book containing two ill-concealed hacksaw blades.

The greatest discomfort I had at Durhamcrest was in trying to get to my bed. So that we would not be awakened in the morning by inmates readying themselves for work, two or three of us were assigned to berths on the third floor. The stairway was narrow, and trying to negotiate it on crutches was quite a challenge. I finally settled for climbing the stairs on my hands and knees, and descending them on my bottom, my sore leg stuck out in front like the bowsprit of a ship.

Finally, my term was up—and I fled to Georgian Bay and the boat. For the next few weeks, we roamed the bright blue waters among the rocky islands, where each new turning presented a vista from a Group of Seven painting. Nights brought midnight blue skies alive with the twinkling of stars and the trembling wash of northern lights. If God had ever intended peace, this was where it was to be found.

Most of that summer was spent that way, exploring new waterways and finding secluded places where we could hide away from the world. There were occasional forays into civilization, places like Parry Sound and Little Current and Meldrum Bay. Sometimes it was just a plain old-fashioned boat ride, for the excitement of the wind in our faces and spray rolling out from the bow; the roar of the motor, and the wake arcing in a wide, bubbly V, leaving the track of our passage.

There is a commonality among boaters, a great levelling. You may be the chairman of the board with a 45-foot motor yacht, or you may be the shipping clerk, with a 21-foot sailboat. But when you sit together at a dock, or on the aft deck at anchor, rank and place disappear. The bank president may bring along a supply of martinis, but they'll be served out of an aluminum bucket. Sailboaters, sometimes a breed apart, show the motorboaters how to properly tie a spring line, and teach them that ropes are lines and sheets, that the steering wheel is the helm, and the pointy end of the boat is the bow. Motorboaters make the fridges and ice-makers available to the sailboaters, who seem always to be stuck with a tiny icebox.

During my period of extreme notoriety, our short visits to civilization were marked by well-wishing people, eager to extend their sympathy and wish me luck. Of course, there were those who were less than sympathetic, too, but I was surprised at how few.

By the end of the summer idyll, I had recovered from my physical injuries. I was now prepared to take stock of my personal situation and ask myself some basic questions. Did I have what is referred to as "a drinking problem?"

The answer to that one was obviously "yes." I clearly drank too much, too often.

Was I an alcoholic?

I didn't know. I didn't think so . . . but then, that's what all alcoholics say.

Did I need some help?

Yes, that seemed to be a good idea.

The questions swirled in my mind, day after day, I talked, compulsively, with Brenda and with my close friends Jack and Lindsey, and I had a long conversation with a lady doctor at the Little Current Hospital on Manitoulin Island, as she removed the cast from my ankle.

I also had the occasional drink, cautiously, tentatively, testing myself. Booze, I knew, is like a crutch with a hinge in it; you never know when the hinge will buckle and drop you right on your ass. I knew I was on the brink of a war with alcohol: surrender was out of the question, but I preferred a negotiated peace to a never-ending battle.

I went back on the air in October, after some long talks with Don Cameron and Murray Chercover. At their suggestion, I enrolled in a day-care program at the Donwood Clinic in Toronto, a world-famous institution which treats alcohol and drug-related problems. I was one of a group of about a dozen patients with drinking problems of varying severity, and we were encouraged to talk about them among ourselves. There were lectures and films, and the horrors of alcohol were made all too clear. We were given Antabuse, a drug that precludes the use of even the minutest amounts of alcohol: to drink booze, even to eat rum cake, while on Antabuse is to risk loss of breath, chest pains . . . all the frightening symptoms of a heart attack. I was afraid even to walk past the open door of a bar.

Don Cameron suggested I attend meetings of Alcoholics Anonymous, and I did. But I had a problem with the "anonymous" part: I wasn't, and that created pressure of another kind. I decided that if I was to stop drinking entirely, or at least bring it under control, I would do it myself.

While I still drink occasionally, it has not been a problem for some years. The potential for disaster is too frightening for booze to ever again be a dangerous challenge.

Chapter 22

I was now approaching my fifteenth year with CTV News, and for the first time, I began to entertain serious thoughts about leaving the newscast. Maybe it was part of the re-evaluating I'd done during the trauma of the court cases—perhaps it was just that I was genuinely tired of working nights.

The combination of Lloyd and I was working better all the time. Lloyd hadn't brought the expected flood of CBC viewers to our audience, but our numbers were building day by day, as though Canadians were cautiously dipping their toes in the CTV pool and finding it pleasing.

I had just returned from an exciting assignment at Camp David, where Menachem Begin, Anwar Sadat, and Jimmy Carter had hammered out the accords that were to lead to a normalizing of relations between Egypt and Israel, and which held out the promise of peace in the Middle East. There were other exciting news developments in the air: the Trudeau government was on the ropes, with Joe Clark's Conservatives looking more and more like a credible alternative—in October by-elections, the Liberals had lost 13 of 15 contests. Quebec was moving inexorably toward a major confrontation with the rest of the country over the separation issue. Beirut was being devastated by civil war. Iran was in the throes of a revolution against the rule of the Shah.

It was not a time to be getting out of the news business.

Tom Gould, who'd done so much to revitalize the newscast, had left the network, to be replaced by Don Cameron. Tom had an unfortunate penchant for taking a back-to-the-wall, all-or-nothing position on any given issue, and sadly, he took it once too often. He left himself too little room to manoeuvre in a dispute over the frequency of preemptions for *W-5* (he felt there were far too many for what was supposed to be a flagship current affairs program), and wound up with no option but to resign. Most of the staff was sorry to see him go. He had presided over some of the strongest growth in the network's news and current affairs department, had fought tenaciously for what he needed to do the job, and was a popular, if sometimes erratic leader.

When Don Cameron moved into Gould's office, we all held our breath. Don was a newsman of the old school— he could have been created for a Ben Hecht play. He covered his office walls with photographs taken on assignment all over the world: Don with GI's on patrol in 'Nam; Don and crew in Biafra; Don in the jungles of Central America. His attitude was: "Keep your suitcase packed and your passport up-to-date . . . you never know where you'll be tomorrow." His credentials for an administrative job like the vice-presidency were not impressive. To his credit, he moved slowly and cautiously, until the mantle fit him comfortably. He has since put his own, indelible stamp on the network news programs. Once in a while though, when a big story breaks in some exotic corner of the world, Don still grabs his pre-packed suitcase and charges off, the old juices pumping again.

Cameron was one of those responsible for one of the most important acquisitions made by CTV News in that period. Tim Kotcheff, a volatile, hyperactive Bulgarian with a solid record in current affairs production at the CBC, had been brought in as executive producer of news and current affairs shortly after Lloyd joined us. He had a Ralph Naderish look about him: his suits appeared to have come off the rack at Woolco, his thinning hair seldom saw a comb, and his ties never sat straight in his collar. He had a laugh like a jackal and eyes that could shatter brick. Kotcheff was a human dynamo who made the newsroom move as it never had before. He took for himself the clout needed to deal with production values, with news judgements, with equipment acquistions, with bureau expansions, and with relations with affiliate newsrooms—in fact, with every element of the national news operation. Right or wrong, his judgement prevailed, and he was more often right than wrong, though some of us thought he had serious failings when it came to dealing with editorial personnel . . . (he had a bad habit of forgetting commitments—perhaps an understandable failing in one so overloaded with responsibility).

As soon as he was hired, Kotcheff went to work on the news operation, adding badly needed support staff to both the assignment and line-up desks, and ordering such elementary necessities as a high-speed photocopier, a telecopier for transmitting scripts and other documents, reliable monitors and recording equipment, an improved telephone system, and even a small research library. At the same time, technical facilities for the bureaus were upgraded dramatically. The newsroom itself was expanded and completely renovated—for the first time, we had carpet on the floor and comfortable chairs to sit in while we worked. What had been an ulcer factory for the people on the desk was becoming a much more humane working environment. At the same time, though, Kotcheff exerted unremitting pressure on performance standards: he was a hard man to please.

Kotcheff's most important innovation in the news operation may have been his organizing something called DNS, short for Daily News Service. It's a closed-circuit microwave feed that links all the affiliate newsrooms with CTV headquarters once a day. News reports prepared by the affiliates or by CTV News reporters are swapped up and down the network for use on the local newscasts. Its establishment led to a dramatic improvement in the quality of many of the affiliate newscasts, but more important from CTV News' point of view, it gave the network the clout in dealing with the affiliate newsrooms that had been so sadly missing during all the network's previous history. The affiliates found that there was much to be gained through co-operation, and their growing dependence on DNS gave CTV News a powerful lever in resolving conflicts between local and network priorities. With the coming of DNS and the political power that devolved to CTV News headquarters, we were able at long last to begin operating like a real news network.

At the same time, Lloyd was gradually taking over the anchor role for almost all the specials we did. That didn't concern me much . . . I felt that while specials perhaps impressed the board of directors, the nightly newscast was where the viewers were, day in and day out. Daily news was our bread and butter.

At the same time, it was becoming tedious to be tied constantly to the anchor desk. I decided to take an aggressive stance on the issue:

"Listen Kotcheff," I ranted. "Lloyd's working on all these specials and I'm constantly stuck on the desk. I want to get out of here once in a while. Shake the cobwebs out of my brain."

That led to a meeting with Don Cameron and results a little more drastic than I'd expected. I was to become a special correspondent, but would not anchor specials: Lloyd would anchor specials, but would not function as a reporter. Lloyd, naturally enough, was not at all happy with the arrangement. It had been just such arbitrary restrictions on his duties that had driven him out of CBC and over to us in the first place.

It did seem like a silly case of overkill. I couldn't see how this artificial division of duties would serve any constructive purpose. All I'd wanted was to get off the desk once in a while. Fortunately, Lloyd and I had worked together long enough to be able to arrange our own accommodation for these kinds of irritants. We discussed it, and decided that we could find our own ways of circumventing such authoritarian measures.

It worked out fine. I went to Cairo and Jerusalem, shuttling between the two cities as the details of the Camp David-inspired peace treaty were worked out. Within an hour of President Reagan's being shot in Washington, I was on a Lear jet at Toronto airport, on my way to the scene. During the 1979 federal election telecast, I moderated a panel that included Don Jamieson, Tommy Douglas, Jack Webster, and some other informed observers, while Lloyd and Bruce Phillips did the anchoring—and I had the best time I'd ever had in an election broadcast. The same happened a year later, when Trudeau returned. In the Quebec sovereignty-association referendum telecast, I tried to keep order between Brian Mulroney, then a suave Tory businessman, and Louis LaBerge, the fiery Quebec labour leader. That was an entertaining, though almost impossible assignment, and I believe Mulroney came out the loser. No one could long withstand the verbal onslaught of Louis LaBerge.

I was doing some network promotion work in Montreal during a Gray Cup celebration, when I casually mentioned to Don Cameron that we should have someone in Belfast . . . that Ian Paisley was talking about raising a private army and was organizing rallies that were likely to turn ugly. Cameron, with characteristic decisiveness, growled: "Well, you'd better go."

I phoned home and had my step-son Michael pack a bag for me and send it with an Air Canada crew to Dorval Airport, where I collected it before catching a taxi for Mirabel and a flight to Belfast. I was there within hours of my conversation with Cameron.

This assignment gave me my first close contact with Clark Todd, CTV News' London bureau chief and general overseas firefighter. Clark was a scholarly-looking man, thin, blonde, rumpled, and, without his thick aviator's glasses, myopic. He walked with a determined stride, his jaw thrust forward as though parting the wind. He was the kind of reporter who headed straight for the thick of the action, who revelled in the excitement of violent turmoil.

I, on the other hand, have always been a firm believer in discretion being the better part of valour. At a Paisley rally outside Belfast, I was rehearsing my stand-up in the supercharged atmosphere at the fringe of the mob, while the crew set up its equipment. A heavy-set man sidled up to me, and out of the corner of his mouth, said:

"Yer not goin' tuh say that, are ya?"

I walked away, a little shaken by his tone. Minutes later, when we were ready to shoot the stand-up, I glanced behind me. There, ranged in a semi-circle, were six of the toughest-looking Irishmen I'd ever seen. I made some last-minute changes in my script, figuring I could always get the tough stuff into the voice-over narration later on.

Not all my foreign assignments went as smoothly. On the way to Iran during the hostage crisis at the American embassy, I got as far as New York before finding out that I could not obtain an Iranian visa. So I spent two weeks, instead, observing the futile deliberations of the United Nations, as that body struggled impotently to deal with the problem.

On another ill-conceived assignment, I was to make a fast trip to Libya during a period of heightened tensions between Tripoli and Washington. There were rumours of Libyan "hit squads" abroad in the United States, and Colonel Ghaddafi had expelled some Americans from Libya. I was called at home, and told to be on a plane to New York immediately. I stayed there overnight, prepared to board a London-bound Concorde early the next morning. London, however, was in the grip of a severe snowstorm, and so the Concorde was held back in New York for several hours. I did eventually get to London that day, but too late to collect the Libyan visa Clark Todd had arranged for me. I picked it up first thing next morning and raced back to the airport. Heathrow had by then been almost completely shut down by the storm: few planes were moving.

I spent the day amid crowds of stranded travellers, as the weather steadily deteriorated. In the meantime, the Libyan story had petered out. In fact, it had never really existed in the first place, except in the fertile imaginations of a few unnamed Pentagon "sources," a couple of gullible American network correspondents and our own, temporarily demented, assignment desk. The Iranian hostage story, though, had heated up, and so I spent the next four days working overnight, re-voicing the narration to film from Teheran, and feeding packaged reports via satellite from London to Toronto. Not what you'd call a glamour assignment.

* * *

We were sitting in the den of our Scarborough apartment in the spring of 1983. Brenda's attention riveted by her favourite TV soap opera. I was reading Cornelius Ryan's D-Day opus *The Longest Day*.

I looked up from my book.

"What do you say we get married?" I said.

"Mmmmmm." Some reply.

"What do you say we get married." I asked again.

"Okay." Her eyes never left the television set. She was a true soap addict. The seconds passed.

"When?" she asked.

I looked at my book: "How about June 6th?"

We'd been living together for five years. We'd talked about marriage before, but it had never seemed important.

"It would make things easier for me," I said. "If we're married, I can introduce you as my wife. I feel a little silly, at my age, introducing you as my girlfriend."

"Okay," she said.

I had done some thinking about this. I thought it would be nice to be married at the Martyr's Shrine, a white, hillside cathedral in Midland. It was close to our marina, and I thought we could have a little party afterward on the boat.

Brenda blew that idea. "First, we're not Catholics. Second, we're both divorced. I don't think we'd be welcomed."

Gord Blake, the rotund, energetic owner of the Wye Heritage Marina, where we docked *Golly Goya*, came to the rescue by offering his house. It was in a magnificent setting on the shore of Midland Bay, and June 6th came up bright and sunny. A handful of close friends and relatives gathered at the marina, and Jack Sherritt and Lindsey Williamson volunteered their boats for the short trip across the bay to Gord's house.

When we'd all arrived, Brenda and I discovered that the Sherritts and the Williamsons had laid on a big spread of food and drink, and Gord and his friend Ted Brady had arranged for a couple of musicians. So after a brief ceremony, everyone set to and we had a marvellous party. It was one of my better, luckier, days.

I made another basic decision about the same time. I was due to sign a new contract with CTV in the fall, and I decided I would sign only until December 3rd, 1983,

215

which would be my twentieth anniversary with CTV News. That would mean I'd surpassed even Walter Cronkite's record for longevity in a network anchor position.

I was tired of the daily grind, most of all with having to force myself to be "up" every night at eleven o'clock. I found I was spending less and less time in the newsroom, taking less and less interest in the content of the program, and appearing only infrequently at the important editorial meetings that marked the transition between the dayside, assignment shift, and the nightly line-up shift. I feared I was falling into the trap of doing the newscast by rote: seeing the script with my eyes, and speaking the words with my mouth, without using my brain in between. It was a condition I abhorred in other performers.

There was also the matter of stretching myself professionally, seeing if I could do something else in the television game. I'd enjoyed my brief appearances on other shows, away from the tightly structured format of the newscast, and I figured that if I was ever going to break out of the mould, I'd better do it quickly: I was no kid anymore.

In the past, I had never negotiated my contracts—I'd arrive at Murray Chercover's office, Don Cameron would be there, and they'd tell me how it was going to be. Since I had no real idea of how to bargain, I'd usually say "fine," and take off. This time, Chercover insisted on a three-year contract, a year more than I wanted. I finally agreed, but insisted on a clause that would allow me to get out at the end of 1983 if I wanted to. The contract was written up, and we all signed it . . . only then did I notice that my option clause was nowhere to be found! I am quite certain that nobody believed I really wanted off the newscast: they took my protestations for a bargaining ploy.

I can't deny that I was still a little ambivalent, and that there were times when my resolve to leave faltered a bit. The newscast was better than it had ever been, the department more efficient, the audience growing. We were now neck-and-neck with the CBC, with about 1,500,000 people watching every night. I was well-paid . . . over-paid, if anything, even if I was working half my time for Revenue Canada.

There were other factors, though. Being a "celebrity" is a wonderful ego trip, but I'd been in that position for quite a few years, and, as our audience increased and our promotion department grew ever more conscientious, I began to feel a growing resentment at being recognized wherever I went. I found myself being snarly with people who wanted nothing more than to say "hello" and wish me well. Brenda and I escaped more and more often to the seclusion of our boat in the wilds of Georgian Bay and Lake Huron's North Channel.

Then there were the unending requests for speeches, and for public appearances. I have always believed that if you've got something good going, you have an obligation to pay back into the system. Over the years, I've tried to do that—but in my own way, and on my own terms. The celebrity auction, for instance, has been the bane of my existence. I believe it is an imposition for a fund-raising group to ask for personal articles to be auctioned, so, for the past several years, I've not even replied to those requests. Sorry about that.

However, the final decision to leave the newscast was made for me in a series of personal tragedies that hit our little news family like so many hammer blows over a period of just a few months. I say "family" advisedly, since we were a small, interdependent group that worked closely together and developed close friendships which had a life beyond the newsroom. When one of us hurt, we all hurt.

Sandra McKenzie, network publicist for news and current affairs, went to the hospital for an appendectomy, contracted an infection, and died. Knut Kurcharski, a big, soft-spoken film editor I'd worked with since my earliest days at CFTO, had a heart attack that killed him instantly. Brian O'Brien—"Obie," we called him—went to the doctor complaining of chest pains and discovered he was riddled with cancer. He'd become almost as much a newsroom fixture as I was, doing everything from writing and line-up to running DNS. I went to visit him, and found him standing, wasted beside the bed, packing a suitcase. "Hey you old fart, you're just in time to drive me home." Obie didn't want to die . . . he told me that with great bitterness. But within a few weeks, he was gone. Not long afterward, our young and talented Ottawa producer, Bruce Galt, was run over by a bus. He lived on for eight months in hospital, then just gave up the ghost. Don Cameron, tough as rawhide, was hit by his third heart attack. He made a remarkable recovery and is once again in the pink, but it shook me. Sandie Rinaldo, who moved through CTV from secretary to anchorwoman on *Canada AM* . . . pert and perky Sandie had a baby boy who died a few days after birth.

Amid all of this tragedy came the death of Clark Todd, in Lebanon. The manner of his dying moved us all, profoundly. Clark was a reporter who sought out action stories. He was never more alive than when he was covering a riot in Belfast or Warsaw, or bribing his way, visa-less, into Togo at a Dahomey border crossing, or in the midst of shelling in Beirut. We were, none of us, very surprised when we heard Clark had been hit while covering the withdrawal of Israeli forces from the Shouf mountains above Beirut.

When the Israelis pulled back, they left a military vacuum in the Shouf, and it was bound to be hotly contested by the Druze and Christian militias. So it was to the Shouf that Clark headed as soon as he arrived in Lebanon on that particular visit—one of many he'd made for CTV. He didn't bother to inform the desk he was heading into what was fast becoming a no-man's land—he wouldn't risk being ordered to stay out of harm's way. He filed two stories, the second from a mountain village called Kfar Mata, which he predicted would be the focus of heavy fighting in the days to come. The town had already been deserted by its war-wise inhabitants. That's where he was hit, caught in the chest by shrapnel in the opening salvos of the battle. In the terror of the moment, the men who were with him— the two ABC camera crews and their drivers—abandoned Clark, leaving him, mortally wounded, to shift for himself in the dubious shelter of a village hovel.

That was as much as we knew for the first week after Clark was hit. There were a hundred rumours—Clark had been evacuated to a Druze hospital; Clark was being cared for by a Druze nurse; Clark was okay, but was unable to get out of Kfar Mata because of the constant shelling . . . .

We were certain he'd pull through. Clark had been in so many scrapes in the past we'd stopped counting. Tim Kotcheff and Don Cameron were already in Lebanon with Jerusalem correspondent Martin Himel, searching field hospitals and, at the same time, trying desperately to get into Kfar Mata. That's what we heard they were doing: in fact they were also picking through makeshift morgues, surviving hours of artillery shelling, enduring the horrors of a front-line dressing station, coping with a wildly erratic Christian militia officer-guide, and a shell-shocked and guilt-ridden survivor of the attack that got Clark. They were living through a personal hell, more certain with each passing day that Clark was dead, but unable to give up the almost suicidal search in the battleground of the Shouf. Theirs is a story of courage and perseverence worthy of a book in itself. In the end, they did find Clark, stiff and bloated, in the room where he'd been abandoned. His body was loaded onto the back of a Red Cross truck during a frantic few moments before a brief cease-fire was due to end. Cameron and Kotcheff escorted the body back down the mountain roads to an Israeli checkpoint, and from there to Tel Aviv, and then to London where it was claimed by Clark's wife and young children.

It had been eight days from the time we heard he'd been wounded to when we learned he was dead. In that time, we'd never given up the hope that he'd survive. In the end, it was the sudden wrenching away of that carefully nurtured hope that hurt so much.

Clark may have bled to death the night he was hit, or he may have lived long enough to succumb to dehydration two or three days later. We'll never know. He was conscious and alert enough minutes after he was hit to tell his companions to leave him, to run for their lives before the shelling started up again. He was still alive and conscious later that same afternoon when, incredibly, two of the ABC men returned to check on him before leaving him a second time, to flee for their lives down the mountain to Beirut.

Months later, when the fighting had ended and the village of Kfar Mata had returned to Druze occupation, a group of reporters was invited to examine the remains of a Christian miltia massacre of civilians that had taken place there, presumably about the same time Clark was killed. Some of the reporters found their way to the house where Clark's body had been recovered. In the room next to the one in which Clark died, they found the charred remains of 20 women and children. In Clark's room, the reporters found a blood-stained pillow case on which Clark had written his name and address and these words: "Please tell my family I love them."

I have had some difficult times in the business. You expect them; bad news is our stock-in-trade. But I have never been so sorely tried in my profession as the night when I had to read Clark's obituary.

The streak of grim luck we'd been experiencing at CTV News had taken on truly grotesque proportions. It seemed as if a black cloud was hanging over us, with lightning ready to strike out at random.

It was not yet over. We still had to endure the bewildering tragedy of David Eibel's death. David, the bright young line-up editor, Columbia grad, who was the brunt of so many of my bad jokes, went to Normandy to help produce our coverage of the memorial services marking the fortieth anniversary of the D-Day invasion. He worked himself to exhaustion, and on his way back home, he fell into a coma on the aircraft. He spent his thirtieth birthday unconscious in hospital, and a few days after that, he was dead. An autopsy showed he'd had viral meningitis.

I didn't go to David's funeral, because I wanted to remember him the way he was. I can still see him the night I'd been riding him about the way he'd lined up the show. He leaped onto his desk and shouted:

"I'm the boss here and I can do anything I want to do!"

He couldn't carry it off though. He began laughing.

Then there was the night he'd got mixed up in a water-pistol fight with a crazy Australian novelist named Derek Maitland who'd been working on the desk. It quickly escalated to the point where David filled a bucket with water, and was poised to drench Maitland as he appeared in the newsroom doorway. There were footsteps in the hallway, a figure appeared in the door, and David let fly. He was dead on target, but the figure in the doorway was Lloyd, returning from make-up. It was probably the only time Lloyd has lost his cool in the newsroom. He breathed fire on David, who raced, white-faced, to a nearby department store to buy Lloyd a new shirt and tie in time for the newscast.

* * *

My mother died, too, during that time of anguish. She'd been wasting away for a long time with Parkinson's disease.

It was a period when it was difficult to avoid reflecting on the fragility of life. I was in my mid-fifties, overweight, and not in good physical condition after a lifetime of booze and cigarettes. I'd had 20 years as a news anchorman, and if a change of career were in the cards, it was going to have to come now. I might not have another chance.

Chapter 23

I told Don Cameron and Tim Kotcheff that I intended to leave the newscast by December, 1983. This time, they took me seriously. But Kotcheff had a problem: Lloyd would be spending most of the following February in Sarajevo, Yugoslavia, hosting the network's Olympic coverage. He'd been anchoring Olympic telecasts since the Sixties, and was head and shoulders above the competition. The trouble was, February is the most important ratings month of the year. Tim suggested I stay with the newscast until spring, to maintain the Lloyd and Harvey team through the rating period, and in return, he would honour my contract until the end of August. It was an offer I couldn't refuse.

And so it was on April 27th, 1984, that I reported the daily CTV News to Canadians for the last time. There was quite a crowd in the studio: George Cowley, a studio cameraman who'd worked on my first newscast when CTV News moved to Toronto, asked to be assigned to our studio that night. Other crew people came in to say goodbye. Cameraman Mike Yurek, our Polish connection, even got a haircut. Jack Miller, the *Toronto Star* TV columnist who'd been a friend since my Hamilton days, was there with his wife, Helen. Jennifer Lynn, who looks after news promotion for the network, was clucking around like a mother hen.

It was a normal newscast up to the end . . . the usual blend of politics, mayhem, disaster, gossip, and information. Then, when we came back from the final commercial break, Lloyd said something like: "This is Harvey's last night on this newscast, and we leave the last word to him." I had written about a minute of copy—a thank you and farewell to the audience—and I managed to get through it, despite a certain blurriness of vision and tightness in my throat. Now, I'm damned if I can remember what I said. Emotion can play tricks on you.

A month later, Brenda and I used up most of our savings to make the final payment on our new boat, the *Fair Passage*.

Years earlier, we'd decided that at some time, we'd like to live aboard a boat, for the summers at least. But much as we loved her, our big Chris Craft, the *Golly Goya*, was simply not suited for long-term living aboard. As gasoline prices climbed, two big engines burning a gallon for every mile-and-a-half wasn't very practical either.

With much sadness, early in June of 1983, we'd put *Golly Goya* on the block. We expected it would be late summer before a buyer would be found. But, in two weeks, one arrived, with considerably more money than we'd paid for her. That's how we came to watch most of the building of our new boat.

We'd rummaged through the boat magazines and visited marinas, searching for something that would better fit our needs. We came upon the Pilgrim. Ted Gozzard, a bearded genius of a naval architect, had spent 13 years designing and building Bayfield sailboats in southwestern Ontario. Now, he'd sold his interest in Bayfield, and was starting to build a trawler-type powerboat, the design of which he'd doodled over for years. It was 40-feet long, on a displacement hull patterned after the rugged little Great Lakes fishing tugs that clawed and rammed their way through the worst of Great Lakes weather. It had a small diesel engine, capable of moving the boat at a hull speed of about ten knots an hour. There was a 110V generator for onboard electricity and even a small freezer below the main deck. It was the first boat I'd seen with a head big enough for me, and there was ample room for a well-equipped galley for my first mate, and chief cook, Brenda.

We spent most of June and July in the lovely little villages and towns that line the east shore of Lake Huron, close to the North Castle Marine factory in Goderich where we watched *Fair Passage* take shape each day. On the backs of place mats from Murphy's Landing restaurant, Ted sketched ideas that later were incorporated in shining, varnished mahogany inside the boat.

Finally, in September, she was ready. She was loaded on a truck, and driven to Bayfield, about 12 miles away, for launching. Lloyd and Nancy Robertson drove up from Toronto. A camera crew arrived from Kitchener TV, and the local newspaper sent a photographer. While *Fair Passage* lay suspended in the slings of the big Travelift, Brenda walked up to her bow, and took a practice swing with the champagne bottle. The workmen who'd put her together cheered. Gozzard and his wife, Jan, smiled, and I got my camera ready. At a nod from Ted, Brenda took a long swipe with the bottle of champagne. It shattered. The boat slowly sank on the straps and then floated gently in the launching bay, bobbing a little as she gained her balance. She was beautiful, straight, high and true, and looking like a champion!

But Brenda looked pained as she walked from the ramp. Blood trickled from the back of her hand. One finger hung slack.

We discovered later that a tiny chip of glass from the champagne bottle had whistled across the back of her hand, leaving a thin cut that severed the tendon of her first finger. She was in a cast for four weeks.

Our first port of call on our summer cruise was Cobourg, a small town east of Toronto, close to the Port Hope home of my friend and co-author, Wade Rowland. We spent seven weeks in Cobourg, tied up at the brand new marina, enjoying the hospitality of the Cobourg Yacht Club and the townspeople. The Mayor bullied and coaxed us into being the official openers of the Cobourg Highland Games. We played hard-to-get but ended up enjoying ourselves immensely.

Then, my trusty little Sharp word processor on board, we set out for a couple of weeks on the Trent-Severn Waterway, cruising up through Trenton, Peterborough, Bobcaygeon, and Orillia to Georgian Bay and our home port, the Wye Heritage Marina at Midland. For much of the time that summer, the boat played second fiddle to the word processor . . . much of this was drafted to the sound of waves rolling into the breakwater in front of our slip.

There was plenty of time for reflection . . . 40, or 30, or even 20 years ago, I never dreamed of being where I am now. I have been extremely fortunate in having had opportunities thrust my way, and in knowing people who had faith in my abilities: Bas Scully in the Sault: Don Insley at CKEY; Art Cole, hunched over his battered desk in the dusty, old *Telegram* newsroom; little Davey Rogers in Hamilton; Murray Chercover and Bill Crampton at CFTO; Murray again at CTV, along with Michael Hind Smith, Charles Templeton, Tom Gould, and Don Cameron.

The associations and friendships I've forged through the years have helped and sustained me in a powerful way. I have yet to find a studio crew that I didn't enjoy. Cameramen, technicians, control room crews . . . it has always been a pleasure to walk into a studio and be greeted by the Barkleys and the Cowleys, the Summers and the Yureks, the Scotts and the Obersons, and old Cam Thomas, the World War Two Mosquito pilot turned technical director, who posted his lampooning poetry on the office bulletin boards around Christmas each year, and George Beck, our prop man, who never failed to place a glass of water on my desk (after George died, his successor Jim Close and I named a water tap in the back shop "the George Beck Memorial Well"). Technical crews, from propmen to videotape operators, are the guts of any television station, and for me, they've been the salt of the earth.

I guess I've made my feelings about newsroom people pretty clear. They are simply the best. Irreverent and bawdy, often world-weary, but seldom truly cynical, they provide television's daily diet of news, agonizing over arcane technical and editorial problems, burdened by the responsibility of telling the truth about complicated issues in fractions of minutes, and doing their best to keep their anchormen looking astute and learned.

And Lloyd Robertson . . . Lloyd went through terrible culture shock when he joined CTV, not simply because he became a news story and the subject of a lot of misinformed media gossip, but because the atmosphere in the CTV newsroom was so different from what he'd been accustomed to at CBC. He found himself in a newsroom that had to scramble every day to find the resources to match the competition: a newsroom that treated news, not with hushed awe, but with an attitude of irreverence and skepticism, particularly where political utterances were concerned. It wasn't long, though, before Lloyd overcame his shock at my occasional outbursts over unctuous copy. In the end he would join me in demanding to know: "Who wrote this shit?"

Lloyd left the CBC in a dispute over proscriptions against his taking part in regular newsroom activities like writing, editing, and reporting. He now writes, edits, and reports on a daily basis and is an integral part of the editorial decision-making process. He presents an interesting picture, hunched over a typewriter, peering at a scrap of wire copy through half glasses, pecking away with two fingers.

I've never met a woman I didn't like, nor had a drink I didn't enjoy. I've faced the consequences where the drinking is concerned—it was not pleasant. I've been married three times, and don't regret a minute of it. My first wife and I grew up together. My second wife taught me many things about the world and living, and about myself. My third wife, Brenda, pulls my strings, but knows exactly when and how far to pull them. She is small, but mighty: she goes along with my whims and impulses with soft good nature, but when she says no, I listen. Most of the time. My three children—Bernie, Tina, and Brenda's Michael, are a continuing source of pride and pleasure.

I've lived through the golden age of television, worked through its growing pains, and now, will continue to work through whatever its future offers—provided, that is, that audiences continue welcoming me into their homes the way they have so generously done for the past 20 years.

I once had a floor manager named Gerry Wilkinson, a short, slight man whose accent betrayed his British background. Each night, as he counted down the final seconds to my "goodnights," Gerry would say to me: "Say goodnight, Harvey," and then give me the on-air cue.

One night, somebody miscalculated and opened a mike too soon (or perhaps Gerry got mixed up on the count). From television sets across the land came Gerry's impeccable accent:

"Say goodnight, Harvey."

I did. And I think it's that time now.

Afterword

This is a memoir, and for most of it, I've relied on my memory. I know that there are discrepancies in the chronology of events, but I hope I've played everybody in the right place in the context of the various anecdotes.

Many events that affected my career took place in boardrooms, and I never got to the boardroom. In those cases, I've relied on the public record, or my personal knowledge . . . neither of which are always completely accurate.

I would be remiss if I didn't thank all the people who answered my badgering phone calls during the months when this manuscript was in preparation. I'm particularly grateful to Agnes Manion, Jack Goddard, Don Cameron, Murray Chercover, Bas Scully, Russ Ramsey, Pete Griffin, and Brian Nolan, who, with many others, stretched their memories for me.

Wade Rowland started me on this whole business of writing a book by suggesting the idea, and, when I objected that I wouldn't know how to go about it, he told me: "It's easy, you just start at the beginning and keep going until you get to the end." What he didn't say was what a lot of damned hard work there'd be in between. I suppose I should thank Wade, even though he almost ruined my summer's cruising plans.

And Brenda. Whenever I sat at the computer, she came round, asking me to print out what I'd done so far. She read every word, commented, and criticized, and always had a coffee at my elbow. Thanks, hon.

On board *Fair Passage*,
Midland, Ontario,
October, 1984.

Index

ABC News, 139, 140, 147
Abraham, Ralph, 148, 149
Academy of Radio Arts, 47
Affleck, Bruce, 203
Aldred, Joel, 73, 82, 98, 111
Aldrin, Buzz, 171
Allen, Helen, 92
Alloway, Bruce, 65
Anders, William, 169
Anthony, Marge, 203, 204
Armstrong, Frank, 73, 78, 79, 84
Armstrong, Neil, 171
Arsenault, Ray, 115, 122, 124, 125, 128, 129

Baker, Carroll, 2
Banas, Carl, 80
Barron, Jim, 49
Barron, Win, 37
Bassett, John, 111, 113, 114, 123, 126, 132, 151
Baton Broadcasting Ltd., 111, 113
Beck, George, 159, 225
Bennett, Pat, 91, 121
Berton, Pierre, 155
Bibby, Sid, 104
Blake, Gord, 215
Board of Broadcast Governors, 126
Bock, Raimund and Ilona, 118
Boliska, Al, 92
Bond, Cec, 30
Borman, Frank, 168, 169, 170
Bradford, Earl, 100
Brady, Brenda, 191, 200, 201, 204, 207; *marriage to Harvey*, 214, 215, 217, 223, 224, 226, 228
Brinkley, David, 107
Bryant, Jim and Kay, 44
Burghardt, Jack, 104, 108, 109, 110
Bushnell, Ernie, 132, 138

Caldwell, Spence, 98, 126, 127, 147
Cameron, Donald, 182, 193, 195, 197, 203, 204, 208, 209, 210, 212, 213, 216, 218, 219, 222, 225, 228
Cameron, Earl, 56, 57, 149, 151
Campbell, Max, 94, 95, 96
Canada AM, 1, 195, 197, 218
Canadian Football League, 126
Canadian National Exhibition, 79
Carmichael, Mike, 92
CBC, 47, 138, 154, 160, 182, 199, 210
CBC National News, 148, 151, 194, 195, 197, 216
CBC Radio, 19, 37, 50, 55, 71
CBC-TV, 97, 98, 102, 128, 141, 156, 159
CBS-TV, 115
CFCF Montreal, 100
CFCF-TV, 153
CFRB Toronto, 19, 100
CFRN-TV Edmonton, 65
CFTO-TV Toronto, 111, 112, 113, 114, 116, 120, 121, 122, 124, 126, 127, 128, 129, 130, 147, 148, 149, 150, 153, 164, 168, 194, 217, 225
Champ, Henry, 151

CHCH-TV Hamilton, 102, 103, 108, 109, 110, 113, 115
Chercover, Murray, 111, 112, 115, 122, 125, 147, 152, 156, 163, 203, 204, 208, 216, 225, 228
Christie, Gil, 97
CHUM Toronto, 61, 84, 85, 86, 87, 88, 90, 91, 92, 93, 94, 99, 100, 102, 104, 112, 121
CJIC Sault Ste. Marie, 51, 53, 54, 55, 56, 57, 58, 59, 61
CJKL Kirkland Lake, 19
CJOH-TV Ottawa, 127, 128, 131, 134, 135, 138, 142, 145, 146, 151, 160
CKBB Barrie, 57, 59, 60, 62
CKEY Drama Workshop, 48, 51, 73
CKEY Toronto, 48, 49, 50, 51, 62, 73, 74, 76, 78, 79, 80, 82, 83, 84, 91, 100, 200, 225
CKOY Ottawa, 73
CKXL Calgary, 62, 63, 67, 68, 69
Clark, Joe, 209
Clooney, Rosemary, 57
Close, Jim, 225
Cole, Art, 92, 93, 225
Collins, George, 66
Collins, Michael, 171
Connaught Laboratories, 38
Conners, Arden and Harvey, 15
Conroy, Bob, 168, 169, 193, 194
Cooke, David, 122
Cooke, Jack Kent, 48, 74, 80, 100
Cooney, Howard, 73, 78, 79, 84
Cooper, Iris, 49
Courrier, Sheila, 121
Cowley, George, 222
Crampton, W.O., 111, 112, 114, 115, 116, 122, 123, 225
Crate, Brian, 200
Creighton, Doug, 92
Crete, Zia, 28
Cronkite, Walter, 36, 216
Crouter, Walley, 74, 100
Crysdale, Joe, 73, 77

CTV National News, 127, 131, 132, 134, 136, 139, 142, 145, 146, 147, 149, 150, 151, 152, 153, 155, 159, 166, 167, 168, 169, 192, 195, 198, 209, 210, 211, 213, 216, 222
CTV network, 112, 126, 127, 130, 147, 150, 160, 163, 164, 175, 182, 193, 197, 199, 200, 215
Cumming, Don, 147, 148, 152

Daily News Service, 211, 217
Daley, Tom, 59
Danielson, Gord, 2
Delaney, E.J., 111, 112
Dempson, Peter, 92
Dennett, Jack, 74, 100
Dennis, Laddie, 98, 99
Dexter, Susan, 182, 183
Dickens, Peter, 100
Diefenbaker, Elmer, 137
Diefenbaker, John, 136, 146, 155, 163
Diefenbaker, Olive, 137
Douglas, Ab, 128, 130, 134, 135, 136, 141, 148, 149, 153, 154
Douglas, Tommy, 212
Dowling, Bob, 196
Drainie, John, 47
Drylie, Bill, 102
Dunsmore, Barrie, 122, 123
Durhamcrest, 206

Eckland, Paul, 137
Edwards, Douglas, 97
Edwards, Peter, 125
Eibel, David, 220, 221
Ellis, Ron, 104
Evans, Bob, 115, 121, 122, 123, 124
Evans, Trevor, 124

Ferrier, Gary, 100
Finlan, Mike, 114, 148, 149
Fisher, Doug, 155
Foss, Ken, 67
Fry, Jeff, 114, 124, 153

Gabereau, Francois, 184
Galt, Bruce, 218
Gibson, Joe, 134, 147
Gillies, Bernice, 196
Gingles, Ray, 94, 96
Global Television, 150
Glover, Elwood, 74
Goddard, Bill, 11, 13
Goddard, Jack, 18, 228
Goodrich, Roger, 115
Gorman, Mary, 168, 169
Gould, Tom, 154, 155, 165, 166, 167, 182, 192, 193, 195, 196, 209, 210, 225
Gozzard, Ted, 223, 224
Graham, Arthur, 2
Grand, Elaine, 97
Greene, Lorne, 37, 47, 73, 78, 79, 81, 82
Griffin, Pete, 60, 62, 63, 64, 66, 68, 69, 70, 71, 228
Griffiths, Phyllis, 92, 93
Griffiths, Stuart, 131, 132, 135, 140, 142, 143, 145, 147
Gulf Oil, 168, 169

Hall, Hazeldine, 49
Halliwell, Harry, 92
Halton, Matthew, 36
Hamilton, Margaret, 15
Harris, Michael, 206
Harrison, Art, 57
Hartley, Norman, 195, 197
Hawkins, Ronnie, 89
Hayward, Dick, 92
Healy, Albert, 15
Heaton, John, 99
Hellyer, Paul, 134
Henderson, Larry, 97, 141
Hendrie Cartage, 32, 34, 38
Hetherington, Morley, 15
Hewitt, Bill, 61
Hewitt, Foster, 19, 20, 32, 39, 61
Hicks, Wes, 92
Higgins and Burke Ltd., 45, 46, 51
Himel, Martin, 219

Hind Smith, Michael, 127, 130, 131, 141, 145, 147, 225
Hines, Orville, 15, 16
Hockey Night in Canada, 20, 61
Holland, Art, 92
Howarth, Dorothy, 92
Hunter, Jim, 19, 32, 39
Hunter, Tommy, 89
Huntley, Chet, 107
Hurricane Hazel, 86, 87
Hyland, Grant, 54

Imperial Bank of Canada, 40
Insley, Don, 73, 74, 75, 77, 78, 83, 84, 99, 225
Irwin, Dave, 54, 55, 56

Jamieson, Don, 212
Jennings, Peter, 127, 128, 130, 134, 140, 147
Johnson, Norm, 92
Johnston, Court, 87
Johnston, Doug, 115, 121, 122, 123
Jones, George, 88
Junkin, Ray, 154

Keeble, Gordon, 98, 147
Keeping, Max, 151
Kelly, Bill, 181
Kelly, Dr. Colin, 174
Kelly, Hal, 73, 77, 81
Kennedy, John F., 129, 130
Kenny, Stu, 73, 77
Kent, Alan, 92, 94
King, Josh, 89
Kirck, Harvey
  Assignments and News Stories:
    "Harvey's People", 1–3;
    1953 CNE air disaster, 79–80; Hurricane Hazel, 86–87;
    Girl with Leukemia, 90;
    Child Murder, 93; Railyard profile, 98; Kennedy Assassination, 129–130;
    Diefenbaker Interview, 136–137; Churchill Funeral, 142–143; Martin Luther King

Assassination, 161; Apollo Moon Missions, 168–171; Film on Nationalism, 182–183
Election Coverage: Hamilton Municipal 1960, 108–109; Federal Election 1965, 145–146; Conservative Party Leadership Convention 1967, 155–156; Federal Election 1968, 163–166; Federal Election 1974, 192–194
Foreign Assignments: Hungarian Refugees 1956, 93–96; West Germany, 107–108; Commonwealth Conference, 138–139; Expo 70 Osaka, 175–178; "Window on the World", 183–187; Camp David Accords, 209; various assignments overseas, 212–214
Kirck, Brenda see Brady, Brenda
(Kirck), Maggie, 47, 49, 51, 52, 59, 64, 66, 71, 91, 101
(Kirck), Renate Bock, 118, 119, 120, 132, 133, 143, 144, 157, 162, 173, 181, 188, 189, 190, 191, 202
Knapp, Bud, 47
Kotcheff, Tim, 210, 211, 212, 219, 222
Krick, Earl, 8
Krick, George, 5
Kurcharski, Knut, 217
LaBerge, Louis, 213
Ladd, Phil, 88
Lambert, George, 25
Langton, Baden, 127, 128, 130, 134, 139, 147
LaValley, Pete, 65
Lawton, Gerry, 193
Lee, Bob and Leigh, 84, 85
Lester, Mickey, 73, 77
Leverre, Orphia May, 5

Lind, Derek, 100
Long, Dr. Marcus, 100
Lovell, James, 169
Luke, Hans and Renate, 117, 118
Lynch, Charles, 36, 127, 128, 139, 145, 146, 176, 177, 178
Lynn, Jennifer, 222

MacFarlane, Doug, 204
Macht, Wally, 150, 160, 175
Macklem, Len, 42, 43
Macpherson, Duncan, 164
Maitland, Derek, 220
Manion, Agnes, 228
Mann, Larry, 97
Mannis, Harry, 56, 57
Marsh, Bert, 147
Martin, Larry, 86, 87
Maynard, Bill, 61
McAuley, Lionel, 54
McCourt, Mike, 196
McDonald, Finley, 132
McDougal, Dick, 97
McGaw, Jack, 175
McGee, Frank, 168
McKenzie, George, 121, 124
McKenzie, Sandra, 217
McKnight, Wes, 39, 74
McLean, Ross, 97
McPherson, Don, 155, 167, 168, 169, 175, 176, 177, 178, 182
Miller, Jack, 222
Milsom, Howard, 48, 49, 50, 51
Moore, Mavor, 47
Mosca, Angelo, 109
Mulroney, Brian, 213
Mungham, Dick, 58
Munro, John, 109
Munro, Ross, 36
Must, John, 153

NASA, 168, 169, 170, 172
NBC News, 151, 168, 169, 170
New Liskeard High School Band, 29
New Liskeard Golf Club, 31
Newspaper Guild, 114, 124

Nickle, Will, 15
Nolan, Brian, 134, 135, 147, 148, 149, 228
Nordheimer, Peter, 87, 89

O'Brien, Brian, 217
Olchowy, Nick, 104, 105
Oliver, Craig, 194

Paizel, Bernie, 196
Parks, Al, 196
Parliamentary Press Gallery, 128, 133, 138
Parrish, Don, 115, 121
Pastor, Tony, 57
Pearson, Lester, 143, 146, 163
Pearson, Marion, 143
Penny, Gordon, 114, 148, 149
Peters, Ray, 132
Pettifer, Clifford, 12, 15, 24
Phillips, Bruce, 167, 192, 193, 194, 212
Phillips, Vic, 150
Platt, Randy, 184
Plaunt, Don and Darryl, 15
Poulton, Ron, 92, 112, 113, 114, 116
Presley, Elvis, 91, 92

Q'Part, Jack, 85, 87

Racicot, Tony, 45, 46
Rae, Claude, 49
Rae, John, 74
Ralph, Gary, 196
Ramsey, Don, 54, 56
Ramsey, Russ, 228
Rasky, Harry, 79
Reade, John Collingwood, 125
Reilly, Peter, 148, 151
Rinaldo, Sandie, 218
Robertson, Lloyd, 197, 198, 199, 200, 209, 210, 212, 220, 221, 222, 224, 225, 226
Rogers, Dave, 102, 103, 104, 105, 107, 108, 110, 225
Rogers, Ted, 111

Rowland, Wade, 224, 228
Royal Conservatory of Music, 72
Rubie, Les, 49, 50, 51
Russell, Andy, 2

Safer, Morley, 115
Saltzman, Percy, 97
Sandy, Keith, 63, 73, 76, 81, 82
Scully, Basil, 50, 53, 55, 59, 225, 228
Sharp, Mitchell, 134
Shaw Business Schools, 40
Shaw, Fred, 65
Shaw, Jim, 135, 136, 142, 143
Sherritt, Jack and Joy, 204, 205, 207, 215
Sinclair, Gordon, 74, 80, 100
Sinclair, Ian, 176
Slaight, Allan, 89, 90, 99
Snelgrove, Ralph, 57, 58, 60, 61, 62
Soble, Ken, 103, 104
Solway, Larry, 49, 100
Southam Newspapers, 167
Spragge, John, 100
Standard Casing, 35
Stanfield, Robert, 146, 163, 164
Star Weekly, 7, 33, 37
Stewart, Jack, 63, 64
Strangway, Dr. David, 170
Stransman, Harry, 38, 39
Stursberg, Peter, 127
Swayze, John Cameron, 97

Taylor, Peggy, 1
Temiskaming Speaker, 25, 30
Templeton, Charles, 152, 153, 155, 156, 160, 163, 165, 166, 167, 225
Texaco Canada Ltd., 167, 168
Thomas Cam, 225
Thomas, Richard, 183, 184, 185, 186, 187
Thomson, Roy, 56
Thoreson, Roy, 2
Todd, Clark, 213, 214, 218, 219, 220

Toner, Gerry, 92
Toronto Star, 37, 38, 45, 80, 102, 164, 222
Toronto Sun, 92, 204
Toronto Telegram, 87, 91, 92, 93, 94, 99, 111, 113, 114, 116, 121, 122, 123, 196, 204, 225
Town, Harold, 49, 51, 52
Trudeau, Pierre, 156, 161, 163, 164, 175, 212
Tumpane, Frank, 92

Van Dusen, Jack, 147
Vaughan, Guy, 125

W-5, 151, 175, 182, 195
Waters, Allan, 87, 88, 89, 90

Watson, Whipper Billy, 22
Webster, Jack, 212
Weekend Magazine, 195, 196, 197
West, Bruce, 36
Wilkinson, Gerry, 226, 227
Williams, Hank, 57
Williams, Johnny, 77, 79, 80, 83
Williamson, Lindsey, 204, 205, 208, 215
Wiseman, Stephanie, 49
Woodman, Steve, 65, 66, 68
Woolford, Dr. Bernard, 174, 175
Wright, Dave, 61

Yellowley, Charles, 153, 195, 198
Young, Dick, 196
Yurek, Mike, 222